Lockheed U-

by Jay Miller

Lockheed-California Company

Prototype TR-1B, 80-1064, poses for Lockheed photographer Bob Ferguson during a pre-delivery test flight off the California coast.

Aerofax, Incorporated
Austin, Texas

PUBLISHED BY

P.O. Box 5337
Austin, Texas 78763

Cover photo:
Lockheed chief photographer Bob Ferguson catches U-2R, 68-10336, as it turns on its downwind leg during a landing at Palmdale, California. This aircraft mounts a SLAR-type radar system in the nose, and is possibly serving as a testbed aircraft for the forthcoming production ASARS (Advanced Synthetic Aperture Radar System).

Lockheed-California Company

Library of Congress Catalog Card Number 83-072828
Library of Congress In Publications Data
Miller, Jay N.
    Lockheed U-2
    (Aerograph 3)
    Bibliography: P.121
    1. Lockheed U-2 (Reconnaissance Aircraft)
    2. Jet Planes, Military.
ISBN 0-942548-04-3 Softcover
    0-942548-05-1 Hardcover

European Trade Distribution by —

 **Midland Counties Publications**

24 The Hollow, Earl Shilton
LEICESTER, LE9 7NA, England
Telephone: (0455) 47256

THE LOCKHEED U-2
by Jay Miller

CONTENTS

Lockheed-California Company

Second prototype TR-1A, 80-1067, cruises serenely over the Palmdale, California area during its pre-delivery flight test program. Note that the flaps are in the gust control position.

Air Force pilot, Deacon Hall, models early MC-2 high-altitude flight suit and MA-2 helmet while standing in front of U-2A, 56-6715. The U-2A is equipped for HASP missions as evidenced by the particulate sampling system intake in the nose. Note the early center-mounted rear-view mirror.

PREFACE

Born, bred, and sustained in a hotbed of secrecy and intrigue, Lockheed's enigmatic U-2 has doggedly carried out its surreptitious surveillance and research missions day in and day out over a period that has now spanned nearly a third of a century. Somewhat surprisingly, age has detracted little from the U-2's mystique and undeniably incredible performance. Capable of routinely cruising at altitudes that had been considered, at its birth, the domain of only the most exotic experimental research aircraft types, the U-2 remains unparallelled in the art of sustained high-altitude flight.

When the high-altitude reconnaissance aircraft program leading to the U-2 was first conceived in late 1953, it was established by the preliminary proposal team that a high-cruising altitude capability in excess of 70,000 feet would be mandatory for the specified mission. The U-2, after "winning" the rather unorthodox design competition, went on to achieve that required altitude, and significantly higher, almost from the day of its first flight. It was, and still is, a feat unmatched and virtually unchallenged in the annals of subsonic aircraft development.

In 1983, although changed considerably from the first configurations to enter production, the U-2, under the TR-1 designator, is once again in series production for the USAF. Additionally, the U-2R, on which the TR-1 configuration is based, has reentered production for sale to the Air Force and several non-indigenous intelligence agencies.

Because of the classified nature and awesome performance capabilities of the U-2, the aircraft has grown in stature and mystique as the years since its first unveiling have passed. What follows is the most authentic and technically accurate history of this precedent-setting aircraft yet published. From design study to present production status, the U-2 story is herein documented . . .

And readers please note: Like many of his colleagues, the author has become sensitized to items that are truly politically and/or militarily sensitive. Readers will not find such material in this book. As a point of interest, every statement, fact, or figure presented in this publication has been gathered from unclassified or declassified documents and all interviewees were given editing privileges. Additionally, it should be mentioned that many aspects of the U-2 program remain classified due to their direct relationship to current sensitive U-2 configurations and mission profiles. Again, nothing about these facets of the program appear in this volume.

Jay Miller
July '83

ACKNOWLEDGEMENTS

The published history of the Lockheed U-2 has been a long time in coming. The reasons for this are seemingly manifest in the aircraft's *raison d'etre*, but suffice it to say that this was only the first of many barriers that had to be overcome. The author found, like many researchers before him, that the aura of secrecy surrounding the U-2 was at times more smoke-screen than legitimate barrier. It was only through the efforts of people who were truly intimate with the program and who had legitimate insight into the author's objectives that the story was eventually told at all.

For the first time, the efforts of many individuals and agencies intimately involved in the U-2 program have been brought together in order to create a virtually definitive work covering all aspects of the aircraft and its history. As readers might expect, there were several contributors who requested that their efforts remain unacknowledged. I grant that wish with regret. To you select few, special thanks. . . .

What follows then, is a list of friends and associates who made innumerable important contributions to this book, and who deserve all the thanks I can bestow through the written word:

John Andrews of the Testor Corporation, Jim Goodall, Bob Lawson, Pat Groves, Bruce Hallock, Don Webster, Tommy Thomason, Chuck Hansen, Ben Koziol, Harvey Lippincott and Harry Keiner of the United Technologies Corporation, Bob Ferguson, Ben Rich, Ray Goudey, and Jeff Fellows of the Lockheed-California Company, Bob Birkett, Bob Schumacher, Robert Archer, Chris Pocock, Tony LeVier, Vinko Dolson, Doug Campbell, René Francillon, Ph.D., Chris Borden and Bob Danielson of NASA Ames, Paul Swendrowski, Dave Menard, Dick Hallion, Ph.D. and Lucille Zaccardi at the Edwards AFB Historian's Office, Brian Rogers, David Anderton, Col. George E. Daniels and the staff at *Air University Review*, Paul Binder of the Lockheed Missiles and Space Co., Danny Schweers, Ted Bear, Walter Boyne of the National Air & Space Museum, Gerald Balzer, Joe Newland of Tracor Aerospace, Lewis and Janet Shaw, Deke Hall, Tom Ivie, Chuck Banks and Aero Publishers, Theron Rinehart of Fairchild Industries, and Chuck Davis (for the outstanding and meticulously executed multi-view drawings that grace many of the pages in this book).

Last but far from least, Susan Miller, Anna Miller, and Miriam Miller are offered a special word of thanks—with love.

Albert Gibb via Chris Pocock

U-2A, 56-6953, landing at RAF Upper Heyford in 1962, during an early TDY assignment in England. Air Force U-2's were still several years away from being painted in all-black, low visibility paint scheme. Note the particulate sampler on port side of fuselage, just ahead of the main gear well.

Majesty in metal—56-6708 shows off well the U-2A's esthetically pleasing high-aspect-ratio wing and the markings seen on most early Air Force aircraft.

Chapt. 1:
SEABERG'S SOLUTION

The initial three contenders for the MX-2147 high-altitude recce aircraft program included, from the left, the Fairchild M-195, the Bell X-16, and the Martin B-57D (identified here as the Model 294). As related in this chapter, Bell's X-16 was the eventual 'unsuccessful' winner.

Reconnaissance and surveillance technique, within the doctrinal philosophies of the USAF and its sister services, can be broken down into three major categories. Basically, these consist of strategic reconnaissance, tactical reconnaissance, and local reconnaissance.

Strategic reconnaissance is concerned with the acquisition of an overview of a large territorial area, with the intent of acquiring details of places and/or things that might affect the long term balance of political and/or military power. Involved in this analytical pursuit is information pertaining to a country's war-waging ability, its cities, its industrial complexes, its recent technology advances, and its environment. Strategic reconnaissance sorties are usually conducted surreptitiously and the data acquisition process does not often require a real-time information delivery schedule.

Tactical reconnaissance is concerned with more immediate concerns such as on-going battlefield situations, enemy troop strength, available firepower, enemy positions, and developing targets. Information gathered during tactical reconnaissance sorties is usually time-sensitive and the quicker it can be delivered to its client, the more useful it becomes.

Local reconnaissance is concerned with localized events and usually demands the services of low-performance aircraft and visual observers who can communicate rapidly with ground forces. Direct communication is, in fact, almost mandatory for this recce type as local reconnaissance tends to have direct and immediate influence on such items as field artillery accuracy, the positions of troop emplacements, and the immediate safety of small pockets of allied troops and equipment.

In the March-April 1982 issue of the *Air University Review*, Col. George E. Daniels summarized contemporary reconnaissance doctrine in an essay entitled "An Approach to Reconnaissance Doctrine." With Col. Daniels' kind permission, and that of the *Air University Review*, this insightful article follows:

Air Force Regulation 1-2 (22 November 1978) establishes the need for a USAF operational doctrine entitled *Reconnaissance* (AFM 2-11), thus emphasizing the lack of current reconnaissance doctrine. It may be indicative of the importance of doctrine in general or, more specifically, the degree of interest shown for the mission of reconnaissance that accounts for the lack of such information. Without an authoritative document to expand the principles established in basic doctrine and provide direction for the employment of aerospace resources, it is easy to see why numbers of reconnaissance assets have dwindled, control has vacillated, and the needs are difficult to define. Thus, because of this obvious deficiency, a new approach to a reconnaissance operational doctrine seems vital.

Surveillance and Reconnaissance

Surveillance and reconnaissance constitute one of the nine basic operational missions of the Air Force established in AFM 1-1. It is especially important to recognize the operational nature of these missions and that the definition of both surveillance and reconnaissance be understood.* According to JCS Publication 1:

Reconnaissance—A mission undertaken to obtain, by visual observation or other detection methods, information about the activities and resources of an enemy or potential enemy; or to secure data concerning the meteorological, hydrographic, or geographic characteristics of a particular area.

Surveillance—The systematic observation of aerospace, surface, or subsurface areas, places, persons, or things by visual, aural, electronic, photographic, or other means.

While surveillance and reconnaissance appear similar in purpose, the main difference is in specification and duration. AFM 1-1 states that surveillance systems collect information continuously while reconnaissance missions are directed toward localized or specific targets. Surveillance and reconnaissance systems are the eyes and ears of the political and military structure through which the necessary information is gained to support the decision-making process. The importance of this mission cannot be overlooked.

Basic doctrine is specific in defining strategic and tactical surveillance and reconnaissance operations and the relationship between them. The important factor to recognize in this relationship is that the function being supported determines if it is strategic or tactical, not the command that performs the mission or trains the crews. Neither is it the department nor agency that funds the platform. Thus the myth of national reconnaissance, strategic reconnaissance, and tactical reconnaissance operating as separate and distinct entities with individual purposes may be dissolved.

AFM 1-1 provides basic guidance as to the nature of strategic and tactical surveillance and reconnaissance.

Strategic surveillance and reconnaissance operations support our needs for national and strategic intelligence. They also help fill the information requirements of the tactical commanders. Through these strategic operations, we can assess the total capability of a foreign nation to wage war, and can monitor the progress of a war. These operations provide information that is essential to:

Identify targets for strategic and tactical attack.

Provide indications and warning of hostile intent and actions . . .

Assess damage to enemy and friendly targets.

Determine force structure.

Determine our requirements for research and development of warfighting systems.

Help verify compliance with treaties and agreements.

Tactical surveillance and reconnaissance operations support the theater and the tactical field commander. When these tactical systems are assigned targets, the resulting information may fill both national and strategic intelligence requirements. Tactical systems provide indications of hostile intent, plus information from which intelligence is derived. These surveillance and reconnaissance systems provide information on:

The disposition, composition, and movement of enemy forces.

The location of enemy lines of communication, installations, and electronic emissions.

Post-strike damage.

Conditions in surface battle areas.

Weather and terrain.

The use to which the information is put determines the strategic or tactical nature of the collection operation. The operational mission of collecting information is known as surveillance and reconnaissance.

Relationship to Intelligence

Surveillance and reconnaissance do not exist for their own purpose. Therefore, it is necessary to discuss the information product, the relationship to intelligence, and disciplines employed. The JCS Publication 1 definitions are important at this point:

Information (intelligence)—Unevaluated material of every description, including that derived from

*All definitions throughout this section are taken from The Dictionary of Military and Associated Terms, JCS Publication 1, 3 September 1974, unless otherwise noted.

observations, reports, rumors, imagery, and other sources which, when processed, may produce intelligence.

Intelligence—The product resulting from the collection, evaluation, analysis, integration, and interpretation of all information concerning . . . foreign countries or areas. . . .

Strategic intelligence—Intelligence which is required for the formation of policy and military plans at national and international levels.

Tactical intelligence—Intelligence which is required for the planning and conduct of tactical operations. . . . tactical intelligence and strategic intelligence differ only in scope, point of view, and level of employment.

While the basic definitions may appear to quibble over semantics, it is important to realize that the basic product of the surveillance and reconnaissance operational missions is information and that it only becomes intelligence after it has been transformed through the process defined above. This does not mean that information has no direct value. The conversion to intelligence is often time-consuming; therefore, information provided to satisfy the needs of combat commanders directly is combat information. It has been defined as combat information.

Combat information—Unevaluated data, gathered by or provided directly to the tactical commander, which, due to its highly perishable nature or the critical timing of the situation, cannot be processed into tactical intelligence in time to satisfy user tactical intelligence requirements.

The interrelationships of surveillance, reconnaissance, information, and intelligence have been extracted from JCS Pub. 1 and AFM 1-1 to provide clarification. The specific expansion of principles and procedures governing the processing, production, and dessemination of intelligence will be addressed in AFM 2-10, *Intelligence* (forthcoming).

Collection Disciplines

The methods used to conduct surveillance and reconnaissance are best described by the intelligence discipline supported. The general categories of imagery and signals intelligence (SIGINT) can be used to describe collection activities that cover the major portions of the electromagnetic spectrum. While each is a specialty unto itself, it is necessary to understand a description in general terms, some applications, and significant capabilities and limitations of each discipline.

Imagery

Imagery, as defined by JCS Publ. 1, consists of "collectively, the representation of objects reproduced electronically or by optical means on film, electronic display devices or other media."

Photography is the oldest mechanical means of conducting surveillance and reconnaissance, dating back to the box camera and balloon. The camera and films of today are highly sophisticated and provide what is generally considered by commanders as the ultimate intelligence product, a picture. While it may be worth a thousand words and serve as hard evidence on the battlefield or at the conference table, it is not totally infallible. Dummy equipment, derelict vehicles, and camouflage are used to deceive the viewer. Optical photography requires sufficient light to expose the film, either daylight or with photoflash augmentation as well as direct viewing of the subject, unrestricted by weather phenomenon. Infrared film is often used to overcome camouflage; at night, because it records variations of relative temperatures, it is passive in nature and does not unnecessarily expose the position of the reconnaissance platform as does photoflash augmentation. The greatest limitation in film-based photo-

graphy is the time required to deliver, process, and interpret the imagery after the target has been acquired. The greatest advantage is the detail so necessary when trying to locate, identify, and determine the size of the enemy force.

Radar imagery is produced by an active sensor that emits and records the reflected signal. Radar provides a standoff capability and is a day/night all-weather sensor. The product requires sophisticated processing and specialized interpretation skills, but because of its electronic nature it is possible to digitize and data link relay the image, thus making it a near-real-time sensor. Radar is a very good wide area surveillance sensor capable of providing target location; however, it is not capable of specific identification unless it is correlated with data collected simultaneously from other disciplines. Dispersal patterns, field formations, and knowledge of enemy tactics provide clues to identify general categories of equipment. Knowing the presence of tanks, artillery, or bridging operations may satisfy the combat information requirements of a commander while other sources and disciplines are employed to gain specifics such as type and caliber. It is possible to improve the identification capability of radar sensors within the constraints of time and fiscal practicability.

Nonimaging infrared sensors provide the battle commander the ability to detect and track missiles and identify impact areas. They may also be used to track certain types of aircraft. The heat emissions of exhausts provide the necessary data, even though the vehicle itself may not be seen. Heat emissions from power generators or distribution lines may aid in locating unit headquarters or communication nodes even without transmission.

Another type of infrared system capable of cockpit display or data link relay is forward-looking infrared (FLIR). This sensor system functions on relative differential temperature measurement but records and displays electronically rather than on film, as in the case of photographic infrared. The system is totally passive and can produce scenes of the battlefield in detail that allow identification of equipment without regard to light level. There are restrictions caused by weather that may totally or partially attenuate the temperature measurement and thus restrict its use.

Intelligence Disciplines

Signals intelligence is "a category of intelligence information comprising all communications intelligence, electronics, intelligence, and telemetry intelligence."

As seen by this definition, there are specialties or disciplines within the broad general category of SIGINT, each of which provides a unique type of information. The definition of each specialty found in JCS Pub. 1 is fairly descriptive.

Communications intelligence (COMINT) is the "technical and intelligence information derived from foreign communications by other than the intended recipients." It is through COMINT that the battle commander is able to gain the most vital information, intent. If the directions being given to enemy forces can be accurately determined in sufficient time to allow the battle commander to take counteractions, the effect of the enemy intention may be negated. This is not without its difficulty or flaws, however. The practice of communication security by the enemy is designed specifically to deny unauthorized persons information of value or to mislead their interpretation. Even though the enemy's intention may be overheard, its accuracy must be determined.

Electronics intelligence (ELINT) is the "technical and intelligence information derived from for-

eign, non-communications, electromagnetic radiations emanating from other than nuclear detonations or radioactive sources." Search and acquisition radars and tracking systems emit electronic signals that when collected may provide the battle commander the ability to locate and identify the enemy air defense systems. Many of the characteristics of electronic systems such as radars are unique and provide reliable identification when properly analyzed. Knowledge of the electronic order of battle (EOB) of the enemy is essential for planning offensive action against him in order that concentrations of firepower may be avoided or destroyed as required.

Closely related to ELINT but requiring uniquely different collection and analysis is a discipline known as *radiation intelligence* (RINT). RINT is the "intelligence derived from the collection and analysis of non-information bearing elements extracted from the electromagnetic energy unintentionally emanated by foreign devices, equipments, and systems, excluding those generated by the detonation of atomic/nuclear weapons."

The key words are "unintentionally emanated." For example, a radar acquisition system may be operating in a standby mode, while the intended target is being tracked optically. The electronics portion of the system may be operating under full power with the exception that the transmitter output has been routed by switch action to ground or to what is known as a dummy load rather than to the antenna. Some of the electronic power inevitably escapes and may be recorded, and even though the enemy is not transmitting, he may be emitting. A much simpler example of unintentional radiation is that caused by the ignition system of the family car and heard in the radio unless an attenuation device is installed. The collection and analysis of these spurious signals provide information to the combat commander when the enemy has no intentions of displaying an active electronic presence.

Telemetry intelligence (TELINT) is the "technical and intelligence information derived from the intercept, processing, and analysis of foreign telemetry."

A study of the guidance and control signals being transmitted to a missile, for example, may reveal much information about the operating parameters of the missile. If such analysis could be done fast enough, it might even identify the location of the intended target.

The mentioned disciplines identify in a broad sense the collection capabilities required by the Air Force. Each is a unique field with specialties and subspecialties of its own. However it is through the application of these capabilities, either independently or in combination, that we are able to acquire the necessary information about the enemy to satisfy the decision-making process at all levels.

The Objective of Surveillance and Reconnaissance

In order for the surveillance and reconnaissance disciplines to be applied effectively, we must first establish objectives. This is more than identification of the enemy. It must first be determined if the information will be used for strategic intelligence, tactical intelligence, or combat information. Within these broad categories, we must then determine the nature of the specific missions being supported. This will assist in determining the accuracy, timeliness, and frequency of the collection. For example, if indications and warning information are required, the collection must be accurate, timely, and nearly continuous. On the other hand, if scientific and technical data are required to determine the status of a foreign nation's research and development efforts, the collection must be accurate; timeliness and frequency of collection may be determined when a testing event takes place. Therefore, collection may be more periodic than continuous.

It is important to note at this point the nature and value of timeliness. For information or intelligence to be of any value, it must arrive at the decision-maker in the proper form and *in time* to impact the decision being made. Information or intelligence that does not or cannot arrive in time may in fact have a negative value. Information that is sent to the decision-maker unnecessarily or after the decision has been made may cause other vital information being transmitted also to be delayed beyond the time when it could have an impact on decisions. Persons working throughout the surveillance, reconnaissance, and intelligence communities must be keenly aware of both the value of information and its negative value.

Tactical Reconnaissance as a Primary Function

It is important to understand the sources of authority for the Air Force to conduct surveillance and reconnaissance and the fact that it is not done solely for the Air Force. Department of Defense Directive 5100.1 and *The Unified Action Armed Forces,* JCS Pub. 2, identify as a primary function of the Air Force to: "Furnish close combat and logistical air support to the Army to include tactical reconnaissance and aerial photography." And "provide adequate, timely and reliable intelligence."

Not only is it important that the Air Force be organized, trained, and equipped to collect information and produce intelligence but, more important, it is recognized that this function is vital to Army operations. The degree to which the Army depends on the Air Force for support is spelled out in great detail in Army Field Manual 100-5, *Operations.* It is not necessary to specify in the same detail in this document the types and methods of support. It is vitally important, however, to recognize that surveillance and reconnaissance systems must provide different levels of support and meet different limitations of timeliness and accuracy, depending on the echelon of command being supported.

The Army has defined the battlefield by zones of responsibility and intelligence needs of the commanders responsible for each zone. The distances given are not exact but can be used for Army planning purposes.

The captain's zone at company level extends from the forward line of troops (FLOT) to 4–5 kilometers (km). Combat information is needed to support direct fire operations, and this information is virtually impossible to provide by other than organic means, such as gun sights and night obeservation devices. Very little outside support is expected, but the Air Force should remain aware of this need by troops in contact with the enemy. Should technology provide a simple solution in the future, integration of support must be explored. Emphasis must remain on simple solutions; otherwise the captain will rapidly receive negative value combat information that could prove fatal.

The colonel's zone at battalion and brigade level extends from the FLOT to the fire support coordination line and includes the captain's zones of the companies under their command. Colonels need both intelligence and combat information in order to see the enemy. They worry about the forward edge of the second echelon of enemy reinforcements, determine the movement, and control the friendly indirect fire weapons, counterfire, and direct tactical maneuver. Air Force surveillance and reconnaissance activities should be capable of providing support in this

HASP-configured 56-6714 sits on display during open house in Australia. Note the four kangaroo markings on the nose and the particulate sampler just ahead of the main gear well.

U-2C, 56-6680, on final with flaps and airbrakes fully extended. Black area between the intakes is the camera-equipped Q-bay. Note the leading edge extensions on either side of the slipper tanks.

ELINT/SIGINT-equipped U-2's are the most elusive birds off all. U-2R, 68-1029, serves to illustrate well the extensive antenna farm often carried by these specialized aircraft.

zone, which is not accomplished without difficulty, however. The problem of sorting out which battalion commander needs which bit of information may prove extremely difficult. Technology in data handling devices may offer some solutions when coupled with procedures such as templating (also described in FM 100-5). The emphasis again must be on simplicity because the battalion operates under extremes of field conditions and cannot be burdened with over-sophistication and negative value information.

In the U.S. Army view, the general's zone at division and corps level extends from the FLOT to 150 km and includes the zones of colonels. From this zone the enemy will provide tactical reinforcement and support. The Army looks to the Air Force to provide surveillance and reconnaissance in this area by either standoff or penetration tactics. While time constraints for reporting information from these areas is not as restrictive, it is important to remember that if the distance from the FEBA that enemy actions can be detected equals time to react, then time cannot be eroded due to poor communications or faulty procedures. The value of information becomes critical because of the volume to be handled from such a large area. It becomes essential that the most important elements necessary for decision-making be identified in advance and that efforts be undertaken to satisfy them as quickly and directly as possible.

While the Air Force is satisfying the surveillance and reconnaissance needs of the Army, it must also do the same for its own forces and possibly for the National Command Authorities and strategic planners. Some of the information will be of use to all organizations, but it is a mistake to believe there is a high degree of overlap. The fine detail required for targeting weapons is unnecessary for strategic planning. The technical information required to satisfy a research and development question may go far beyond the needs of a combat soldier or airman who only needs to know what is where, when, and how many.

A workable management system should be established to satisfy a wide variety of users; it must be able to integrate the needs of all users and match them with appropriate collection resources. Tactics must be developed in coordination with the organizations being supported to assure that the needs are understood and the best system capability is applied to each task.

Tasking of Collection Resources

Within the Department of Defense, the procedures for tasking collection resources are governed by JCS Publication 2. The flow of intelligence requirements follows command channels with the Director, Defense Intelligence Agency (DIA), having validation authority. Requests are forwarded from component commands, through the unified and specified commands, to the Director, DIA, acting for the Joint Chiefs of Staff. Once requests have been validated, the tasking for collection is passed to the agency or command responsible for operation of the particular collection resource.

Assets operated by Strategic Air Command are tasked through the joint reconnaissance center in the Pentagon to the strategic reconnaissance center at SAC Headquarters, and hence to the operational unit. Some assets are tasked through specific procedures established by the intelligence community, and these vary by discipline. For specific details refer to AFM 2-10.

Collection resources assigned to a specific theater of operation must be managed through a centralized collection management office (CMO). The CMO is responsible for receiving requests, determining the most appropriate resource for collection, tasking the unit operating the resource

(either directly or through applicable procedures), and maintaining a follow-up on request satisfaction through feedback. While it would be highly desirable to have a single CMO in each theater of operations, it is ofen not possible due to command arrangements or combined operations. In such cases the Air Force component should establish a CMO to coordinate the collection activities with other component commands to ensure maximum use of available resources and preclude unnecessary collection duplication.

System Requirements

The Air Force must pursue the surveillance and reconnaissance mission because it supports the intelligence needs of the NCA, DOD, and our allies. Without knowledge of what is happening in the world around us, we will be unable to identify our potential enemies, know the threat they pose to us, or be able to defeat them should the need arise.

To have a viable surveillance and reconnaissance capability, we must identify in detail the information needs of those we are tasked to support, determine the conditions under which the data must be collected, and assess the continuous or periodic nature of the collection. Technology must then be applied by discipline to determine the specific sensor required to accomplish the collection and under what operating parameters. Then and only then should we begin to evaluate the platform necessary to accomplish the mission. Technology must not be allowed to drive collection simply because it is possible. If there is no requirement, information collected under those conditions is of negative value.

Starting with a platform and trying to determine what surveillance or reconnaissance missions it could perform has been done successfully several times—in fact, it is our normal method. The fallacy is that we often spend valuable and scarce resources in an attempt to make sensors operate under less than optimum conditions or develop an operational profile that is unrealistic for the mission. Serious consideration must be given to the needs of those being supported. When quantified in even gross terms and coupled with templating procedures to streamline the transformation of information to intelligence, it will be possible to develop the rudiments of force structure.

The size of the surveillance and reconnaissance force must be determined by the importance placed on the need for information. Indeed, this need may be greater than bullets or bombs or the platforms that dispense them. The Air Force must vigorously pursue this important mission with creative and innovative ideas. Technology must not be chased but effectively applied to ensure that the information collected and delivered to the requester always retains its value.

Air War College,
Maxwell AFB, Alabama

Contemporary high-altitude strategic reconnaissance philosophy was born during the months of October, November, and December of 1952, when an Air Force major by the name of John Seaberg, then Assistant Chief of New Developments Office, Bombardment Branch, at Wright Field near Dayton, Ohio, placed on paper ideas he had for achieving sustained flight at ultra-high altitudes. Seaberg, who because of the Korean War had been called back to active duty following a stint as an aeronautical engineer at Chance Vought's Grand Prairie, Texas facility, had noted that the new generation of turbojet engines, with their inherent high altitude potential, could be mated to an aircraft of extremely efficient high-altitude-optimized wing and achieve cruising altitudes far in excess of any aircraft then in service. The ramifications of this conclusion

were multiple. It was obvious that an aircraft operating at the altitudes Seaberg predicted possible would make detection extremely difficult and interception virtually impossible. Obviously, reconnaissance and weapons delivery were two ideal candidates for an aircraft with such unique performance potential.

Soon after organizing his ideas and presenting them to his superior, William Lamar (then Chief of the New Developments Office), Seaberg began to formalize a proposal calling for the development of a high-altitude recce aircraft utilizing a high-aspect ratio low load wing and a state-of-the-art turbojet engine. By March of 1953, Seaberg's high-altitude aircraft idea had led to a formal specification, the contents of which were:

Design Study Requirements
Dated March 27, 1953

Objective: To determine the General Design Specification and a proposed work statement for a Phase I Program for a special reconnaissance aircraft weapon system.

Statement of Work: The Contractor shall conduct a design study as required by WADC Document, "Design Study Requirements," Identification No. 53WC-16507, dated 27 March 1953 in order to achieve the above stated objective.

1. Purpose:
The purpose of this design study is to determine the characteristics of an aircraft weapon system having an operational radius of 1,500 n.m. and capable of conducting pre- and post-strike reconnaissance missions during daylight, good visibility conditions.

2. Study Requirements:
a. Performance
The following parameters will be considered:
(1) Radius—1,500 miles
(2) Speed—optimum subsonic cruise speed at altitudes of 70,000 feet or higher over the target.
(3) Payload—100 to 700 pounds of reconnaissance equipment.
(4) Crew—one.
(5) Powerplants—current production engines with modifications, if necessary, for very high altitude operation. Investigate both jet and turbojet engines.
(6) Gross weight—as low as possible, commensurate with the desired characteristics.
(7) Fuel Requirements:
(a) Consideration will be given to the glide potential inherent in this type of aircraft.
(b) The MIL-C-5011A reserve fuel requirement will be waived for this mission. A 10% fuel reserve is considered adequate.
b. Navigation:
A non-emanating system capable of providing reasonably accurate navigation of the vehicle to the limit of its operating radius will be required. Equipment will be kept to a minimum. Consideration will be given to a ground position indicator system or an inertial system. A simple viewfinder will be provided to permit the pilot to fly a flight line.
c. Communication:
The weapon system should include a two-way communications system of the simplest UHF command type. No emanations from the aircraft will be permitted over enemy territory.
d. Armament:
No defensive armament will be required.
e. Data sensing elements:
The search mission will be accomplished with a tri-camera installation of 9" by 9" cameras of 6" focal length. The target analysis mission will utilize either one or two 9" by 18" format cameras of 36" focal length. Investigations will be con-

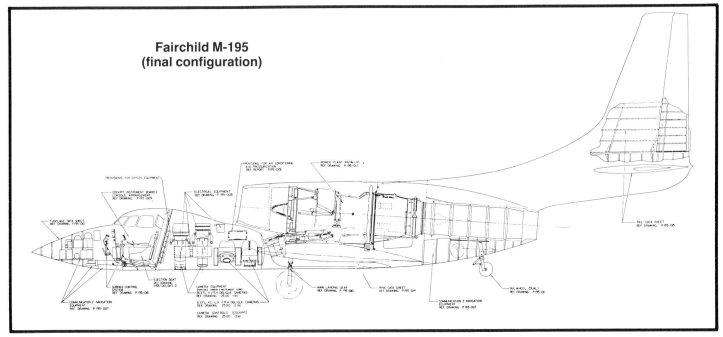

**Fairchild M-195
(final configuration)**

ducted to determine the feasibility of carrying cameras for the accomplishment of both target analysis and search missions, simultaneously.

f. Crew accommodations and escape:

(1) In addition to the normal pilot seating position, the prone pilot position will be investigated.

(2) The pilot must remain with the aircraft under any emergency condition at altitude, therefore, effective modes of fire extinguishing must be considered. No pilot ejection will be required.

(3) The weapon system should operate as automatically as possible to reduce the work load of the pilot.

(4) Pressurization and temperature control of the pilot and camera compartments is required.

g. Detectability:

Consideration will be given in the design of the vehicle to minimize the detectability by enemy radar.

3. Concept of Operations:

a. Employment:

The specialized aircraft weapon system will be operated over the target during the hours of daylight under good visibility conditions. It will provide a capability for conducting photographic reconnaissance missions, including search and target analysis. It will penetrate singly at optimum cruise speed to a target altitude of 70,000 feet or above.

b. Vulnerability:

(1) Base System:

The aircraft normally will operate from available bases considerably removed from enemy borders or front line action.

(2) In flight:

It is anticipated that the enemy will have limited methods of detection and/or interception of a vehicle of the required performance. The greatest opposition to the operation of this aircraft can be expected to be encountered from guided missiles.

4. Program Recommendations for Components and Complete system:

a. Time and cost estimates:

This study will determine the time and funds necessary for the various phases of development of the weapon system and for the complete weapon system to become operational.

b. Recommended sources:

The contractor will recommend sources of suitable powerplants for this type of aircraft.

Seaberg would later recall: "I immediately moved out on the preparation of the planning and program documentation we needed to get higher level support for starting a development effort which had been generated at the grass roots level. There was no AF requirement at the time. The first document I produced was a standard format paper stating the objectives, the approach, the payoff or potential value to the USAF and schedule/cost estimates. We requested $200,000 to contract for design studies. We talked to no one in industry until months later when we got positive reactions from the ARDC (Air Research and Development Command)."

Seaberg and Lamar, as was their prerogative, elected to avoid soliciting the major airframe manufacturers. The new project was expected to result in a very small production contract, at best, and it was assumed that a smaller company would give the new project a higher priority and would therefore produce a better end product, quicker. They also elected to avoid the pitfalls of bidding. Accordingly, they selected three relatively small airframe manufacturers and requested that representatives be sent to Wright Field in order to discuss the project (which had, by now, been assigned the MX-2147 designator under the classified code name of *Bald Eagle*). All three companies responded by sending representatives and on July 1, 1953, study contracts were let to each: Bell Aircraft Corporation (contract #AF33[616]-2160) of Niagara Falls, New York; Fairchild Aircraft Corporation (contract #AF33[616]-2182) of Hagerstown, Maryland; and Martin Aircraft Company (contract #AF33[600]-25825) of Baltimore, Maryland. The contracts were to run through December 31st.

"Bill Lamar and I talked it over and decided that we should not consider any of the larger primes (contractors) like Boeing, Convair, North American, Douglas, and Lockheed. But rather go to two of the smaller contractors because we did not envision large production and we felt we would get higher company priority out of Bell/Fairchild, who also had some very innovative engineers and had done things like it before. So we called each of the three contractors in and asked if they would be interested, which they were. We talked to no other contractors."

Only the Bell and Fairchild teams had been asked to submit proposals calling for the design and construction of a totally new aircraft. Martin,

in fact, had been asked to take their B-57 (which had been developed in Great Britain by the English Electric Company as the *Canberra* for RAF service) twin-engine attack bomber and examine the possibility of improving its already exceptional high-altitude performance (several stock B-57's were already in Air Force use as specialized recce aircraft flying "Sneaky Pete" missions in the Far East) through a major redesign effort. The stock B-57 was already a pressurized, readily adaptable high-altitude aircraft, and it conveniently resembled some of the early configuration sketches drawn by Seaberg while working on the original project requirements. Seaberg considered the B-57 option an interim, near-term solution to the mission problem, but not a complete panacea.

By January of 1954, the three companies had completed their studies and submitted them to Wright Field for evaluation. Martin had, as requested, developed a big-wing version of their B-57 under the in-house designator of Model 294; Fairchild had developed their single-engine M-195 design calling for an over-the-fuselage intake and a stub-boom mounting for vertical and horizontal tail surfaces; and Bell, under project chief Richard Smith, had devised their Model 67, a twin-engine, rather fragile-looking aircraft that was the essence of lightweight airframe design.

Although the powerplant type to be used in the new high-altitude design was undecided at the beginning of the studies, in-house research conducted by Pratt & Whitney under the auspices of the AF convinced the Wright Field engineering team reviewing the proposals that the new P&W J57 axial flow turbojet engine had the best potential for achieving the high-altitude performance required. Proposed modification to the stock J57 engine were expected to permit sustained operating thrusts 7% of the available sea level total at the desired cruising altitude. Though far from being an impressive figure, even by the standards of 1954, it was sufficient in the rarified atmosphere above the tropopause to keep any one of the three aircraft under consideration in sustained horizontal flight. Though other powerplants (i.e., the General Electric J73 and the Wright J67) would be considered during the course of the program study period, the Pratt & Whitney J57 was never seriously contested and all three design submissions listed it as the preferred powerplant (with high-altitude modifications, the original

The first RB-57D completed by the Martin Company was 53-3977. A total of twenty RB-57D's were built as interim aircraft to serve until the introduction of the U-2.

designation for the specific J57 model involved was the J57-P-19; later this designation would become J57-P-37).

By March of 1954, evaluation of the three contending designs had been completed by Seaberg and other engineers at Wright Field. Preparation of a detailed report with a recommendation calling for hardware procurement was then begun for submission to higher headquarters. The Martin and Bell proposals had been chosen as the two most suitable for the mission, with the former serving as an interim aircraft and the latter as the long-term operational type. Fairchild's proposal was never in serious contention.

Seaberg would later recall the decision making process as follows: "I had the data evaluated by the Wright Field labs during January-March 1954. I prepared an analysis, picked Martin and Bell as preferred, wrote an abbreviated development plan, and prepared a concise briefing for the higher headquarters."

In mid-March, Lt. Col. Joseph Pelligrini, attached to a reconnaissance unit at Air Research and Development Command headquarters, visited Wright Field and met with Seaberg and several of his aides. Pelligrini was impressed with the on-going high-altitude recce airplane program, but felt that the delays involved with the design and development of a totally new airplane could be more easily rationalized if acquisition and service integration of an interim aircraft could be expedited. The proposed B-57 modification, by now tentatively referred to as the B-57D, appealed to Pelligrini and during his visit he recommended that Seaberg send a list of necessary B-57 modifications to ARDC headquarters in no more than seven days following their meeting. Pelligrini felt that the proposed B-57 modification could provide a fast way of meeting the urgent Air Force intelligence need in Europe.

The following month, Seaberg flew to ARDC headquarters in Baltimore, Maryland and gave a briefing to Air Force commanders on the three aircraft studies. Among those attending was Lt. Gen. Thomas S. Power who had just succeeded Lt. Gen. Donald Putt as ARDC commander. Powers was impressed by Seaberg's presentation and requested that he give the same briefing at Strategic Air Command headquarters in Omaha, Nebraska, the following day.

This presentation, too, generated serious interest and it was now apparent to Seaberg that he was gaining strong support for his project and that it had a good chance of proceeding to the hardware stage if political and technological pitfalls could be tactfully avoided. In May of 1954, Seaberg was again asked to make a presentation, this time to Air Force headquarters in Washington, D.C.

Following the Washington presentation, Seaberg received immediate approval to forge ahead with the B-57D program and tentative approval to consummate the Bell Model 67. The latter, because it was a totally new aircraft and therefore in need of significantly more time for development, was temporarily delayed while further

studies were conducted.

On May 18, 1954, some two weeks after returning from Washington, a new proposal for a high-altitude cruise aircraft, from Lockheed's well-known advanced design bureau chief, Clarence L. "Kelly" Johnson, arrived on Seaberg's desk for review. The birth of one of the world's most politically and historically significant aircraft was about to take place.

"Kelly" Johnson, even in 1954, was one of the few aerospace engineers in the business who truly could lay claim to being a legend in his own time. His design talent was well known throughout the aerospace industry and defense department, and his work on such exceptional Lockheed aircraft as the P-38, F-80, Constellation, and Mach 2-capable F-104, to name just a few, was without peer.

It therefore came as no great surprise to Seaberg and his fellow Wright Field staffers when a proposal from Johnson was placed on his desk. Johnson, as it were, had acquired the confidence of many high ranking military personnel and he was accustomed to dealing with them at all levels of the bureaucracy. It was almost inevitable that one would take the liberty of telling him about the classified high-altitude recce airplane program that was quickly developing at Wright Field.

Seaberg had, in fact, known of Johnson's proposal (Lockheed Report No. 9732) for several weeks prior to its arrival in his office. Word had been passed that Johnson was extremely interested in the program and thus Seaberg had expected a submission from Lockheed in due course. Seaberg's recollection of the Johnson submission's arrival was, "It descended to my level when I got it in the mail on 18 May 1954 requesting my evaluation. You can see from this timing, that in the preceding month I had briefed three levels of General officers and received their approval to proceed with my recommended program."

Seaberg and his fellow Wright Field engineers spent three weeks evaluating the Johnson proposal. Known under the company designator of CL-282, it consisted of a slightly-modified early-configuration XF-104 fuselage and associated vertical and horizontal tail surfaces, and a large span very-high-aspect-ratio wing. Fuel was to be carried in four wing tanks and one fuselage tank together providing a total capacity of 925 gallons. The powerplant was to be a General Electric J73-GE-3 non-afterburning turbojet engine with a sea level static thrust of 9,300 lbs. In a serious break from the norm, which was always a distinctive trait of Johnson aircraft designs, the CL-282 did away with conventional landing gear. Early in his design effort Johnson had concluded that the proposed aircraft would be extremely weight sensitive and accordingly, he elected to exorcise the landing gear completely. Though his solution to the gear problem was not new, it was fairly novel for jet powered aircraft—two skis would replace the conventional landing gear and a jettisonable wheeled dolly would be used for take-off.

Other features of the CL-282 included an unpressurized single-seat cockpit and a 600 pound sensor system payload. The latter was to be carried in a 15-cubic foot bay behind the cockpit. The wingspan was 70' 8", the length was 44' 0", and the wing area was 500 sq. ft. Maximum altitude capability was estimated to be just over 70,000' with payload, and range was estimated to be approximately 2,000 miles.

Other important CL-282 specifications included: a horizontal tail area of 47.5 sq. ft.; a vertical tail area of 34.7 sq. ft.; a wing aspect ratio of 10; a horizontal tail aspect ratio of 2.98; a vertical tail aspect ratio of 1.10; a wing taper ratio of .25; a horizontal tail taper ratio of .31; a vertical tail taper ratio of .50; a wing root chord of 136"; a horizontal tail root chord of 73"; a vertical tail root chord of 112.5"; a wing tip chord of 34"; a horizontal tail tip chord of 22.7"; and vertical tail tip chord of 43". The wing root section was a NACA 64A409 with an incidence of plus 3-deg.; the wing tip section was a NACA 64A406 with an incidence of plus 1-deg.; and the tail surfaces had a NACA 64A008 section.

Seaberg and his Wright Field engineering team rejected Johnson's CL-282 submission for several reasons, not the least of which was his powerplant choice. The J73 was an unknown (and eventually, unsuccessful) powerplant, and its capabilities at altitude were considered limited. Because of the tremendous thrust losses suffered by turbojet powerplants at the cruising altitude being proposed for the new recce aircraft, it was determined by Seaberg and his associates that the J73's thrust loss would be too great to provide the performance required. They strongly supported use of the Pratt & Whitney J57 in any contending high altitude aircraft design and because of this, they felt that the CL-282 was unsuitable for consideration. Additionally, the configuration as submitted by Johnson could not easily be enlarged to accommodate the preferred J57-P-37. Seaberg would later summarize the evaluation team's position as follows: "The evaluation letter I wrote (in late June 1954) did recommend not buying the Johnson design. As far as I know, this position was accepted all the way up the line to the Gen. Putt level."

When the Air Force, upon Seaberg's recommendation, turned down Johnson's CL-282 proposal, Johnson did not give up. In fact, further development of the project as an in-house Lockheed study continued unabated inside the confines of the obscure advanced development projects facility at the Burbank, California plant while Johnson scurried around Washington, D.C. drumming up support for the CL-282 at all levels of the Pentagon—and, as it turned out, elsewhere.

Elsewhere, of course, was the Central Intelligence Agency (CIA). There, Johnson met with Dr. Joe Charyk, who was the main operative in charge of programs such as the high-altitude recce airplane project now being generated under the auspices of the Air Force. Johnson's timing was decidedly perfect as numerous intelligence sources had begun to input data into the US intelligence community indicating that the Soviet Union was moving quickly toward the completion and flight test of an extensive family of liquid fueled, nuclear warhead-bearing, ballistic-capable missiles. There was great concern in the Department of Defense and the various security agencies concerning this new development and it became a priority of the utmost urgency to obtain information concerning the new missiles.

As a fall-out over this great fear of new developments behind the Iron Curtain, the Department of Defense, with President Eisenhower approving, took the mid-1954 initiative of forming a number of advisory groups to examine the various aspects of military planning and weapons both here in the US and around the world. James R. Killian, then president of the Massachusetts Institue of Technology, became chairman of one of these committees, which was saddled with the responsibility of determining the possibility of a surprise attack by the Soviets. Thanks to the efforts of a peripheral intelligence panel, the Killian Committee was soon introduced to the Air Force's new high-altitude recce airplane program and shortly thereafter, on November 18, 1954, was briefed by Seaberg on the four contending configurations proposed by Bell, Fairchild, Lockheed, and Martin.

The Seaberg briefing took place in the DoD office of Lt. Gen. Donald Putt, Air Force deputy chief of staff for development. Seaberg recalls that he was not introduced to the 15 or so distinguished scientists making up the majority of the Killian Committee, but he recalls that there were a number of prominent faces in the crowd. "Nobody announced who they were (tight security measures were really starting to close down). But from the technical questions I got I could tell there were aerodynamicists, propulsion, optics or camera, and other experts in the group. Dr. Edwin Land may have been there, but I really met him as an individual much later (1957 or 1958). This group was aware of Johnson's (CL-282) proposal by the time of this meeting. What I did was present the results of my comparative analysis of all four designs. I showed the relative high altitude performance capabilities of all four. I pointed out that aerodynamically the Bell, Fairchild, and Lockheed designs were close. Martin's B-57, being a modification, was not quite as capable. I stated that, in my opinion, the J73 would not be good enough to do the job in Johnson's airplane. And further, I overlaid a curve showing that with the J57 installed, it would then be competitive with the Bell and Fairchild designs."

Because of Johnson's ability to move freely within the confines of the Department of Defense (DoD) and intelligence communities, his contact with the CIA's Charyk proved an important foot in the door during the critical decision making period that led to the high-altitude recce airplane program hardware contract. While work on the Bell Model 37 and RB-57D programs moved ahead rapidly under the direction of the Air Force, Charyk and CIA director Allen Dulles saw, with a little prompting from Johnson, that Lockheed's CL-282 proposal had merit and might, indeed, prove to be an exceptional sensor system platform on its own if mated with the proper powerplant. They also concluded that a far more clandestine intelligence community effort might be more appropriate than the Air Force's and that a diversionary program, in the form of the Model 67, might not hurt the intelligence community's proposed project. The latter, to all intents and purposes, offered the same intelligence gathering capability with substantially less red tape.

The Killian Committee was not long in being convinced that the Lockheed aircraft, with a change in powerplant, was ideal for the proposed mission. Johnson, by that time, had agreed to completely redesign his CL-282 and incorporate the recommended J57 powerplant. Conveniently, a decision to uprate the F-104 to the new General Electric J79 was also in the mill in the Lockheed advanced development projects office at this time, and though the J79 and J57 were not related in any way, the redesign of the F-104's fuselage laid the groundwork for the redesign of the J57-powered CL-282.

Johnson's CL-282 design team consisted of some twenty-three select engineers including his immediate assistant design chief, Dick Boehme.

The team operated out of a small facility within the confines of Lockheed's Burbank, California plant. Nicknamed the "Skunk Works" after Hairless Joe's foul smelling Dogpatch Kickapoo Joy Juice factory in the Al Capp Li'l Abner comic strip that appeared regularly in newspapers around the world for almost half a century (Al Capp referred to it as the "Skonk Works;" Lockheed has since trademarked the name Skunk Works to avoid a conflict of interest with the Al Capp title) the operation had been in existence as Lockheed's advanced design projects office since the days of the company's P-80. Low key and ruled absolutely by Johnson, the "Skunk Works" was (and still is) one of the most efficient in-house design and production plants in the US.

The Killian Committee's opinion was soon delivered to Secretary of Defense Charles Wilson and Central Intelligence Agency Director Allen Dulles. In late November, convinced of the merits of the program, Wilson and Dulles decided to brief President Eisenhower. Eisenhower would later recall, "Back in November 1954, Foster Dulles, Charlie Wilson, Al Dulles, and other advisors had come to me to get authorization to go ahead on a program to produce twenty special high-performance aircraft at a total cost of about $35-million. A good deal of design and development work had already been done. I approved this action."

At this time, Charyk brought Richard Bissell, an economist who had taught at both Yale and MIT, in to direct the CIA side of the new program. Bissell recalls, "Towards the end of November (1954), I was summoned one afternoon into Allen's (Dulles) office and I was told, with absolutely no prior warning or knowledge, that one day previously President Eisenhower had approved a project involving the development of an extremely high-altitude aircraft to be used for surveillance and intelligence collection over "denied" areas in Europe, Russia and elsewhere. And Allen, after perhaps 15 minutes of explanation of the background of this undertaking told me that in half an hour I was to go over to the Pentagon and present myself in Trevor Gardner's (Under Secretary of the Air Force for Research and Development) office. When I arrived, Trevor Gardner, Gen. Don Putt, Gen. Irvine, and several others were already there. We were to decide, between us, how the project was to be organized and run. My most vivid recollection of this meeting is of the telephone call put through at the end by Trevor Gardner to Kelly (Johnson) in which he gave him

a go-ahead on a program to develop and produce 20 aircraft."

Eisenhower had agreed that the funding and direction of the project, soon to be code-named Aquatone, would be through the offices of the CIA with Richard Bissell selected to head it. Though some Air Force money was to be utilized in the acquisition of J57 powerplants for the program, the service's main job (with Jean Kiefer working under Bissel as the chief liaison between the service and the Agency) initially would be to act as a front for the Agency and contract with Lockheed for development of the aircraft. The special engines would be mixed in with a contract for conventional J57's ordered to power Boeing B-52's, North American F-100's, and Convair F-102's. Because of the sensitivity of the project, the Air Force would handle its part directly from headquarters.

At a later date, it was expected that the Air Force would absorb U-2's into its inventory, these coming both directly from the Lockheed production line, and also from the CIA inventory. Additionally, a decision was also made to create cover publicity by releasing information stating that the aircraft had been developed as a high-altitude research tool for use primarily by the National Advisory Committee for Aeronautics (NACA).

Funding for the new aircraft, the contract for which was signed on December 9, 1954, was to come from a secret CIA special reserve fund. Eventually, some $54-million was allocated, with $8-million being returned by Lockheed following a 15% underrun (yet another example of Kelly Johnson's masterful program directorship).

On November 9, 1954, Trevor Gardner visited with Lockheed President Robert Gross and Kelly Johnson at Lockheed's Burbank, California facility. Following a review of the full-scale U-2 mock-up, Gardner gave them official confirmation of project approval. As both parties knew that Bell's Model 67 (by now officially designated X-16 as a cover by the Air Force) program was moving ahead rapidly, it was agreed that the completion date and first flight of the new Lockheed aircraft would have to be expedited. Johnson promised that the first aircraft would be in the air no less than eight months after the first metal was cut. Finished drawings were already rolling from Lockheed drawing boards and actual construction of the first aircraft was scheduled to begin in early January. "Kelly's Angel," as the new aircraft would soon be called, had just taken wing.

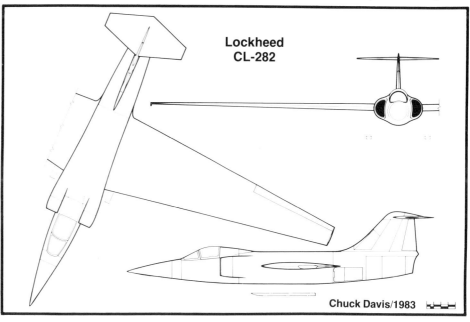

Lockheed
CL-282

Chuck Davis/1983

RB-57D's, such as 53-3972, were extensively modified on several occasions during the course of their respective operational careers. General Dynamics' Fort Worth division accommodated many of these modification programs and later developed the related, but almost totally new, RB-57F.

One-fiftieth scale Bell X-16 model gives a good impression of this aircraft's twin-engine design and its impressive high-aspect-ratio wing. Wing-tip placement of pogos was later discarded in favor of a mid-wing locatin. Runway considerations dictated the change.

Chapt. 2:
THE UNKNOWN CONTENDERS

As has already been mentioned prominently in the preceding chapters, three other companies had developed aircraft design studies for consideration in the Seaberg-conceived Air Force high-altitude recce airplane program prior to the birth of the Lockheed U-2. Due to the extensive publicity generated by the U-2 program over the years since its first service introduction, little has been published concerning these three aircraft. What follows then, is an abbreviated account of each:

FAIRCHILD M-195

The Fairchild M-195 proposal, which would soon prove to be the least attractive of the three submissions, was the end result of parametric design studies that had encompassed everything from subsonic turboprop high-aspect-ratio wing configurations to rocket and ramjet powered supersonic deltas. Through a conventional process of elimination and a thorough study of the original John Seaberg specifications, a jet-powered high-aspect ratio wing configuration was chosen, much along the lines of the two other contenders. Fairchild's process of design option elimination was officially reduced via the following steps:

1. General Configuration Study—was initiated to determine the optimum configuration for the desired mission and to determine the maximum altitude obtainable. Supersonic configurations were eliminated after a very cursory examination because the design and development time required would exceed the 1956 operational date.

2. A very preliminary analysis resulted in narrowing the spread of wing loadings to 10–30 lbs. per sq. ft. The remaining configurations were analyzed for two J57 powerplants at 65,000' altitude to further narrow the field.

3. As a result of the above analysis the field was narrowed by elimination of swept wings and aspect ratios of 6.0. Altitudes were tied down to 65,000' for any J57 installation (absolute max. altitude was 67,200' full nominal rated power). The best powerplant selection of J67, J73, and J57 tied in at this point. Further analysis of the remaining configurations were with J57 and J67 powerplants.

4. The final airplane was chosen with area and aspect ratios selected by a point of diminishing returns. Construction weight v/s aerodynamic gains made the final determination. The wing thickness/chord ratio was set by aerodynamics, performance, and stall pattern. The basic design based on the J57 was due to the design requirements; but alternate powerplants considered were the J67 and the J73. The two-engine aircraft was eliminated even though it could perform the mission as well as the single engine. This was because it resulted in a considerably larger and heavier design.

Estimated performance of the M-195 was as follows:

SEA LEVEL

Take-off distance ground roll	809'
Total take-off distance over 50'	1,112'
Structural limit speed at take-off wt.	150 kts.
Stall speed at take-off weight	65 kts.
Rate of climb at nominal rated power	5,008'/min
Landing distance ground roll	688'
Total Landing distance over 50'	2,006'
Structural limit speed mission landing weight	90 kts.
Stall speed mission landing weight	52 kts.

35,000 FT.

Rate of climb at nominal rated power	3,188'/min.
Structural limit speed	269 kts.

65,000 FT.

Rate of climb at military rated power initial cruise weight	137'/min.
Rate of climb at nominal rated power average cruise weight	178'/min.
Cruise speed	398 kts.
Glide potential from 65,000'	232 n.mi.
Maximum radius attainable	1,500 n.mi.

Structurally, the M-195 was fairly conventional. Both the airframe and external structure was aluminum, and all internal electrical and environmental control systems were stock items. The sensor system bay was located behind the single-ejection-seat-equipped pressurized cockpit, and all communications and navigation equipment was located in the nose. The normal sensor system bay complement consisted of two Fairchild 36" EFL (equivalent focal length) oblique cameras and two 6" EFL oblique cameras. The landing gear was somewhat unconventional consisting of a steerable aft-fuselage tail-wheel arrangement and two mains that retracted into the wings. The wings were equipped with a gust relief system that elevated the flaps and ailerons to a positive trailing edge attitude (see U-2 technical description). Aircraft weight was critical and the following M-195 summary breaks down the weight by group:

Wing group	2,623 lbs.
Tail group	418 lbs.
Body group	1,232 lbs.
Alighting gear group	500 lbs.
Main gear	(425 lbs.)
Tail gear	(75 lbs.)
Surface controls group	225 lbs.
Propulsion group	4,550 lbs.
Engine (P&W JT3-J)	(3,920 lbs.)
Engine aux. systems	(630 lbs.)
Instruments & navigation	80 lbs.
Electrical group	175 lbs.
Electronics group	150 lbs.
Furnishings & equipment	280 lbs.
Air conditioning group	200 lbs.
Photographic group	480 lbs.
Estimated contingencies	30 lbs.
Total weight empty	10,943 lbs.
Useful load	8,073 lbs.
Crew weight	(300 lbs.)
Fuel weight	(7,728 lbs.)
Oil weight	(45 lbs.)
Gross weight	19,016 lbs.

The powerplant installation was perhaps the most unconventional design aspect of the aircraft. The installation itself, incorporating a dorsal intake behind the cockpit, permitted the intake and exhaust duct lengths to be kept at a minimum, thus providing the most efficient utilization of available thrust. Less important, but of some significance, was the fact that the engine arrangement permitted short pressurization ducts to the cockpit and sensor system compartment thus lowering their weight and improving their efficiency.

The M-195 mission profile called for an initial ascent to 61,100' at 150 kts over a distance of 139 miles. The slow climb to 65,000' would then take another 161 miles at which time the aircraft

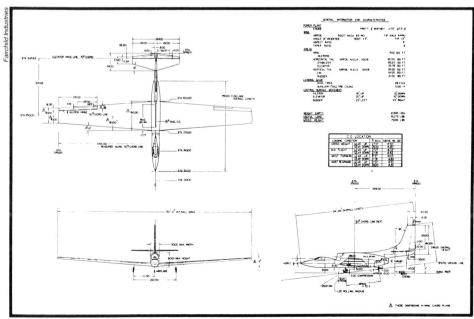

Fairchild Industries

Fairchild's M-195 was the least attractive of the initial three contenders in the Air Force's MX-2147 program.

RB-57D's were some of the first Air Force aircraft to be equipped with roll-control and lift-dumping spoilers. All but the first six aircraft were equipped with inflight refueling receptacles.

The fact that the majority of the RB-57D's built were inflight refuelable has rarely been documented. Note extended spoiler on starboard wing.

would level off and cruise for the following 1,200 miles to its target. Cruise speed at 65,000' was expected to be 390 kts. The return to base would be at the cruising altitude and a spiraling descent would begin as near to the home base as desired. Weight at the time of return to base would be 12,106 lbs.

Though the Fairchild design was a viable approach to the high-altitude recce aircraft requirement, it was definitely not as capable as the design being offered by Bell, nor less risky than the B-57 modification being offered by Martin. Accordingly, it was shelved and contracts were let to the Bell and Martin teams.

MARTIN RB-57D

As mentioned earlier, the Martin company had been approached by Seaberg and Lamar with the idea of building an interim high-altitude recce aircraft to fill the gap that would exist until the definitive X-16 could enter the inventory. In order to expedite construction and flight testing of this interim design, it had been proposed that an off-the-shelf type be modified to the high-altitude recce configuration. Ideally, the type chosen would be an aircraft that would involve the least amount of work to accomplish the mission objectives. A thorough analysis of available configuratoins quickly narrowed the choices down to one— the Martin B-57. Having a commodious fuselage and already possessing an exceptional high-altitude performance, the B-57 was an ideal platform for the modification program the Wright Field team had in mind.

Following Pelligrini's initiative, on June 21, 1954, the USAF under the highly classified "Black Knight" program directed the Air Material Command to procure six Martin Model 294 aircraft. These were new aircraft utilizing the basic fuselage design of the stock B-57A configuration. Two 10,000 lb. thrust J57-P-9 turbojet engines were utilized in place of the stock J65-W-5's, and the stock wings of 64' 0'' span were replaced by totally new wings with a span of 106' 0'' (107' 6'' with wing-tip sensor pods) and a gross wing area of 1,500 sq. ft. The wings were also equipped with internal fuel tanks and there were attachment points in order to accommodate leading edge sensor pods.

The Martin Model 294 was officially designated B-57D on September 29, 1954, and in April of 1955, it became the RB-57D. Three versions of the RB-57D were eventually built. The initial program, calling for six Model 294 aircraft was

increased to 20 in early 1955. The original six, plus seven of the additional 14, were single-seat RB-57D's. These aircraft were equipped with two K-38 and two KC-1 split vertical cameras and accommodations were available for more refined sensors as specific missions required. This sensor gear was located in the space normally occupied by the second crew member, behind the pilot.

The single RB-57D-1, which was the first Model 796, was equipped with an AN/APQ-56 hi-resolution, side-looking radar for day or night radar mapping reconnaissance. It also was a single-seat aircraft.

The remaining six aircraft, known as RB-57D-2's, and also Model 796's, carried a crew of two (the backseater being an "EWO," or electronics warfare officer) and served as dedicated ELINT/ SIGINT (electronics intelligence/signal intelligence) types optimized for the classified ferret mission. Martin undertook the development of this gear, which was designated the Model 320 or SAFE (Semi-Automatic Ferret Equipment) equipment. It was tested during 1956 and 1957 under the *Blue Tail Fly Project* and following this, was placed on operational status and utilized routinely.

All but the first six RB-57D's had inflight refueling capability which was necessitated by the type's limited endurance of approximately 5 hours. The receptacle was mounted on top of the fuselage, just behind the cockpit canopy. The aircraft was refueled by KC-97 tankers.

Curiously, Martin's in-house model designation system did not follow a conventional pattern. The first six aircraft, for instance, were known as Model 294's and were designated RB-57D's. The Model 744 series aircraft which basically consisted of a second batch of seven RB-57D's, were essentially the same as the first six machines. And finally, the Model 796 designator applied to a final batch of seven aircraft which included the six RB-57D-2's and the single RB-57D-1.

Flight testing of the first RB-57D's to roll from the Martin production line took place during late 1955 and early 1956. Because of the urgency of the program for which the aircraft were built, only a limited flight test program was possible. Initially, the immense wing caused serious problems; the wing spar was found to be prone to fatigue cracking and had to be strengthened; and a similar

condition, and corrective action, affected certain wing panels. Additionally, the Martin-developed honeycomb wing skin construction suffered from a problem related to water seepage and wing stress.

The first of the RB-57D aircraft was delivered to SAC under *Project Black Knight* in March of 1956. Two Strategic Fighter Squadrons, the 31st and 508th, furnished the majority of the pilots (most of the senior captains, the majors, and the lt. cols. were from SAC B-47 units) making up the newly formed 4080th Strategic Reconnaissance Wing (formed April 1, 1956). Its 4025th Strategic Reconnaissance Squadron was assigned the RB-57D, which by the summer of 1956, was training crews at Turner AFB, Georgia following a move from Lockbourne AFB, Ohio, and the arrival of a training RB-57C (53-3842). Some four months after activation at Turner AFB, the 4025th made its first deployment. Under *Operation Sea Lion,* a portion of the 4025th set up an Operating Location (OL) at Yokota AFB, Japan, for one year. Another OL was established briefly at Eilson AFB, Alaska in the fall of 1956.

The majority of the missions flown by RB-57D's during *Operation Sea Lion* were of the ELINT/ SIGINT and sampling variety. The former consisted of the collection of communications and electromagnetic energy data, and the latter, of the collection of airborne particulates related to nuclear weapons testing. The objects of this intense surveillance were various targets in Communist China, and several nuclear test sites inside the borders of the Soviet Union.

The last of the twenty RB-57D's ordered was accepted by the Air Force in March of 1957 and no further production was undertaken. Following a move from Turner AFB to Laughlin AFB, Texas in February of 1957, the 4025th, from March through August of 1958, flew air sampling flights from the Eniwetok Proving Grounds on the Marshall Islands. In early-1959 under the auspices of *Operation Bordertown,* they were deployed to Europe in order to undertake ELINT/SIGINT and sampling missions. In mid-1959, following its return to Laughlin AFB, the 4025th was inactivated, and its RB-57D's were dispersed to units in Germany, at Kirtland AFB, the NASA, and various units including the 4677th DSES (Defense Systems Evaluation Squadron) and the 4677th RES (Radar Evaluation Squadron). It should be noted that before deactivation the 4025th served as the training unit for Nationalist Chinese RB-57D pilots (more information concerning this activity is provided later in this book).

In 1963, the wing fatigue problem that had plagued the RB-57D at the beginning of this program reappeared and all remaining aircraft were grounded. An extensive modification program to a select few RB-57D-2's in 1966 resulted in the EB-57D configuration, this model serving as an electronic countermeasures target until the type was permanently removed from the inventory in 1970.

Following retirement, the EB-57D's were flown to Davis-Monthan AFB and there placed in temporary storage alongside the remaining RB-57D aircraft (as a point of interest it should be mentioned that the RB-57D series aircraft had an excellent safety record, none are known to have been lost to enemy action—with the possible exception of Nationalist Chinese-operated aircraft—and none were lost during training sorties; at least four aircraft were eventually written off due to accidents, but none of these caused a fatality). By 1973, the majority of the aircraft that had not been converted to the RB-57F configuration had been scrapped, and only one is known to have been saved for museum display purposes.

All RB-57D's manufactured are listed below:

General Dynamics

During <u>Operation Bordertown</u>, most RB-57D's were painted in an unusual white-on-black camouflage pattern with the upper surfaces off-white and the lower surfaces (and vertical fin) flat black.

Serial No.	Build Sequence	Designation	Subsequent Use
53-3963	14	RB-57D-1	unknown
53-3964	15	RB-57D-2	to 4677th DSES 8-11-66
53-3965	16	RB-57D-2	to 4677th DSES 6-12-61
53-3966	17	RB-57D-2	to 4677th DSES 6-26-61
53-3967	18	RB-57D-2	to 4677th DSES 7-3-61
53-3968	19	RB-57D-2	to 4677th DSES 7-6-61
53-3969	20	RB-57D-2	to 4677th DSES 7-17-61
53-3970	7	RB-57D	mod'ed to RB-57F (63-13502)
53-3971	8	RB-57D	to 4677th DSES 5-13-60
53-3972	9	RB-57D	mod'ed to RB-57F (63-13500)
53-3973	10	RB-57D	unknown
53-3974	11	RB-57D	mod'ed to RB-57F (63-13503)
53-3975	12	RB-57D	mod'ed to RB-57F (63-13501)
53-3976	13	RB-57D	unknown
53-3977	1	RB-57D	to 4677th RES 11-30-59
53-3978	2	RB-57D	unknown
53-3979	3	RB-57D	unknown
53-3980	4	RB-57D	to 4677th RES 12-8-59
53-3981	5	RB-57D	to 4677th RES 9-6-61
53-3982	6	RB-57D	to 4677th RES 12-2-59

BELL X-16

Bell's response to the high-altitude recce airplane program had proved to be the winning design among the three configurations initially submitted. Under the direction of chief project engineer Richard Smith, the Bell design team, operating inside a special tent-like structure at Bell's Niagara Falls, New York plant, had created a delicate configuration that offered cruise-altitude performance potential far beyond any aircraft then flying or known to be on the drawing boards. Known in-house at Bell as the Model 67 and officially designated X-16 by the Air Force, the new aircraft came to life in May of 1954 following official program approval. Contract signing took place in September and eighteen months were estimated to be necessary for prototype completion. The serial numbers allocated by the Air Force, 56-552 to 56-579, called for a total of 28 aircraft.

The X-16 design effort had resulted in an extremely light high-aspect-ratio wing configuration offering twin-engine safety and a cruising altitude in excess of 70,000'. In order to conserve weight, a light weight zero-track bicycle landing gear arrangement was created that involved the services of two outrigger gear for balancing.

Power was to be provided by two Pratt & Whitney J57-P-31 turbojet engines with modifications for improved high-altitude performance. Early in the program it was shown that at throttle cruise settings, these engines would develop 743 lbs. thrust at 65,000'. Thrust losses would increase at higher altitudes and it was therefore a significant challenge for the Bell team to keep the total aerodynamic drag penalty down to twice the single-engine thrust figure. It was proposed that the J57-P-37 be installed in the prototype aircraft, but cancellation of the program curtailed this exercise.

The airframe and structure of the X-16 were significantly more flexible than those of other military aircraft then in service. This was the end result of stringent weight restrictions which had been levied in consideration of the serious negative effect excess weight had on the aircraft altitude and range performance. With an extremely low structural dynamic capability, the X-16 was rated at plus-3 and minus-1 g's during maneuvering flight. The wing, because of its flexibility, was predicted to suffer from aeroelastic divergence as it reached critical Mach number, and in order to negate this, a quarter-chord sweep angle of 15-degrees was incorporated and the ailerons were moved inboard from the wingtips. These "aero-isoclinic" solutions were thought to be effective, but concern that the full-scale aircraft might encounter difficulties remained high throughout the program.

Though the X-16 was designed to be inflight refuelable, its unrefueled range was an impressive 3,300 miles. Mission radius was 1,500 miles and its camera system, consisting of two KA-1 or K-38 12" EFL search cameras, and two KA-1 or K-38 36" EFL target analysis cameras, could photo everything in a path that was 50 miles wide and up to 795 miles long.

Modifications to the J57's were extensive, but subtle. The compressor section was built to extremely close tolerances in order to improve its efficiency and minimize compressor section leakage, the hydraulic pump was uprated, the engine accessory box was changed, the oil cooler was uprated, the oil ring cooler was uprated, the starter was modified, and the alternator and constant speed drives were uprated. All of these changes were made in order to improve the engine's dependability at high-altitude. Static sea level thrust performance remained essentially unaffected.

The X-16 was equipped with an upward ejection seat, a pressurized cockpit (comp. press. 7.5 or 4.5 psi), pressurized sensor system bays (comp. press. 1.25 psi), a periscopic sextant, a standby magnetic compass, a photographic navigation viewfinder, a control stick (not a yoke), an ARN-6 receiver, a liquid oxygen converter, a jettisonable hinged canopy, UHF and IFF systems, and an APN-79 doppler radar navigation system.

David Anderton collection

The fatigue life of the RB-57D was originally estimated to be less than a thousand hours. The original wing design was a simple single-spar configuration not initially designed for a long life or high dynamic loads ("high-Q"). Though there were no fatal accidents attributable to the spar problem, several aircraft, such as this one, were permanently removed from the inventory when their wings separated following landing.

The weight statement for the X-16 was as follows:

Wing	6,375 lbs.
Tail	874 lbs.
Fuselage	1,809 lbs.
Landing gear	1,845 lbs.
Surface controls	573 lbs.
Engine nacelles	1,026 lbs.
Engine and fuel system	8,598 lbs.
Fixed equipment	2,266 lbs.
Photographic equipment and controls	389 lbs.
Crew	230 lbs.
Liquid oxygen	21 lbs.
Fuel (1,860 gallons)	12,080 lbs.
Oil	150 lbs.
Empty weight	23,330 lbs.
Landing weight (approx. 25% fuel)	27,000 lbs.
Gross weight	36,200 lbs.

Dimensional and miscellaneous data for the X-16 included the following:

Length	60' 10.3"
Height	16' 6.9"
Wingspan	114' 10"
Horiz. tail span	20' 8.2"
Wing area (including ailerons)	1,100 sq.'
Aileron area	43.3 sq.'
Wing root airfoil section	NACA 64-210.5
Wing tip airfoil section	NACA 64-206
Wing mean aerodynamic chord	119.16
Wing incidence (root & tip)	0-deg.
Wing sweepback (@ 25% chord)	15-deg.
Wing dihedral	neg. 2-deg.
Wing aspect ratio	12
Wing loading (@ gross wt.)	32.9 lbs./sq.'
Wing loading (@ landing wt.)	24.5 lbs./sq.'
Vert. tail area	95 sq.'
Vert. fin area	68 sq.'
Rudder area	27 sq.'
Vert. fin sweepback (@ 25% chord)	35-deg.
Vertical fin airfoil section	NACA 64A-006
Horiz. tail area	110 sq.'
Horiz. stabilizer area	88 sq.'
Elevator area	21 sq.'
Horiz. tail incidence (root & tip)	neg. 4.5-deg.
Horiz. tail sweepback (@ 25% chord)	25-deg.
Horiz. tail dihedral	10-deg.
Horiz. tail aspect ratio	4
Horiz. tail airfoil section	NACA 64A-006

Construction of the first aircraft got underway in September of 1954, and during the following twelve months, progressed smoothly. In the meantime, unknown to the Bell hierarchy, two things had happened in Washington that would greatly affect the future of the X-16. The first, and perhaps most important, was that, independent of the Air Force, the Central Intelligence Agency had become enamored with the idea of surreptitious high-altitude overflights of unfriendly territory in order to gather intelligence data; and the second was that Lockheed's inimitable Kelly Johnson had gotten wind of the high-altitude recce aircraft program and had decided to develop a responding proposal.

Though both events were covered in more detail elsewhere in this book, it is germane to the history of the X-16 to mention that the CIA's involvement eventually caused its demise. An initial decision on the part of the CIA to fund its own high-altitude recce aircraft in the form of the Lockheed Model 282 in parallel with the Air Force's X-16, following a series of briefings relating to both projects, would soon cause the Air Force to step out of the picture and leave the high-altitude recce program in CIA hands. Once the decision to turn over the Air Force mission had taken place, the X-16's purpose was eliminated and the program was cancelled; there simply was no sense in spending money on two aircraft designed for the same mission—particularly when one, the U-2, was already flying.

The death of the X-16 occurred in October of 1955, some two months after the prototype U-2 had taken to the air for the first time. It was a serious economic blow to Bell, and one from which the company would not soon recover. Though a relatively small contract, the X-16 had been important to Bell's economic future at a time when the company had few other major projects in the mill. To this very day, many Bell employees involved in the X-16 program remain bitter that the aircraft was so hurriedly, and mercilessly, terminated.

X-16 full-scale mock-up was virtually complete when this photo was taken in mid-1954. Size of the wing prevented its being completed in mock-up form.

Full-scale mock-up of engine nacelle, with full scale J57 mock-up inside, was built alongside X-16 fuselage mock-up.

Actual X-16 aluminum wing panel is evidence that construction of aircraft was progressing smoothly at the time of program cancellation.

Chapt. 3:
KELLY'S ANGEL

In November of 1954, with the new recce aircraft approved for production, Johnson and a small team of about fifty engineers began putting in 100-hour weeks in order to meet the promised 8-month first flight date deadline. From a design standpoint, the new aircraft was technologically demanding. Because of the extraordinary cruise altitude requirement, weight and drag became the overriding design considerations. Every facet of the airframe, structure, and external shell design was governed by its relationship to the basic empty weight of the aircraft and its total drag at cruising altitude.

Among the unique weight-related accomplishments of the design program were the following: wing weight was kept to an almost unbelievable 4 lbs. per sq. ft.; the landing gear was a bicycle arrangement with the heaviest component consisting of a single main strut (jettisonable pogos mounted mid-span on each wing were provided for balance); the tail assembly was attached at the empennage section to the fuselage by only three bolts; the side-opening canopy was manually opened and closed; the control system was unboosted; hydraulically actuated systems were kept to the bare essentials; there was no cockpit pressurization; and the pilot emergency egress system was manual—there was no ejection seat.

The Agency had agreed to the acquisition of an initial batch of twenty aircraft. These were to be built at the Burbank plant (and later, as additional orders for the aircraft were placed, in a plant at a small town called Oildale, near Bakersfield, California) and then transported to a newly dedicated secret flight test facility in south central Nevada on the southwest corner of the three-and-a-half-miles-in-diameter Groom Dry Lake.

The Groom Lake operation was the end result of a decision to conduct the flight test program, and later, the pilot training program, under the tightest security constraints possible. While construction of the first aircraft got underway at Burbank, Lockheed test pilot Tony LeVier, who had been assigned to the high-altitude recce aircraft project as chief test pilot, had been given the responsibility by Johnson of locating a suitable site ("remote, but one not *too* remote") for the forthcoming flight test program.

Before embarking on the search and find mission, LeVier spent several days plotting a circuitous route covering hundreds of potential test base sites in southern California, Nevada, and Arizona. Taking chief Skunk Works foreman Dorsey Kammerer with him, he commandeered a company Beechcraft *Bonanza* and departed Burbank on a two week mission to photograph and explore desert areas offering potential as flight test bases. The search eventually led LeVier to the Groom Lake site. After returning to Burbank, he reviewed the many areas he and Kammerer had visited, and, following a detailed appraisal, placed his conclusions on paper in the form of three prioritized choices. Groom Lake, approximately 100 miles northwest of Las Vegas, Nevada, and literally within rock-throwing distance of the nation's largest nuclear weapons test facility, was ranked number one.

Johnson's initial reaction to the site was decidedly negative. He was not at all excited about conducting a flight test operation near an active Atomic Energy Commission nuclear weapons test site, and the lakebed was significantly farther

The inimitable Clarence L. "Kelly" Johnson poses with Central Intelligence Agency-operted N-803X. Agency aircraft were the first to be painted black overall. Note "sugar scoop" under exhaust nozzle.

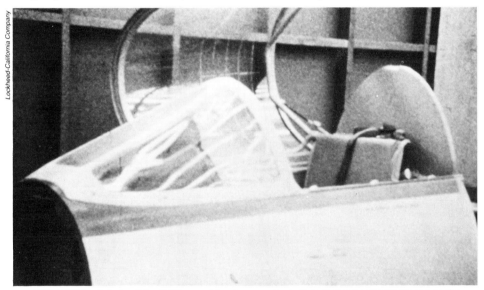

First published photo of the U-2 forward fuselage mock-up. Note that canopy was hinged on the starboard side of aircraft and that there was no ejection seat.

Still, taken from Lockheed film about the U-2, shows the first two prototyupes (top center) under construction inside Lockheed's Burbank, California Skunk Works facility. Wing jigs are visible in the lower left of photo.

Lockheed-California Company

Starboard side of Article 341 (number 1 aircraft) while under construction in early 1955. Note airbrake well and powerplant section oil cooler intake.

Lockheed-California Company

Skunk Works personnel hand-carry the vertical fin for Article 341 prior to installation on the aircraft. Article 341 fuselage is in the background.

from Burbank than what he had in mind. Following a reappraisal, however, and the realization that the AEC security restrictions would, in effect, act as an umbrella for the Groom Lake operation, Johnson recanted and agreed to accept LeVier's recommendation. Shortly afterwards, LeVier, Johnson, and Bissell flew to Groom Lake for a more detailed inspection.

Similar in most geological and environmental respects to the well-known flight test facility at Edwards AFB, Groom Lake offered the attributes of an expansive dry lake bed and exceptional remoteness. Flight test operations from the site would definitely not draw much attention—unless Johnson was concerned about the spying activities of tarantulas and tumbleweeds.

Once the site was located and approved, a construction team volunteered by the AEC was sent to Groom Lake in order to build a single north/south runway and rudimentary accommodations for the flight test team. These were placed on the southwest corner of the dry lake along with several water wells, two large hangars, several fuel storage tanks, and several temporary buildings. Unfortunately, most of the Groom Lake construction took place during the hottest part of the year in Nevada and work crews suffered tremendously in the 100-plus degree heat.

While work on the facility took off at a high rate of speed, LeVier spent nearly a month driving around the lakebed in a pick-up truck cleaning up rocks and other surface debris. At this time he also put together a proposal calling for four 3-mile long runways (technically giving a total of eight different take-off and landing directions) to be marked on the lakebed. LeVier knew from experience that such visual references would be important during the forthcoming flight test program as dry lake beds offered few visual clues for depth perception during landing. Somewhat surprisingly, when Johnson was presented with the runway idea and the fact that it would cost a nominal $450 to accomplish, he turned it down. The money, he said, simply was not available in the budget.

By July of 1955, the first aircraft was nearing completion. Due to the security surrounding the project, an official designation had yet to be allocated, so in-house at Lockheed and the Agency, it was simply referred to as the "Angel" or the

"Article" (the Agency had assigned a series of in-house article numbers to the new Lockheed aircraft; the first aircraft was Article #341). Additionally, pilots were called "drivers," and the Groom Lake site was known as "home plate." The latter would later be semi-officially designated Watertown Strip and still later, nicknamed "The Ranch," but for now, secrecy prevailed and the officially allocated sobriquets, stuck.

In early July, the number-one aircraft (assigned in-house Lockheed number 001 temporarily and flown without it), was loaded in a disassembled state aboard two Douglas C-124's and flown to the Groom Lake test site for final assembly and the initiation of the preliminary flight test program. Upon arrival, the main fuselage and wings were off-loaded via special transport trailers and moved into one of the two large Groom Lake hangars. Once inside and devoid of the special canvas covers protecting the wing and lightweight aluminum skin from damage, Lockheed technicians flown in from Burbank began the task of final assembly.

Some two weeks were consumed in the final assembly process, and after completion, the aircraft was pulled from its metal hangar by truck and trailer for the first time. Unpainted and unmarked except for the US insignia on the intakes and a small 001 on the vertical fin (the only released static photo of the U-2 prototype shows these numbers at the top of the fin, but there is some evidence to support claims that they were airbrushed on the photo, and actually were not on the real aircraft), it was now prepared for the first static engine runs.

Being a prototype, Article 341 was significantly different in detail from its successors to follow. Among the more noticeable prototype indicators were a canvas sunshield mounted on support cords (later aircraft would have the sunshield painted on the inside of the canopy); skid fairings that extended to the wingtip trailing edge; no drag chute housing above the engine exhaust port; no driftsight dome; no tracking camera dome or fairing; no fairing on the main landing gear door; and no bolt access panel forward of the empennage section break line.

Static engine tests were initiated in late July and these were followed on July 29th by preliminary taxi trials. The runs were made about 100 yards off to one side of the single north/south runway, on the lakebed proper. As LeVier recalls the event, Johnson had requested that the first run be made at a speed of 50 knots. After ingressing the aircraft and strapping in, LeVier started the engine and signalled that all was in the green in the cockpit.

The first run was in a northerly direction, roughly parallel to the runway. With the aircraft manually aligned by the tow truck, LeVier now advanced the throttle and watched as the airspeed indicator wound rapidly to the 50 knot mark. The throttle was then retarded and the brakes gently applied. LeVier noted immediately that brake response was poor, and commented to that effect when Johnson and the other team members drove up in a chase car. Johnson claimed the brake problem was due to the fact that the brakes had not yet been broken-in. He commented to LeVier that there was nothing to worry about.

A second run to 60 knots, in an easterly direction, was now requested. Moments later, LeVier and the "Angel" were again on their way. Sixty knots was reached without difficulty and when LeVier attempted to decelerate, he again noted the brake problem. When Johnson and his observers arrived after LeVier had rolled to a halt,

LeVier again mentioned the faulty brakes.

On the third run, which Johnson requested be made to 70 knots, the aircraft was aimed in a southwesterly direction. LeVier advanced the throttle again, and watched as the airspeed indicator needle moved toward the 70 knot mark. As 70 knots was reached, the throttle was retarded and LeVier began to work the ailerons in order to develop some feel for how they might perform during a real landing. It was only then that he became aware of the fact that the control response *was* for real—the "Angel," sometime back, had quietly parted company with Groom Lake.

LeVier's lack of depth perception on the lakebed, and the lakebed's glassy smooth surface, had failed to give him any sensory indication that he was actually airborne. Unfortunately, the realization of flight occurred after the throttle had been retarded—and as many "Angel" pilots to follow him would soon discover, the J57 was not an engine noted for quick throttle response at low airspeeds. Nevertheless, LeVier now slammed the throttle forward in an effort to accelerate. Stall buffetting had begun to shake the aircraft and as LeVier quickly discerned, he was headed for trouble unless he could make a prompt recovery. Seconds later, the "Angel" returned to earth, hitting the lakebed hard and blowing both main gear tires before bouncing back into the air one or two more times as the engine surged to life. The throttle was now retarded again, and this time, the "Angel" settled to earth to stay. Brake application netted little response, and the airplane rolled for over a mile before coming to a stop.

All of this had, of course, been witnessed by Johnson and the other team members on the lakebed. By the time they arrived at the stationary aircraft, LeVier had begun to extricate himself from the cockpit and had already reached several conclusions. A debriefing session followed, at which time he placed heavy emphasis on the fact that the brakes were extremely poor and that the lack of runway markings was extremely hazardous. That evening, work was initiated on the installation of dual brakes on the main gear assembly while the runway marking request remained undecided.

On the morning of August 1, 1955, Kelly Johnson, Ernie Joiner, Glen Fulkerson, Bob Murphy, and several other team members watched as LeVier climbed into the prototype "Angel" in preparation for its first legitimate flight. Given the call sign of "Angel 1," the aircraft was to be chased by a company-operated T-33 with Johnson and test pilot Bob Matye (who was soon to become the second pilot to fly the "Angel") as observers.

LeVier recalls that prior to the first flight he had several conversations with Johnson concerning the landing technique to be utilized. Because of its unique zero track landing gear, Johnson insisted that the "Angel" be landed main gear first. LeVier, antithetically, had argued that it should be stalled-in with the tail wheel touching first. Johnson rebutted, insisting that the "Angel's" high-aspect-ratio wings differentiated it from the landing characteristics of such bicycle gear equipped aircraft as the swept wing B-47 (pilots of which, LeVier had interviewed at some length in order to prepare for the first "Angel" flight). In the end Johnson's philosophy prevailed, and at take-off time, LeVier promised to attempt to land the aircraft as Johnson had recommended.

LeVier recalls that the first take-off and climb went perfectly and that he encountered no problems or difficulties during the ascent. Leveling at 12,500', he spent the following 45 minutes cycling the landing gear, deploying and retracting the

Wings for Article 341 are off-loaded from a Douglas C-124 at Groom Lake on arrival day. In the background the fuselage is being off-loaded from a second C-124.

One of the least-known major flight test facilities in the world, Groom Lake is located about 100 miles northwest of Las Vegas and just south of 9,000´ tall Bald Mountain.

Draped fuselage of Article 341 is towed into hangar at Groom Lake for final assembly following arrival by C-124.

Unheralded Jeep-towed roll-out of Article 341 occurred at Groom Lake in mid-July of 1955. Aircraft bore no markings and was mounted on a ground transport dolly.

First engine run-up took place on same day as roll-out. Note initial smoke of first combustion. Kelly Johnson is seen standing to the right.

Initial powerplant ground checks were made with aircraft mounted on special ground transport dolly. In photo, Tony Levier is in the cockpit and lower Q-bay hatch has been removed.

flaps, testing stability and control, checking engine temperatures and pressure ratios, and practicing power-off stalls. Everything functioned according to plan.

As LeVier entered final following base leg, he noted that almost everyone from the Groom Lake operation was lined up on one side of the landing area. As he crossed the threshold and cut the throttle the aircraft began to settle in the nose-level-main-gear-first attitude Johnson had requested. Flying on one side in the chase T-33 were Johnson and Matye, watching as the aircraft approached touch-down. As LeVier had predicted, the Johnson landing scheme did not work. The "Angel" touched, skipped, and then bounced into the air again, never once giving any indication of not wanting to fly.

A second approach was now made and LeVier decided to give the Johnson argument another chance. This time, he attempted to "spike" the main gear onto the runway by suddenly pushing the control wheel forward and aerodynamically forcing the airplane onto the lakebed. This too, failed, and LeVier was bounced into the air for a third try.

By this time, Johnson was getting extremely excited and was communicating with LeVier almost constantly. To make matters even worse, the sun was rapidly disappearing over the horizon and a summer rain shower was closing in almost as fast as the darkness.

With Johnson dominating the communications channel and mother nature controlling the environment, LeVier decided to get "Angel 1" back on the ground using a conventional tail wheel landing technique. Several days before the first flight, in preparation for making the first landing on the deceptive dry lakebed, LeVier had placed two strips of tape on the canopy parallel to the horizon (this had been accomplished with the aircraft elevated to a level flight attitude while sitting statically on its transport trailer). Now, while watching these canopy marks closely, he sailed over the "threshold" at approximately 75 knots and let the aircraft settle into a controlled stall. As LeVier expected, the tailwheel touched lightly and was followed a few seconds later by the mains. Though the aircraft porpoised a bit following contact, it quickly settled into a smooth roll-out and an uneventful full stop.

After "Angel 1" was pulled back to its hangar, it was discovered by the ground support crew that an anti-porpoising element controlling gear geometry had been left out inadvertently. This was corrected the following day, and further test flights failed to produce any further occurrences of the porpoise phenomenon.

LeVier made an additional nineteen flights in the "Angel" before moving on to other demanding Lockheed flight test programs. His U-2 flights completed Phase I testing, explored the stall envelope, took the aircraft to its maximum g loading (2½ positive and 1½ negative), and explored the speed envelope and took the aircraft to its maximum Mach number (.85). Additionally, LeVier became the first pilot to take the aircraft to 50,000'. In order to accomplish the latter, he was required to wear a partial pressure suit. This had led him, at 42, to become the oldest pilot to successfully complete the Air Force partial pressure suit training program at that time.

The Air Force-assigned U-2 designator became official during this flight test period, though none of the aircraft in the first production series were adorned with "utility" category designators on the fuselage data panels. In fact, except for small Article numbers on the vertical fins, these early Agency-operated aircraft remained unmarked.

LeVier was now transitioned back to his slot as

The only available high-quality photo of the prototype aircraft (Article 341) was probably taken prior to its first flight at Groom Lake. Note early tip skid configuration and lack of drag chute housing. Also note fabric sunshield under canopy.

director of flight test at Burbank following the completion of U-2 Phase I testing. There he became immersed in the rapidly expanding F-104 program and never again flew the U-2. He was replaced at Groom Lake by two other highly experienced Lockheed test pilots, Bob Matye and Ray Goudey. They became the second and third pilots to fly the U-2, respectively, and their efforts explored all facets of the aircraft's performance envelope.

A number of other Lockheed pilots joined the program shortly after Matye and Goudey, including Robert Schumacher and Bob Sieker. Schumacher proved instrumental in clearing the U-2 for maximum altitude operation and in proving the viability of the aircraft's early sensor system payload configurations. Additionally, Schumacher, in 1963, became the first pilot to fly the U-2 from an aircraft carrier.

Unfortunately, Robert Sieker became the first fatality of the high altitude test program when his partial pressure suit helmet faceplate blew out and he succumbed to anoxia. With Sieker unconscious and no longer in control, the aircraft (prototype Article 341) stalled at high altitude and flat spun in. It was three days before the destroyed U-2 and Sieker could be located and it was only by chance that Lockheed test pilot Herman "Fish" Salmon and Ray Crandall, in a borrowed Las Vegas-based Beechcraft *Bonanza,* managed to find them. Other search parties, operating out of nearby Indian Springs Air Base, had previously explored areas of Nevada thought most likely to

be where Article 341 had crashed. Until Salmon and Crandall made their chance discovery, however, the aircraft had remained missing.

The flight test program during the remaining months of 1955 progressed smoothly and by the beginning of the following year, four of the first five aircraft had been delivered to Groom Lake. Altitudes that were incredible for 1955 were now being achieved by the aircraft on an almost routine basis. On one occasion, three consecutive altitude flights made by Matye broke, by significant margins, the then-extant world altitude record of 65,890' set by British test pilot Walter Gibb in an English Electric *Canberra* during an August, 1955 test flight from Filton Bristol, in England.

In early 1956, the first small group of six Agency pilots, following their extensive Agency testing, schooling, and interview sessions in Washington, D.C., arrived at Groom Lake for U-2 flight training. All had undergone an Agency process called "sheep dipping" wherein their military backgrounds were disguised and their full-time employment was officially listed as being with private industry—in this case, Lockheed Aircraft Corporation (where they worked as "flight test consultants"). Additionally, they were given the unique privilege of being able to apply their time spent with the Agency toward their normal military advances and retirement.

The flight training program proved to be a fairly rapid process with piloting difficulties encountered primarily during final approach and

touchdown. The U-2 was an extremely difficult aircraft to land, particularly for pilots who were used to tricycle landing gear and power-on approaches. Fortunately, the pilots selected for the Agency's U-2 program were above average in proficiency, and the majority adjusted to the new flying techniques in fairly short order.

Groom Lake's not insignificant distance from Burbank had led, early in the U-2 program, to an abbreviated shuttle service between the two facilities. Unfortunately, there was some disagreement between Kelly Johnson and the Air Force as to who was responsible for the shuttle, and both fought to control it. By mid-1956, the Air Force had managed to convince the various parties involved that they were fully capable of servicing the short route, and accordingly, a C-54 was dedicated to the project. This aircraft, with a sizable Lockheed team aboard, later hit a mountain during a departure out of Groom Lake and effectively wiped out many key members of the U-2 support group. Johnson immediately replaced the aircraft with a Lockheed-controlled shuttle service using an available company-owned Douglas DC-3, and the right to the shuttle franchise was never again questioned. In the 1960's, with Lockheed still in control, the shuttle service was improved by exchanging the DC-3 for a Lockheed L.749A "Constellation."

By April of 1956, the initial flight test and flight training objectives had been accomplished and the six pilots and their aircraft were ready to embark on the first operational sorties of the program. Kelly's "Angel" was about to ascend.

First flight photo of Article 341 taken by Kelly Johnson from chase T-33 on August 1, 1955.

Test flight work with initial batch of articles remained steady at Groom Lake throughout 1956. Note "howdah" to protect crew members from sun's heat.

This is the first officially released photo of the U-2 and it appeared in February of 1957. It is almost certainly the prototype aircraft (note tip skids) with a fictitious NACA 320 painted (or airbrushed) on the vertical fin. Note drag chute housing above the engine exhause nozzle.

Early photo of 56-6680 shows the aircraft in its original unpainted scheme. This aircraft, though seen in Air Force markings, was actually the property of the Central Intelligence Agency. In July of 1956, this aircraft made the first overflight of the Soviet Union.

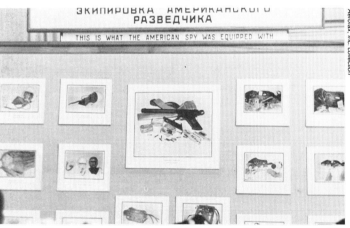

Photos of Power's accouterments were placed on display in Moscow next to the surviving parts of his U-2.

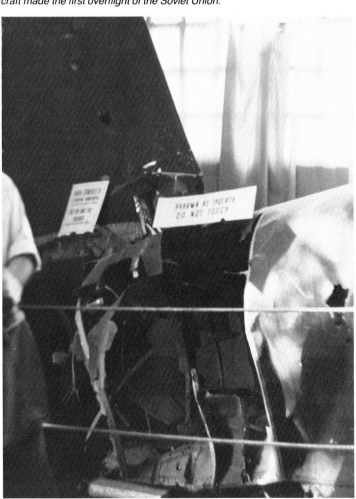

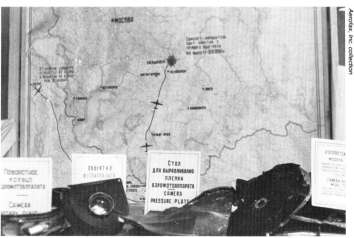

Map showing the route Powers took can be seen behind Type B camera lens and other miscellaneous camera parts.

Empennage and vertical fin sections were just a few of the many U-2 parts placed on display in Moscow in 1960.

Chapt. 4:
THE OPERATIONAL HISTORY—CIA

With operational deployment of the U-2 eminent, and the sensitivity of its proposed mission obvious, it is not surprising that President Eisenhower, in mid-1955, still had grave reservations concerning its use in overflights of denied territory. Eisenhower, however, was a strong believer in the undeniability of evidence in photographs and accordingly, at the suggestion of Nelson Rockefeller and a study committee he had assembled, Eisenhower proposed, on July 21, 1955, during the Geneva Summit, an "Open Skies" plan. This proposition stated that all participating countries would present to each other blueprints of their respective force structures which could be used as reference and base line data for a limited number of annual recce overflights by each of the participants. These flights would be used to verify the blueprint claims and provide assurance to each country that all military activity was being kept at an equitable level.

Though obviously surprised by the Eisenhower proposal, the Soviet Union's Summit delegation reacted favorably to the idea and agreed to immediately confer with Party Secretary Khrushchev.

Unfortunately, Khruschev's reaction proved markedly reserved, and accordingly the Soviets made no decision. Though the "Open Skies" proposal was approved one month later by a majority of the members of the United Nations, the Soviet Union continued to refuse to commit. Shortly afterwards "Open Skies" died a quiet death.

In June of 1956, with the first group of Agency pilots in final preparation and some 10 U-2's available for operational sorties, Richard Bissell and Allen Dulles arranged a meeting to discuss the overflight option with President Eisenhower. Secretary of State Foster Dulles and Eisenhower aide, Col. Andrew Goodpaster, were also in attendence when the meeting convened. The conclusion was simple—overflights were authorized, but only for an initial period of ten days.

With the official sanction in hand, Bissel quickly returned to his Agency office and relayed the information to the U-2 operations team in England. The first flight was tentatively scheduled for July 1.

In preparation for the *Operation Overflight* program, the first two U-2's had been disassembled and airfreighted in April to RAF Lakenheath, England from Groom Lake. There the first Agency U-2 detachment was formed under the spurious 1st Weather Reconnaissance Squadron, Provisional (WRSP-1) designator. A hangar on the far side of the airfield, remote from the majority of the main base activities was set aside by the RAF for WRSP-1 activities. After the two U-2's were reassembled and quietly flight tested, the unit moved again, this time to Weisbaden, in Germany.

The move to Germany had been brought about by political as well as tactical considerations. Due to less than ideal foreign relations with the British during this period, a decision was made to move the U-2 base closer to the Soviet border. Germany, through diplomatic liaisons, agreed to permit operations out of Weisbaden (Despite the move to Germany, the British were kept in touch with U-2 developments. A CIA aircraft visited the Royal Aircraft Establishment at Farnborough in November of 1956, and British links with the program later became intimate in May of 1958, when four Royal Air Force pilots, John MacArthur,

Early Agency-operated U-2A was placed on display for the press shortly after the Powers incident. NASA 55741 registration was totally fictitious.

Agency-operated aircraft were almost always distinctive due to their black paint schemes. U-2B is seen during test flight out of Van Nuys airport in California.

Agency U-2B, N-804X, is prepared for a test flight while mounting a somewhat unusually configured ventral antenna. Ventral antennas were seen on several aircraft during the early and mid-1960's and were probably used for ELINT work.

U-2B operated by the Agency on temporary loan to Lockheed is used to verify cross-wind landing characteristics of the aircraft during Lockheed-sponsored test program.

Agency U-2B, N-805X, displays minor modifications undertaken during IRAN (inspect and repair as necessary) at Lockheed's Van Nuys airport facility. Small blade antennas at 10 and 2 o'clock positions on fuselage, behind wing trailing edge, are particularly notable.

Agency operated U-2F, N-807X, taxies out for test hop at Van Nuys following systems modifications. Note large ventral antenna and dorsal spine extension.

U-2F, N807X, heads skyward from Van Nuys with a 100-gallon pylon-mounted fuel tank slung under each wing and unpainted replacement panels on its nose and at the base of its vertical fin leading edge.

U-2F, N-808X, taxies without rear panels on dorsal canoe modification. Note also that the words "Air Force" are barely visible on the fuselage just ahead of the horizontal stabilizer.

David Dowling, Michael Bradley, and Christopher Walker, were sent to train in the U-2 with the Air Force at Laughlin AFB, Texas.).

The new location for WRSP-1 from a security standpoint was hardly an improvement over RAF Lakenheath. Wiesbaden was a large town and the base was only fifteen miles from the city of Frankfurt. Conveniently, however, it was close to *Camp King*, the CIA's major West German intelligence facility. There, reports from agents and defectors from behind the Iron Curtain were sifted and analyzed and then used to form the basis for U-2 overflight requests.

On July 4th, the first operational overflight was flown. Taking off from Weisbaden, the aircraft, Article 347, headed northeast, eventually overflying Moscow, Leningrad, and the Soviet Baltic seacoast. It was a long, circuitous mission, and the target areas proved significant. Moscow and Leningrad were heavily defended areas and the industrial activity surrounding both cities was of great interest to defense analysts.

The film footage from this first overflight quickly verified the viability of the concept. The imagery was extraordinary and the ability to collect usable information was now undeniable.

Because of the element of surprise, the first overflight failed to garner a reaction from the Soviets. The second overflight, however, did. In a secret communiqué, the Soviet Foreign Ministry lodged a heated protest with the State Department acknowledging the airspace violation and hinting that action would be taken if further overflight activity occurred.

There was no response from the US. Four more flights over a period spanning four months now followed. Unfortunately, one of the Agency's U-2's crashed during this period near the town of Kaiserlautern and the pilot was killed. This accident generated significant publicity and eventually led to a short cessation of overflight activity in order to protect the security of the mission.

In late May of 1956, the second class of CIA U-2 pilots entered U-2 training at Groom Lake and completed the course in August. From there they were shipped to Incirlik air base, near Adana, Turkey, where they became WRSP-2 and operated as "Detachment 10-10". Francis Gary Powers was part of this unit and as such, was later able to describe the compound and its facilities in his book, *Operation Overflight*. Security was the order of the day, he would recall, and the group's entire operational and living accommodation was contained within its own fenced compound inside the base. Even within this compound certain areas were further restricted to just a few key individuals. The photo lab and communications section (which housed the cryptographic unit through which instructions for missions and other classified objectives were relayed from CIA headquarters) were particularly sensitive.

Detachment 10-10 comprised about 100 personnel in total. There were up to seven pilots and five aircraft available at times, with those figures varying from week to week, depending on maintenance requirements and duty schedules. Detachment 10-10 was a combined CIA/Air Force operation with the military providing logistical support and the squadron commanding officer, and the Agency providing the executive officer and manning the key slots in operations and planning. Obviously, much of the squadron organization reflected Air Force practice.

In February of 1957, the last CIA U-2 pilot class finished its training at Groom Lake and dispersed to the various Operating Locations (OL's). By now, WRSP-1 had again been moved, this time to a remote airfield at Giebelstadt, in the hills south of Wurzburg in Germany. After another relatively short stay, the squadron moved again and this time was merged in late 1957 with WRSP-2 at Incirlik. Flights from Germany continued, however, in the form of detachment aircraft, but Incerlik was now the main OL.

When Agency aircraft required major servicing or major systems updates or changes, they were ferried or shipped back to the US where Lockheed Aircraft Services located at the Van Nuys airport near Los Angeles did the required work. Lockheed also had a service operation at Groom Lake, and later, Warner-Robbins AFB, in Georgia, and the destination of the aircraft to be repaired or reconfigured often depended on what kind of work was required and where the work could most efficiently be accommodated. Warner-Robbins eventually became the main logistics support depot for the U-2 and was also the headquarters for the *Senior Year* Project Office (SYPO). All logistical needs of the aircraft were serviced from this Agency-operated facility under priority 1-1 requests.

Agency U-2 operations continued in sporadic fashion throughout 1957, 1958, and 1959. During this time, a total of some 30 overflights were undertaken, with the vast majority of the remaining missions being of the peripheral or training variety. Peripheral flights were significantly less risky than overflights and in many cases, were just as effective in the information gathering role. With the improved sensors developed for the U-2 program, close proximity to a target was not absolutely necessary. Imagery obtained with opti-

Agency U-2B, N-809X, cruises during post-modification test flight over California. Markings seen on this aircraft were typical of Agency operated U-2's.

Rare photo of Agency-operated U-2C, possibly N-806X, mounting "super pods." Pod on starboard wing appears to be carrying particulate sampling equipment.

The Agency was allocated six U-2R's, including N-810X. Early U-2R's, presumably the six allocated the Agency, had white sun shades. Later aircraft were provided black sun shades.

N-803X was prototype U-2R and, as originally built and test flown, was unpainted. Only visible marking was registration on vertical fin. First six aircraft were operated by the Agency.

27

Five of the first six U-2R's are seen at the Agency's facility at Edwards AFB North Base. Aircraft in foreground is N-803X. Note camera port in nose of N-803X.

Agency Aircraft rarely carried markings other than tail numbers, as exemplified by 68-10330, shown. Both Agency and Air Force aircraft were known to fly with bogus serial numbers.

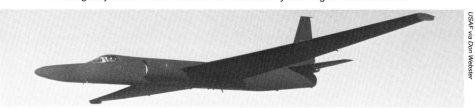

The U-2R is a graceful aircraft in flight and has a wing that is some 23 greater in span than that of its predecessor.

U-2R, 68-10333, during roll-out following a successful landing. U-2R is significantly more stable than its predecessor during landing.

cal systems was usable when taken obliquely at ranges approaching 100 miles, and electronic intelligence systems were equally as sensitive.

The system used for determining recce flight targets was as complex and sophisticated as the aircraft itself. Many factors were brought into play before a mission could be successfully executed, and even mother nature played a big role. As the majority of the overflights at this time were of the optical sensor type, weather conditions and sun positions were of tremendous importance. Accordingly, both the weather and the sun had to cooperate for a flight to result in usable imagery, and delays in takeoff schedules could sometimes lead to flight cancellation.

Photo coverage requests , usually eminating from the various security agencies, were routed through Richard Bissell's Agency office where they were screened by an Ad Hoc Requirements Committee. This clearing group, which had been formed during the summer of 1955, consisted of representatives from the CIA, the State Department, and the various armed service intelligence groups. Taking weather and other elements into consideration, they put together quarterly U-2 overflight programs and passed these on to the White House for approval. Missions were then cleared with Foster Dulles through Robert Murphy, his assistant secretary of state. The requests were then returned to Bissell who then turned them over to Col. Goodpaster at the National Security Council. From there, they were routed directly to the President, who would then confer with his secretaries of state and defense before giving them a final stamp of approval.

The U-2's incursion into Soviet airspace had, of course, upset the Kremlin greatly. Though a number of secret protests were filed during this period, the US refused to respond and the overflights were continued. In a not-unexpected move to counter the aircraft, which in its early lightweight versions was penetrating Soviet airspace at altitudes approaching 72,000', a massive program to develop an effective countermeasure was initiated.

At its beginning, members of the US intelligence community participating in the overflight program had predicted that the U-2 would have a usable overflight life of about two years. Beyond that time, countermeasures would almost certainly negate the security provided by high-altitude operation and the likelihood of an aircraft loss would be great. At the end of two years, however, no discernable improvement in Soviet anti-aircraft capability had been noted. And though attempted intercepts by Soviet MiG-19 and MiG-21 fighters and SA-1 (or SAM—Surface-to-Air-Missile) anti-aircraft missiles were known to be taking place, the U-2's extraordinary altitude capability continued to place it well above the 60,000' altitudes these intercepts were reaching. Additionally, it was found that the thin high altitude air made it extremely difficult for these intercepting aircraft and missiles to maneuver. The small aerodynamic surfaces found on most air-to-air missiles simply did not provide enough area to be effective—launches went ballistic and inevitably resulted in a miss.

In 1958, the Soviets began to gather momentum in their efforts to develop an effective anti-aircraft countermeasure. The SA-2, an improved surface-to-air missile eventually code-named *Guideline* and equipped with a warhead that had a kill pattern with a diameter of about 400', was pushed into service and for the first time, a weapon with the U-2's altitude capability was actually on hand. Unfortunately, the missile's beam following radar-directed guidance system was not up to its performance, and though it was obviously a threat, its 2% probability of kill (PK) was still of no great concern to the Agency. In consideration of the new missile, however, flight plans during 1958 and 1959 began to take SA-2 launch sites into consideration and accordingly, they were given a wide berth (usually around 30 miles).

When the first U-2 overflights were initiated in July of 1956, the Iron Curtain was still very firmly drawn against the western intelligence community. Vast areas of the Soviet hinterland still remained closed to travellers, and attempts to gain intelligence through conventional HUMINT (human intelligence) in-country spy techniques had been generally unsuccessful. As an example of the US intelligence community frustrations, an awkward attempt to gather data on a catch-as-catch-can basis was undertaken in the form of a bizarre recce technique using small, helium filled balloons mounting small cameras with automatic shutter releases. Depending on the whim of the winds, these balloons, of which several hundred were eventually launched under project *Moby Dick*, were to fly at 60,000' over the Iron Curtain and arbitrarily take photos of whatever passed underneath. This project resulted in a small amount of virtually useless imagery, and minor embarrassment for the Agency (at that time still the Office of Strategic Services) when several of the balloons were retrieved by the Soviets.

In the late 1940's, the advent of large, high-performance aircraft and their ability to transport powerful sensors eventually permitted closer examination of activity behind the Iron Curtain, but the price was high. During a ten year period, nearly fifty allied aircraft were lost to Soviet anti-aircraft activity, and along with them, nearly two-hundred crew members.

With the birth of the U-2, the intelligence community at long last felt it had obtained a reliable sensor system that could produce data of the most revealing kind. It was now in a position to analyze Soviet military strengths and weaknesses first hand utilizing an analysis process that would eliminate the guessing game that had gone on for so many years.

The results of the Agency's overflight efforts were indeed, impressive. During the first few missions out of Germany, U-2 flights quickly revealed that the long-argued Soviet jet bomber threat, represented by the Myasishchev Mya-4 *Bison*

U-2R, 68-10330, seen during a TDY deployment to Cyprus. Aircraft is configured for ELINT/SIGINT mission and mounts non-standard systems pods and related antennas on both wings.

U-2R, 68-10330, taxies to a halt at RAF Akrotiri, Cyprus. Special ELINT/SIGINT equipment was used during peripheral flight work. Note "Snoopy" logo on vertical fin.

Another view of 68-10330 taxiing in after mission from Cyprus. Note wing walkers lying on port wing tip to compensate for lack of starboard wing pogo.

Rare close-up view of ELINT/SIGINT/COMINT dedicated U-2R configuration. Airfraft 68-10329 mounts special sensor system pods and associated antenna farm for collecting communications and signal intelligence.

and Tupolev Tu-95 *Bear*, was relatively small. They also revealed, however, that Soviet activity in the ICBM field was accelerating, and that forthcoming missile developments would have to be countered, and rapidly.

The Soviet missile test areas were known to be in the remote southern areas of the USSR, with concentrations around the Caspian Sea and Kazakhstan. Detachment 10-10 was ideally placed to examine these sites and accordingly, in 1957, WRSP-1 was moved from Germany to Incirlik and there, while working out of OL's at Lahore and Peshawar in Pakistan, was tasked with the missle site overflight missions. Soviet SS-3 and SS-4 IRBM's (intermediate range ballistic missiles) were tested during this period and later, the ICBM (intercontinental ballistic missile) test base at Tyuratam, just east of the Aral Sea, was discovered to be the primary test facility for the new R-7 ICBM (later known as the SS-6 *Sapwood*). Often the launch countdowns for these missiles were picked up by ground sensors (particularly the giant installation at Samsun on the Turkish Black Sea coast) and the border surveillance flights, and it was not unusual for a U-2 surveillance mission to be launched in response.

For every overflight, there was at least one border surveillance mission that did not lead to a penetration of Soviet airspace. Many of these flights were of the ELINT (electronics intelligence), SIGINT (signal intelligence), and COMINT (communications intelligence) type utilizing dedicated receivers and recorders to monitor Soviet and East European communications, and electromagnetic energy generation equipment (i.e., radar systems).

A typical U-2 mission of this type normally covered approximately 3,700 miles and was routed out of Incirlik to Van in eastern Turkey, then across Iran and the southern Caspian Sea as far east as the Afghanistan-Pakistan border, and then back to retrace a similar track. Such missions would often last for seven hours or more, depending on weather conditions.

In 1958, a U-2 detachment was sent for three weeks to Bødo, Norway, and there tasked with the gathering of nuclear debris blown into the atmosphere by Soviet nuclear tests then being conducted on the Arctic islands of Novaya Zemlya and Franz Joseph Land. This mission proved very successful and gave the US intelligence community its best insight to date into the Soviet nuclear weapons program.

The task of sampling Soviet (and other countries') nuclear weapons debris was eventually to become a major task of the Agency's U-2 operations (and as noted in the next chapter, it was also a responsibility assigned to Air Force aircraft). The Agency's Atsugi-based (WRSP-3) operation proved particularly adept at the gathering of this material, due in part to the wind patterns and upper atmospheric conditions surrounding Japan. This OL was ideally placed for intercepting particulates blown into the atmosphere by Soviet tests deep within the confines of Russia's borders.

Agency U-2 overflight activities were not confined to the Soviet Union during this period. In late September of 1956, Gary Powers flew across the eastern Mediterranean and gathered intelligence data on the positions of British and French warships as they prepared to aid the forthcoming Israeli invasion of Egypt. Further flights followed during the Suez crises and later, during crises involving Syria, Iraq, Saudi-Arabia, Lebanon, and Yemen,—all to gather intelligence data on military activity and the eternal warring between these various Mid-eastern powers. Additionally, U-2 flights over the Chekiang and Kaingsi Provinces in China occurred as early as December 6, 1958.

Premier Khrushchev visited the US in September of 1959 and followed this with a reciprocal invitation to President Eisenhower to visit the Soviet Union in 1960. In the interim, it was agreed that there should be a summit in Paris in which the British and French would participate. Surprisingly, though there had been a lull in U-2 overflights during the course of Khrushchev's US visit, the forthcoming Paris summit did not merit similar consideration.

Eisenhower, during the first few weeks of 1960, had approved the flights for the first quarter of that year. By the time of the Paris summit, scheduled for May 14th, the mission profiles had been worked out by Col. Stanley Beerli (Agency U-2 mission planner along with a small team of assistants—and immediate past commander of Detachment 10-10) and passed on to the Agency for review. Secretary of State Christian Herter became the first to connect the significance of the mission dates and their proximity to that of the forthcoming summit and he relayed the information to Allen Dulles. Eventually it was decided that the missions, depending on the weather, could be flown any time up to two weeks prior to the May 14th meeting.

On April 9, 1960, an overflight by an Agency U-2 apparently revealed that major work on an ICBM program was moving along much faster than expected. The priority of this discovery led to a decision to schedule another flight over the same targets and accordingly, a mission was approved and tentatively scheduled for late April or early May, dependent upon weather.

Francis Gary Powers had flown some twenty-seven Agency missions following his arrival at Incirlik in mid-1956. Though the majority had been of the peripheral variety, he had penetrated Soviet airspace on several occasions and was familiar with the risks. Because of scheduling, Powers had been assigned the follow-up recce mission after the flight of April 9th. Three attempts on April 28th, 29th, and 30th were made to launch the flight, but it wasn't until May 1st that the weather over the target areas was good enough for photography.

May 1st, International Labor Day, was a major Soviet holiday. For this reason it was considered a "safe" day for Powers to fly his mission. It was assumed that defensive anti-aircraft systems would not be at peak readiness and radar and other observation facilities would be minimally manned. Powers' targets were Sverdlovsk and Plesetsk, two major ICBM test sites and also the locations of some of the Soviet Union's heaviest anti-aircraft missile concentrations.

Powers' flight had been scheduled in conjunction with another, peripheral flight in the hopes that the latter would create a diversion, of sorts, for Soviet anti-aircraft defenses. Powers flight on this particular day was to originate from a base near Peshawar, Pakistan and terminate 3,788 miles later at Bødo, Norway. The diversionary flight was to leave from Incirlik.

Interestingly, Powers' aircraft (Article 360) had developed somewhat of a "hangar queen" reputation during the course of its service career with the Agency. It had been plagued with a number of seemingly insoluble problems, not the least of which was a propensity for compressor section stalls and associated powerplant flame-outs at altitude. These problems had yet to be overcome at the time of Powers' May 1st mission, but they had not been considered serious enough to lead to an aircraft change.

On May 1st, both flights took off on schedule and shortly afterwards, Powers' aircraft, leveling off at 67,000', initiated his penetration of Soviet airspace. Powers' flight was routine in every respect until he reached Sverdlovsk. During the course of the photo run, while still at altitude, Powers recalls that suddenly the sky turned bright orange and there was a dull explosive noise somewhere underneath and behind his aircraft. Seconds later the right wing began to drop and Powers responded by turning the control yoke to the left. This brought the aircraft back to a wings level position, but moments later, the nose began to pitch downward—apparently because the empennage section had separated from the main fuselage. By this time, Powers was aware that something was terribly wrong with his aircraft. At this same moment, it pitched forward violently and both wings separated as the primary wing structure overloaded.

Powers would later recall that his first rational thought while the aircraft was coming apart around him was to reach for the sensor system destruct switches (which were located on an extension on the left side of the instrument panel in line with the windscreen railing, and which actuated a seventy second time delay in the associated pyrotechnics). In later interviews he would not be able to ascertain whether the system was activated (the system, contrary to popular myth, was not designed to destroy the entire aircraft, but rather to "melt down" the various classified sensors such as the "B camera", and any ECM equipment onboard), but he would recall that following the attempt, he began getting into the proper seat position for ejection.

Unfortunately, what remained of the U-2 was now in an inverted flat spin and the g forces were pushing Powers forward so that his legs remained pinned under the instrument panel. He knew that an ejection in this position would cause serious injuries to his knees, so the following seconds were spent trying to force his body back into the seat for proper positioning.

At that time, Powers began to realize that it was not absolutely necessary for the ejection seat to be utilized. The aircraft was not supersonic and the canopy could be opened manually. Glancing at the rapidly unwinding altimeter, he noted that he was passing through 34,000' and that something had to be done soon. He immediately reached up and pushed open the canopy, which folded over to the left side of the aircraft. The seat belts were then manually unlatched and as they disconnected, Powers was thrown forward and half out of the cockpit. When this happened, he became painfully aware that he had forgotten to disconnect his oxygen hoses—and that these were preventing his egressing the aircraft.

After an attempt to get back into the cockpit, Powers gave up and began pulling on the hose in an effort to make it break. Several strong tugs finally snapped a connector and moments later, he was floating free. At approximately 15,000' the barometric sensor in his parachute pack actuated the chute's release, and with a jerk, Powers was at last suspended in space, slowly heading earthward toward an uncertain future—and world headlines beyond his widest dreams.

In 1965, *The Penkovsky Papers* (Doubleday) were published and in them, the author, Oleg Penkovsky (some sources spell it Penkovskiy), a colonel who had worked for years in Soviet intelligence, gave some insight into the downing of Powers' aircraft. Penkovsky claimed that 14 SA-2's had been fired at Powers in a shotgun-type attack, and that the shockwaves generated by the explosions at Powers' altitude had led to a structural failure in the U-2. The post-crash investigation by the Soviets failed to reveal any indication of contact by any of the SA-2's and there was apparently nothing to indicate that the aircraft had been hit by shrapnel. Penkovsky also claimed that a MiG-19, attempting to intercept and destroy the U-2, accidentally had been destroyed by one of the 14 SA-2's.

Like all overflight pilots, Powers had been given a small coin with a hidden pin that had been dipped in "shell fish toxin" (some early news releases stated that the poison involved was curare, a blackish resinlike substance from *Strychnos toxifera* and other tropical plants of the genus *Strychnos*, and from *Chondodendron tomentosum,* used as an extremely toxic poison which works by arresting the action of motor nerves). The Agency had supplied this device as an alternative to torture in case a pilot was forced to leave his aircraft over unfriendly territory. The pin was discovered in Powers' flight suit not long after he landed, and as events worked out, he never had any need for it anyway (some sources claim that the "shell fish toxin" on the pin was so powerful that half-milligram quantities inserted under the skin were potentially fatal).

Powers was captured shortly after hitting the ground. Four days later, as the political importance of the event began to dawn to the international news bureaus, the destruction of the U-2 became front page news in virtually every major newspaper in the world. What had once been the most secretive clandestine reconnaissance operation in the world was now one of the world's most highly publicized.

The political and diplomatic ramifications of the Powers incident would soon gain world wide attention. Due to Powers' ensuing trial in the Soviet Union as an espionage agent, which was publicized to the hilt by the Soviet news agency, the event remained in the spotlight for months after its occurrence.

Though the political and diplomatic events are beyond the scope of this story, it is important to note that fall-out from these two factors led to the immediate cessation of further U-2 overflights, and also the retraction of all U-2 operations world wide. With the demise of the overflights in 1960, the US intelligence community found itself in a difficult situation. U-2 successes had led to an over-dependence on the system and at the time Powers was lost, fully ninety-percent of all hard data on Soviet military developments was being generated from the aircraft's overflight imagery. This material was released to the intelligence community not only in conventional photo form, but also in the form of manuals. These included AFM 200-62 on guided missile systems; AFM 200-40 on airfield installations; AFM 200-56 on atomic energy installations; AFM 200-59 on mechanical processing industries; and AFM 200-61 on military installations. It was to be nearly two years before the intelligence community fully recovered.

Powers was eventually released, but only after spending nearly two years behind the Iron Curtain and only after US agents completed negotia-

tions with the Soviets in which it was agreed to trade a spy for a spy. In 1958, the FBI had apprehended Soviet spy Rudolf Abel who had been the chief operative for the Soviet KGB secret police in the US for nearly a quarter century. Though one of the all-time biggest spy figures ever caught by the US government, it was decided to exchange Abel for Powers as a sign of serious intent. In later years, an unnamed FBI agent would liken the trade to exchanging Mickey Mantle for an unspectacular farm team catcher—with Powers being analogous to the latter (Powers was "just a pilot of a spy plane; Abel was a spy"). On February 10, 1962, Powers and Rudolf Abel passed each other on the German Glienicker Bridge—each returning forever to the haven of his respective country.

Contrary to popular belief, the U-2's career did not abruptly lend on that fateful May 1st day in 1960. Though Detachment 10-10 was withdrawn along with WRSP-3 at Atsugi, Japan, and the Turkish, Pakistani, and Norwegian governments all claimed to be extremely embarrassed by something they claimed to know nothing about, the U-2's usefulness as a sensor system platform was far from over.

As the dust began to settle following the Powers incident, all U-2 OL's were quietly inactivated and the aircraft and crews returned to the US. Air Force U-2 activity at this time was on the rise, and though Agency missions remained significantly more sensitive, the majority of the sampling missions were now being flown by Air Force aircraft.

Somewhat surprisingly, while U-2 exposure to publicity was being minimized throughout the world by the Agency, the Air Force, in 1962, made a point of notifying the press of the deployment of three aircraft to RAF Upper Heyford in England. Observers, of which there are many in England, also noted that mysterious all-black U-2's, obviously of the non-Air Force variety, were still operating in and out of a small field at Watton, some ninety miles to the east. These were, of course, Agency U-2's and they shared hangar space and other facilities with the RAF's Central Reconnaissance Establishment, which was responsible for the British ELINT and photo-recon effort while operating specially modified *Comet's* and *Canberra's*.

It was an Agency U-2, and not an Air Force one, which on August 29, 1962, brought back the first photos of the Russian military build-up in Cuba. The Agency at this time had been flying two missions a month over the island, but this rate was increased to one a week once suspicions of a major military build-up began to increase. The Air Force now lobbied the White House in an effort to take over the mission that had been so rigidly controlled by the CIA. Their efforts, due to a deterioration in the viability of the "plausible denial" theory and a refusal by the

Agency to up the frequency of the overflights, proved successful and the first Air Force flights over Cuba were finally approved on October 9th. Following the check-out of two Air Force pilots from the Strategic Air Command's 4080th SRW in Agency aircraft, the first, and as it turned out, fateful Cuban missile discovery mission of October 14th, was flown.

(Until October 9th, the primary justification for the continuing dichotomy in the Air Force/Agency U-2 operation had been the so-called "theory of plausible denial." This held that if a military aircraft and pilot were shot down, the overflight could be construed as an act of war; an Agency aircraft and pilot, on the other hand, if lost, were not only "civilian," but were also "officially disownable" by the US Government—and a foreign country would, theoretically, be hard-pressed to declare war over a "civilian" intrusion. As this argument was beginning to weaken, the Air Force saw an opportunity to gain control of an assignment it had long coveted. When the Air Force agreed to meet President Kennedy's overflight frequency requirement, which had been refused by the Agency, Kennedy made the fateful decision to task the Air Force with the Cuban overflight assignment.)

Nineteen-sixty-two proved a major turning point in the Agency U-2 story, as official Air Force involvement led to a slow takeover of many missions that had heretofore been under the Agency's absolute control. Cuba mission responsibilities were only the beginning, and others were soon to follow.

There was one assignment, however, that was retained by the Agency long after the Air Force's incursion into its sacrosanct U-2 domain. Due to its political sensitivity and secondarily to its direct relationship to the intelligence community, it was to remain outside Air Force jurisdiction in perpetuity. This was the Nationalist Chinese U-2 operation in Taiwan, which produced valuable intelligence about Communist China's nuclear weapons and missile tests and produced the first hard intelligence on Communist Chinese military activity.

The Agency had first conceived the idea of using the "free Chinese," as the Nationalist Chinese/Taiwanese were called, in an overhead reconnaissance effort in 1958. After a lengthy instruction program undertaken with Air Force supervision during 1958 and 1959 at Laughlin AFB near Del Rio, Texas, three RB-57D's were turned over to the Taiwanese following ferry flights to Tao Yuan AB, near Taiwan. Additionally, two stock B-57C's joined this unit to be used as trainers, and along with them went a small contingency of Air Force pilots and support team members. At least two more Taiwanese pilots, in addition to the original class of six, were later brought into the program and instructed in the B-

Nationalist Chinese operations were maintained under rather trying logistical and political conditions. Two U-2R's, maintained by the Agency and flown by Nationalist Chinese pilots, were assigned to the program. Here, N-8032X is prepared for a mission. Note logo on Jeep door.

Rare photo of U-2R, 3925 (Nationalist Chinese serial number) bearing Nationalist Chinese markings visible just behind open speed brake on fuselage. Following service with the Nationalist Chinese, both Agency-owned U-2's were returned to the U.S. and absorbed into the Air Force inventory.

Another view of 3925 in flight over Taiwan. There were no radical modifications incorporated in the two Nationalist Chinese U-2R's and the sensor system complement was primarily optical.

The two Nationalist Chinese U-2R's were maintained in the original flat black color scheme used by the Agency and the Air Force. The only changes were the tail number and the addition of the Nationalist Chinese insignia on the fuselage.

57C's and RB-57D's.

The first operational sorties by this very secretive unit proved relatively successful and in 1959, it played a key role in gathering usable intelligence for the Nationalist Chinese about the Taiwan Straights Crisis. Unfortunately, it was at this time that the RB-57D began again to suffer from its wing fatigue problem, and the aircraft was soon withdrawn from Nationalist Chinese service.

The US intelligence community, having been the beneficiary of some rather unique intelligence data gathered by the Nationalist Chinese RB-57D effort, elected to fill the gap left by the demise of the RB-57D program by "selling" to Taiwan, under the auspices of Lockheed, two U-2A's in 1959.

For the Agency, the Nationalist Chinese U-2 operation was an ideal arrangement. The US needed information from behind the "Bamboo Curtain" and the Nationalist Chinese were willing to take the responsibility. Additionally, the Nationalist Chinese maintained that as the rightful government of the mainland, their aircraft were entitled to fly over that territory; therefore, if an aircraft was lost over the mainland, it would be an argument between the Communist Chinese and the Nationalist Chinese—US involvement would be absolutely minimal.

In March of 1959, six Nationalist Chinese pilots began their U-2 training at Laughlin AFB under the auspices of the Air Force. Following their graduation, they returned to Taiwan where a number of training missions were flown in preparation for the arrival of the two Nationalist Chinese (Agency) U-2A's in 1960. The first recce missions of the program were initiated early in the year and the first overflights were routed directly over mainland China at a rate of about three flights per month.

The main areas of interest to US intelligence agencies at this time were beyond the Tibetan plateau. Among the sites of highest priority were the Lop Nor nuclear test site in the Sinkiang province and the Chiuchuan intermediate ballistic missile range in the Kansu province. Such missions involved flying northwest from Taipei for more than 1,800 miles and then turning near

Yumen, on a return course that paralleled the outbound track at a distance of approximately 200 miles. With occasional deviations to cover other military installations, the roundtrip distance for such a mission could easily exceed 3,000 miles—with almost all of it being over hostile territory. Fortunately, the withdrawal of Soviet military aid to mainland China in 1960 had led to a decline in the quality of the Communist Chinese air defense system and the risk to the Nationalist Chinese U-2 pilots was considered minimal, as long as the aircraft functioned properly.

Following a lengthy series of successful overflights, a Nationalist Chinese U-2 was finally destroyed by the Communist Chinese over Nanching in September of 1962. Prior to this success, they had resorted to bribery, offering over a quarter-million dollars in gold to any Nationalist Chinese who would defect to the mainland in his U-2! There were no takers.

Two more Chinese pilots commenced training at the 4080th's new home at Davis-Monthan AFB near Tucson, Arizona, during June of 1963, as part of the Air Force's U-2 program, and a further two followed in September. Following the loss of another U-2 in November over Shanghai, two more aircraft were supplied as replacements and the overflights continued. Data obtained from these flights proved instrumental in the ability of the US intelligence community to monitor Communist Chinese nuclear weapons activity. Though the first bomb was not actually exploded until October of 1964, the program had been photographed regularly by U-2's for over two years and it proved possible to predict, within a matter of days, when the first test was to take place.

In 1964, shortly before the first Communist Chinese nuclear weapon was exploded, the Nationalist Chinese U-2 program was stepped up. Still with the Agency in firm control, five more pilots were sent to Davis-Monthan AFB for training between March and September, and three more followed in January. Surfacing sporadically during this period were reports of further U-2 losses over China, including three in 1964, and one in January of 1965.

In August of 1965, the pieced-together remains of four downed U-2's were placed on display at the Peking People's Museum near the heart of the city. By this time, there had been another nuclear test at Lop Nor, and a third device, which was ten times more powerful than the first two of 20-kilotons, was demonstrated the following May. Additionally, it was now apparent that the Communist Chinese were attempting to develop a delivery system, and in October of 1966, a medium range ballistic missile (based on Russian SS-3/-4 missile technology) carrying a nuclear warhead was flown 400 miles downrange and detonated.

The Communist Chinese claimed another U-2 in September of 1967 and at least one more was lost in March of 1969. By this time, there had been at least eight nuclear weapons tests at Lop Nor, and the development of a Communist Chinese intercontinental ballistic missile was just being initiated. Nearly a dozen Nationalist Chinese pilots had now lost their lives while flying U-2's.

The Nationalist Chinese U-2 operation was again uprated in 1968 when the first of two advanced U-2 configurations, designated U-2R, was delivered to Taiwan. These aircraft, representing one-third of the entire Agency U-2R consignment (a total of twelve aircraft were ordered with six going to the Agency and six to the Air Force) permitted significantly heavier and more sophisticated Agency supplied sensor payloads to be transported over longer ranges, and thus

A significant number of U-2C's were lost over Communist China during the 1960's, including the four aircraft shown on display at the Peking People's Museum near downtown Peking. It has been reported that several of these aircraft have now been on display for over 15 years.

greatly improved the program's data gathering capability.

Nationalist Chinese U-2R operations continued unabated, with both Agency and Nationalist Chinese pilots flying missions, until October of 1974, when the Nixon accords (PACPRO) with the Communist Chinese led to a cessation of all U-2 Chinese overflight activity. All Agency U-2 operations, including the U-2R facility at Edwards AFB North Base, were now downgraded and shortly afterwards, phased out.

The demise of the Agency's U-2 mission was a boon for the Air Force's. All Agency U-2's and support gear were brought in from the various Agency OL's and transferred. Interestingly, this created somewhat of a problem as all equipment acquired by the Agency had been left unmarked and unidentified. The Air Force logistical system, highly dependent upon identification numbers and other means of inventory control, found the unmarked gear virtually impossible to absorb!

In what may have been some of the most graceful carrier landings ever made, Lockheed, under the auspices of the Agency, demonstrated the then-new U-2R's carrier suitability aboard the USS America (CVA-66) off the coast of Virginia during closely guarded secret sessions in late 1969. Lockheed test pilot Bill Park (now director of Skunk Works Flight Operations), made the landings during a short three day carrier ops test program from November 21st thru November 23rd, 1969.

Park's efforts aboard the USS America had, in fact, been preceded by Agency tests conducted in 1963. Under Project Seeker, two Agency U-2A's were cleared to practice touch and goes on the USS Kitty Hawk (CV-63). More definitive trials took place in February and March of 1964, when two modified U-2A's, incorporating arrester hooks, special spoilers, and landing gear geometry modifications (and redesignated U-2G, accordingly), were launched and arrested aboard

Closeup of displayed Nationalist Chinese operated U-2C reveals that impact damage to this aircraft was reasonably extensive. Reassembly of surviving parts is only approximate.

The U-2R was carrier qualified in 1969 aboard the USS America (CVA-66). These tests had been preceded by a series of tests and operational missions in the early and mid-1960's using earlier U-2 variants.

Very few modifications to the U-2R were required to make the aircraft carrier compatible. The most significant were the addition of a "strap-on" arrester hook and wing tip skid extensions.

With flaps and spoilers extended, the U-2R was found by Company test pilot Bill Parks to be relatively docile during carrier landings. The aircraft also had plenty of power to meet wave-off requirements.

the *USS Ranger* (CV-61). Landings were made using the World War 2 carrier technique of "Cut 1, Cut 2"—as the U-2 passed over the edge of the carrier deck in the proper attitude and at the proper altitude, the pilot was told to "Cut 1" (retard throttle); and as he crossed the arresting cables, he was told to "Cut 2" (deploy the spoilers). "Cut 2" killed all lift and the U-2G hit the deck and cables in a hurry.

These trials led later to a number of classified operational Agency sorties from aircraft carriers including one covering French nuclear tests in the South Pacific in late 1963. Additionally, plans to fly missions from a carrier operating in the Black Sea were entertained, but apparently never executed.

Details of the 1969 U-2R demonstration have only recently been released. During a recent interview for THE HOOK magazine (c/o The Tailhook Association, P. O. Box 40, Bonita, California 92002) test pilot Park, along with Programs Manager Fred Cavanaugh, and Ken Weir, Chief Project Pilot for the U-2 program, discussed some of the unclassified portions of the *USS America* tests. With THE HOOK editor Bob Lawson's permission, it is reprinted as follows:

Park, a former Air Force fighter pilot, described his first venture into the world of carrier aviation: "The purpose of the landings was to demonstrate the carrier suitability of the U-2R. Having no experience in carrier landings, I first went to Pensacola for training in the regular T-2B student syllabus. I think the most impressive part of the program down there was the students themselves, making carrier landings and cat shots with so little flying experience. I remember after we came back from the carrier, some of the kids asked me what I thought of it. They, of course, were all excited. Well, here I was, the big-time test pilot trying to maintain my image, so I said something like, 'Oh, nothing to it!' Hell, I'd never seen anything like a cat shot in my life!"

Continuing on to the training and preparation phase with the U-2 itself, Park returned to California and worked with a Navy LSO (Landing Sys-

Because of the U-2R's exceptional thrust-to-weight ratio, its expansive wings, and its abnormally high l/d (lift over drag), it did not require catapult assists during launch. Wind-over-deck factors were usually more than sufficient to get the aircraft off the deck in less than 300 feet.

tems Officer) flying FCLP's (Field Carrier Landing Practice) while experimenting with various approaches, using flaps, no flaps, speed brakes, etc. A 45-degree flap setting was finally selected and an approach speed of 72 knots with 20 knots wind over the deck was used for the *USS America* landings. The U-2 has no angle of attack indicator so the approaches were flown relying solely on indicated airspeed and "feel."

The big day finally arrived for the first landing and the stage was all set with the actors in place. Support personnel, test pilot and machine were on the beach with the admirals, while other big brass and the ship were off the coast steaming under clear skies in a fairly rough Atlantic sea state. All was ready. Park manned up and launched for the big event, a culmination of many months of planning and preparation. Arriving overhead at his Charlie time, he began his first approach. All eyes were focused on the broad-winged black bird as it gracefully slid into its approach. Suddenly Park pulled up and circled, radioing his waiting audience that he was returning to the beach for some additional "checks." Unknown below, it seems that someone had forgotten to remove the locking pin from the newly installed tailhook prior to launch.

A quick turnaround soon had the U-2 back over the ship and a rather anticlimatic series of landings and waveoff demonstrations was made. "I flew standard approaches and took a cut for the landings with no problem," stated Park. "The airplane demonstrated good waveoff characteristics and I felt at the time that landings could be made without a hook. We required very little special handling and even took the airplane down to the hangar deck. The outer 70" of the wings fold and by careful placement on the elevator we could get it in with no problem. One of the things that amazed me was the stability of the ship. The sea was fairly rough but the ship was as smooth and stable as could be."

One of the most unique aspects of the U-2 landings was the fact that Bill Park, a civilian contractor pilot, made the suitability demonstrations. This work is a task normally left to the carrier suitability guys at Pax River. However, due to the unique flying characteristics of the U-2, Park made the flights. As for the airplane itself, it required no special modifications for the carrier work other than a specially designed tailhook with a locking pin.

As noted earlier, Agency U-2 missions and programs continued until 1974 in both Taiwan and around the world, but Air Force involvement had now reached the point where it was foolish and wasteful to continue what amounted to two totally separate U-2 operations. Additionally, the gradually improving quality of intelligence data being gathered by recce satellite systems (*SAMOS* and *Discoverer*, to name just two of many) operating under Agency direction had, since 1962, overtaken much of the strategic recce capability provided during the heyday of the U-2 program. With the transfer of the last items in the Agency U-2 inventory to the Air Force, the Agency's U-2 chapter was quietly closed.

At least four U-2A's, as U-2F's, were modified to be inflight refuelable. A U-2F is seen taking on fuel from a Boeing KC-97J.

A Boeing KC-135A, 59-1510, refuels a U-2F during early trials over Edwards AFB. Receptacle was mounted on the front end of the dorsal canoe.

U-2F's inflight refueling capability was only marginally necessary, as pilot fatigue factors, more than range, often dictated duration of flights. Missions in excess of 10 hours were rare.

Until the advent of the Vietnam war, and the introduction of Air Force U-2's into that theatre, all Air Force aircraft remained unpainted. U-2A, 56-6701, is seen in standard Air Force markings. The "no step" borders marked on the wings were in red and the serial numbers on the vertical fin were in black.

Exceptional view of U-2A, 56-6715, reveals its red-painted flaps, elevators, and rudder, and unit citation on the vertical fin.

From the ground, the U-2 was a stunning sight. During an Australian HASP deployment, U-2A 56-6714 spreads its wings.

THE OPERATIONAL HISTORY—USAF

The Air Force had been intimately involved with the high-altitude recce aircraft program since its birth in 1953. Though direct contact with the U-2, the offspring of this program, would occur after the Agency's, Air Force money was being spent and the aircraft was a high-priority item in the Air Force budget. Air Force money had, in fact, paid for the J57 powerplants that had equipped both Agency and Air Force aircraft, and nearly all the Agency's pilots had originally been Air Force fighter pilots. Additionally, in the beginning the three extant U-2 squadrons were combined Air Force/Agency operations and the Air Force provided almost all logistical support.

RB-57D operations had preceded the U-2's Air Force introduction and accordingly, the service already was familiar with the idiosyncrasies of high-altitude aircraft. The Strategic Air Command's 4080th SRW had been flying the RB-57D above 60,000' for some two years by the time the first Air Force U-2's (actual delivery of Air Force-owned and operated U-2A's began a year after the first aircraft were delivered to the Agency) began to arrive at Laughlin AFB in 1957, and initial Air Force pilot training had started the preceding year at Groom Lake.

The first U-2 assigned to Air Force use was delivered by Col. Jack Nole from Groom Lake to Laughlin AFB, Texas on June 11, 1957. Bearing standard Air Force markings and a bare aluminum finish, his aircraft was in marked contrast to the all-black scheme by then being seen with great regularity on Agency aircraft.

The 4080th SRW's operating squadron at Laughlin was the 4028th SRS. This unit was normally equipped with approximately fifteen aircraft and pilot strength was about twice that figure. In September of 1957, five more U-2's were delivered to the 4080th with dedicated gas and particulate sampling systems in place of the more common accommodations for optical and electromagnetic sensors. These aircraft, later referred to as WU-2A's, had a "hard nose" containing a small intake and valve at the very front. Gaseous samples were gathered through this intake and then stored in three containers located in the forward nose compartment. On the lower left side of these aircraft was another intake, located just ahead of and underneath the port engine intake. This intake was significantly larger than the one in the nose and was faired in order to lower its aerodynamic drag factor. Particulates collected through this intake were then removed from the incoming airstream and deposited on a series of retractable round fiber filters.

The five WU-2A's bacame the first Laughlin-base aircraft to be assigned a long term Air Force project. Known as HASP (High Altitude Sampling Program), it was to take no less than five years to complete and involve some 45,000 flying hours (almost all in U-2's). Sponsored by the Defense Atomic Support Agency, HASP had been initiated in 1954 to determine the role played by the stratosphere in the world-wide distribution of fission products from nuclear explosions. Additionally, and perhaps most importantly, the above-ground testing of nuclear weapons invariably resulted in a significant quantity of radioactive material being ejected into the troposphere and stratosphere. Significant insight into the type, structure, and mechanics of a nuclear device could be obtained by collecting such material.

HASP eventually provided the most detailed and extensive study of radioactive material in the stratosphere ever conducted. Over 150 million standard cubic feet of stratospheric air were sampled, from the North Pole to the South Pole. A meridional network for coordinating program coverage proved sound and sampling in this network provided inventories and distributions of material which helped explain the major features of surface fallout noted by other programs both in the US and abroad. The various DASA HASP reports were assembled by Isotopes, Incorporated who integrated the HASP data with that gathered by Department of Defense/Atomic Energy Commission aircraft.

The 4028th nicknamed their participation in HASP, *Operation Crowflight*. Their first deployment was Ramey AFB, Puerto Rico, and after a short stay, they began what was to be a long series of temporary duty assignments to miscellaneous OL's throughout the world. In September of 1958, three aircraft went TDY (temporary duty) for a year to Ezeiza AB near Buenos Aires, Argentina, and following their return to the US, later returned to Buenos Aires for two months in May of 1960.

On March 15, 1960, Capt. Roger Cooper distinguished himself during a HASP mission when he experienced simultaneous engine and electrical system failures at mission altitude. Flying near Saskatchewan, Canada, Cooper elected to stick with the aircraft, rather than bail out. Prior to the flight, he had been briefed on weather conditions in the area, and he knew that there was overcast with blowing snow and low visibility at either of two emergency airstrips along his flight path. Although his partial pressure suit had actuated at the time of the engine failure, Cooper managed to function inside the cramped cockpit and had communicated his problem to ground stations. The overcast was penetrated at 20,000', and cleared

at 10,000'. At what was now a relatively low altitude, Cooper attempted to communicate with a beacon station which unfortunately proved unmanned. Some 42 miles further, he spotted a frozen dry lake and elected to use it as a landing field. There he executed an almost perfect landing that resulted in only minor damage to the aircraft.

A rescue team, alerted to Cooper's predicament and location, arrived shortly afterward. A maintenance team arrived the following day and after repairing the powerplant and correcting other minor systems problems, the aircraft was powered up and flown off the frozen lake back to Eielson AFB in Alaska.

The northern hemisphere was covered by operations out of Eielson AFB, and Minot AFB, North Dakota and on August 25, 1962, an Eielson-based WU-2A, 56-6675, during an operation entitled *Northern Record* and piloted by Capt. Donald Webster, made the first U-2 flight over the North Pole in a 3,121 nautical mile mission which lasted some eight hours and forty minutes. The flight, which was pre-flight planned by 4028th navigators, Capt. Robert Yates, Capt. Billie Bye, and 1st Lt. Frederick Okimoto, and crewed by SSgt. Anson Hokett, placed Webster over the Pole at exactly 4:25 p.m.

The first of at least six HASP detachments to Australia was made in October 1960 with three aircraft, these being based out of RAAF Laaverton, near East Sale. During their first visit in November of 1960, the U-2 was displayed publicly for the first time abroad at the Laaverton open house. This display, a rather futile attempt to underscore the peaceful purposes of the deployment, occurred less than six months after the Powers' incident. Another three-aircraft detachment visited Laaverton in October of 1961, but later deployments were to RAAF Avalon— these including the very last HASP assignment in

U-2A, 56-6705, undergoes preflight checkout following display at East Sale, Victoria, Australia on May 14, 1961. This aircraft was configured for HASP mission at the time.

Another view of U-2A, 56-6705, during landing. Note cartoon character on vertical fin, and unit citation.

Surrounded by flight crew and ground support team, U-2F, 56-6680, poses for a photographer during one of several deployments to Vietnam. Aircraft is equipped with large ELINT-type rams horn antennas.

U-2F, 56-6680, in flight over Vietnam. Aircraft was inflight refuelable and carried an exceptionally sensitive SIGINT/COMINT monitoring system. Grey paint scheme was used during early 1960's.

Late in U-2C 56-6680's life the aircraft was painted in subdued camouflage to give British civilians the impression that it was no longer invoilved in covert activities.

Assigned to the 6512th Test Group at Edwards AFB, U-2A 56-6682 sits on its ground transport dolly with its main gear and tailwheel extended and its pogos pinned into their respective wing holes.

February of 1965. Other HASP USAF bases used during the program, apart from Laughlin AFB, were Plattsburgh AFB, New York; Hickam AFB, Hawaii; Anderson AFB, Guam; Kadena AFB, Okinawa; and the Panama Canal zone fields of Howard and Albrook. Program segment codenames included *Star Dust* (Laughlin AFB, Texas) and *Ashcan* (San Angelo, Texas and Sioux City, Iowa).

Typical HASP missions lasted seven and a half hours. Cruising altitudes were usually between 50,000 and 70,000 feet. In addition to particulates and gases, the U-2 gathered information about cosmic radiation, ozone accumulation, and upper atmospheric jetstreams.

The 4028th SRS operated alongside RB-57D's of the 4025th SRS. Both squadrons mounted sensitive reconnaissance missions in addition to the more public HASP flights, many in conjunction with missions being flown by Agency U-2's. The RB-57D, because of the serious wing fatigue problem that had plagued it from the beginning of its service career, was forced into retirement from the strategic recce role in 1959, and promptly replaced by the U-2. Following this, the U-2 assumed all reconnaissance duties for the 4080th SRW, including the classified *Toy Soldier, Green Hornet,* and *Sky Shield* programs.

While Agency U-2's continued their extremely sensitive peripheral flights and overflights of China and the Soviet Union, the Air Force quietly began to take over more and more Agency U-2 missions of a supposedly less sensitive nature, including the continuing surveillance of Cuba.

In July of 1962, the first of an increasingly ominous series of intelligence reports describing a rapidly growing Soviet presence in Cuba began circulating within the confines of the US State Department. Noticeable increases in military shipments to Cuba were perhaps the most obvious sign of a buildup, and in-country spies had also noted that the number of Soviet military personnel on hand had grown dramatically. Unfortunately, a supposed Cuban propensity for exaggeration cooled any strong concern the State Department might have had about a military build-up, and for another few weeks, little was done.

Finally, reports of a much more serious nature, carrying descriptions of very large missiles, began appearing with a regularity that merited further examination. CIA chief John McCone quickly deduced the veracity of these reports based on information he had concerning military shipments to Cuba, and inputs from other intelligence sources, and with this in hand, on August 22nd, he went directly to President Kennedy and stated that the Cubans were receiving intermediate range ballistic missiles. Kennedy, unfortunately, was skeptical of McCone's information and set it aside until further intelligence could offer stronger proof. Meanwhile, work continued quietly in Cuba as more intelligence data was gathered by agents and through interviews with newly arrived exiles.

CIA information gathering activity was now increased and a daily Cuba situation report was initiated under the codename of *Psalm*. Additionally, U-2 flights were increased in frequency and on August 29th, an Agency flight out of McCoy AFB in Florida brought back photos verifying that at least two advanced surface-to-air missile sites were operational and a further six were under consideration. Most alarming was the fact that these sites were designed in the same Star-of-David pattern noted in conjunction with IRBM (intermediate range ballistic missile) and ICBM (intercontinental ballistic missile) launch facilities in the Soviet Union.

Further recce work by a US Navy P-2 produced

photos of the Soviet freighter *Omsk* on September 8th, these indicating that there was very unusual cargo onboard in the form of oblong canvas covered crates. Unfortunately, the quality of the imagery was not good enough to produce a definitive evaluation and poor weather over the following several days curtailed further photography of the ship.

President Kennedy now requested that U-2 overflight activity be increased to a rate of one mission per week. Complicating this overflight decision, however, was the fact that on August 30th, a HASP U-2 mission had resulted in an inadvertant overflight of the Soviet-held Sakhalien Island and on September 9th, a Chinese Nationalist U-2 was lost over Communist China.

These incidents caused significant State Department concern over the safety of further U-2 incursions into Cuban airspace, and for a period of about three weeks, there as a moratorium on overflight activity. During the moratorium and unknown to anyone in US intelligence, the first shipment of Soviet MRBM's (Medium Range Ballistic Missiles) arrived in Cuba on September 8th and was moved out of Havana during the following six day period. A second shipment arrived on the 15th.

Shortly after the missiles hit Cuban shores, the pace of reports arriving on the desks of the various US intelligence agencies picked up considerably. Many exiled Cubans entering the US now reported seeing the large offensive weapons moving through city streets and down country roads. This data was relayed to the Agency and then to the State Department.

The overflight moratorium was lifted during the first week in October, and on October 5th and 7th, U-2's overflew the island and gathered updated information. This new intelligence revealed that further work had been done on the SAM sites and additional construction of an undeterminable nature was underway.

While activity was picking up over Cuba, HASP missions continued to create their share of problems. Lt. Col. Forest Wilson, while flying a HASP sorty more than 300 miles to the southwest of the Alaskan coast, experienced a complete electrical system failure. Using a flashlight and a standby compass, Wilson elected to fly to the Kodiak Naval Air Station in order to make an emergency landing. Arriving at Kodiak, he was distressed to discover that the runway lights were not on and no one at the field could be aroused. With no other choices available, Wilson then headed for Elmendorf AFB, more than 200 miles away. By this time he was beginning to suffer from fatigue and cold as he had been flying the aircraft manually and functioning without cabin heat since the beginning of the electrical system failure. To make matters even worse, his helmet faceplace had begun to frost over and his vision was being slowly obscured. Three hours and fifteen minutes after the onset of the failure, Wilson successfully landed his U-2 at Elmendorf—safely completing a mission that easily could have ended in disaster.

On October 10th, President Kennedy approved, for the first time, overflights using Air Force pilots in place of Agency pilots. Accordingly, two pilots from the 4080th, Maj. Rudolph Anderson, and Maj. Steve Heyser, went TDY to McCoy AFB and there were checked out in Agency-operated U-2's (Being U-2E's, they differed from Air Force aircraft primarily in the fact that they were equipped with sophisticated defensive countermeasures systems—and were therefore heavier.). They were followed, several weeks later, by other available pilots from the 4028th SRS.

Seconds away from touchdown, U-2A 56-6682 flares for a full-stall landing. Note unpainted Q-bay lower hatch and special 6512th Test Group paint scheme.

Sitting in hangar at Laverton, Victoria, Australia, U-2A 56-6690 takes a break between HASP missions. This aircraft was destroyed on September 20, 1964.

Bearing special grey on grey camouflage, U-2C 56-6692 is seen in flight over southern California. This was the last major paint scheme change applied to early variants of the U-2.

HASP-equipped U-2A, 56-6696, seen during deployment to RAAF Laverton in Australia, in September of 1963. Note lack of rearview mirror.

U-2A, 56-6696, formates for photo session over Davis-Monthan AFB. Early Air Force all-black paint scheme left the canopy sun shade in its original white paint.

The U-2's accident record has never been particularly good. Photo shows the remains of 56-6697 following an unscheduled, and final, landing.

Landing at RAF Wethersfield in England in July of 1975, U-2C 56-6700 pops its drag chute to shorten its roll-out. Aircraft is painted in grey on grey camouflage.

U-2C, 56-6700, turns final during an early morning practice session over Davis-Monthan AFB in April of 1975. Note extended airbrakes and bulged Q-bay lower hatch.

Bad weather prevented the consummation of an Air Force mission for several days, but finally, on October 14th, the first Air Force flight was initiated. The pilot, Maj. Heyser, shortly after achieving his predetermined mission altitude of 70,000', headed southwest toward the Isla de Pinos and then flew north over the Cuban mainland. The run from San Cristóbal, perhaps the most critical part of the mission, lasted no more than five minutes. When it was over, Heyser headed back to Patrick AFB—and as it turned out, into history.

Heyser's film, (shot at approximately 7 a.m. in order to take advantage of the 20-deg. sun angle) contained the first images ascertaining beyond any doubt that Soviet MRBM's were on Cuban soil. After landing, the film had been off-loaded out of Heyser's U-2 and immediately placed on a transport and flown to Washington for processing at the National Photo Intelligence Center. By the middle of the next day, prints from the negatives had been processed and analyzed, and copies showing at least one MRBM on a trailer and several support structures including a launch pad, were distributed to select members of the intelligence community and the State Department.

By October 16th, word of the stunning discovery had spread throughout the intelligence community and President Kennedy had been briefed at the White House. Stepped up U-2 overflight activity was immediately ordered by Kennedy, and low-altitude missions utilizing RF-101C's were also approved. On October 17th, new photos indicated that MRBM launch facilities were under construction at Sagua la Grande, Remedios, and Guianajay. Additionally, there were also indications that SS-4 *Sandal* IRBM (Intermediate Range Ballistic Missile) facilities were under construction.

U-2 overflight activity was now accelerated again, this time to a rate of six or seven flights a day. The 4080th logged some twenty sorties between October 14th and October 22nd, each mission being followed by supporting film transport flights to Washington.

On October 22nd, 1962, President Kennedy made his now-famous speech announcing that Cuba had acquired an extensive offensive weapons capability including MRBM's and IRBM's. In an unquestionably threatening tone of voice, Kennedy declared that *any* Cuban missile launch would be regarded as an attack by the Soviet Union on the US and that massive retaliatory action would result. He also declared a "naval quarantine" of Cuba until all Soviet offensive weapons were removed from the island.

U-2 overflights continued at a very high daily rate with most emanating from either McCoy AFB in Florida or Laughlin AFB in Texas. Due to the proximity of the island, flights direct from Laughlin AFB proved well within the range of the aircraft. Many missions were laters flown from Barksdale AFB (OL-19) near Shreveport, Louisiana. Between October 22nd, and December 6th, no less than 82 Air Force U-2 missions took place.

With SA-2's and Mig-21's in Cuban service, the Cuban overflight assignment was not without its dangers. On October 27th (following several weeks of "cat and mouse" with MiG-21's), while overflying the Cuban naval installation at Banes, Maj. Rudolph Anderson was shot down by an SA-2 surface-to-air missile. This loss wreaked havoc in the Air Force Cuban overflight community and led to significant changes in overflight policy. SAM sites were now given priority consideration during flight planning, and countermeasures equipment was reevaluated and improved.

Two other Air Force pilots would be lost while flying the Cuban overflight mission, though not to enemy action. Following the most critical days of the crisis, Capt. Joe Hyde disappeared near the southwest Florida coast in the Gulf of Mexico during a flight on October 20, 1963. In another accident, occuring nearly three years later, Capt. Robert Hickman, flying out of Barksdale AFB, Louisiana, was killed when he inexplicably lost consciousness at cruising altitude.

Hickman's death, as a matter of record, was officially attributed to an oxygen system failure, but there was later cause to believe that the real problem had been physiological. His aircraft had wondered uncontrolled for nearly 3,000 miles before running out of fuel and descending into the mountainous jungles of Bolivia. The aircraft and pilot were later recovered by an Air Force search party.

On October 24th, US patrol aircraft in the Atlantic Ocean noted that a number of Soviet merchant ships bearing what appeared to be military cargos bound for Cuba had stopped in mid-Ocean and turned around. On October 26th, communications with the Soviets indicated that they would begin dismanteling the Cuban missile sites, and on the 28th, this was confirmed. The Cuban missile crisis, as it became known to the world, began to wind down.

One incident during this two day period near the end of the crisis is worthy of note. Maj. Charles Maultsby, who had taken off from Eielson AFB in Alaska on a routine HASP assignment, experienced navigation problems during the latter part of the mission and inadvertently strayed into Soviet airspace. Unfortunately, Maultsby's aircraft was also running low on fuel and he was far from a friendly emergency landing field. Maultsby's mistake was understandable, but his timing was abysmal. The incursion into Soviet airspace led the Soviets to place their air defense and ICBM forces on a maximum alert status—the first time they had done so since the crisis began. Suddenly the world was once again on the verge of war. Fortunately, a KC-135 navigator, overhearing Maultsby's plight, told him to fly east toward the "Belt of Orion" constellation. With this information, Maultsby was able to accurately reverse his course, move back into friendly airspace, and eventually land safely at a small airstrip on the west coast of Alaska. It is of some historical importance to note that this particular flight, lasting 10 hours and 25 minutes, was the longest ever flown by a U-2 at the time.

Throughout the crisis, it had been known that the MRBM's and IRBM's were not the only offensive weapons in the Cuban arsenal. In fact, a large number of Soviet-built Ilyushin Il-28 medium jet bombers had also been delivered, and these now became a source of some contention during the days immediately following the main crisis diffusion. U-2 photo missions, still taking place as a monitoring activity on a daily basis, indicated a sizable number of Il-28's at several Cuban air bases.

Conveniently, the naval blockade was still in effect and Kennedy used this as leverage to get the Il-28's off the island. In exchange for removing the Il-28's, Kennedy promised to dismember the blockade in thirty days. The Soviet Union agreed and shortly afterwards the Il-28's began to disappear. For the following several months Kennedy monitored the execution of the Soviet promises religiously via the high-quality, high-resolution imagery generated by the cameras in the high-flying Air Force U-2's. Very little could sneak past these awesome optical sensors and over a period of weeks they recorded the IRBM site at Remedious abandoned and dynamited and the IRBM site at San Cristóbal similarly dismantled.

It is interesting to note that a surreptitious agreement between the US, the Soviet Union, and Cuba cleared the way, at this time, for safe

Edwards-based U-2's, such as 56-6701, due to their test and research missions, were usually the most colorful. Note small sensor protruding from Q-bay upper hatch. Painted panels are daglo orange.

Turning final at Davis-Monthan, U-2C 56-6701 (066701 on vertical fin) is seen without paint, yet bearing all the standard Air Force markings. Note wing flex as aircraft banks.

U-2C, 56-6701, is seen with an all-black paint scheme and special dorsal ELINT antenna. The only markings on this aircraft are the serial numbers—which are painted in red.

At least six U-2C's, including 56-6701, operated in and out of Europe on a regular basis in the late 1960's. Most were painted in grey on grey camouflage.

Rene Francillon collection

Aerofax, Inc. collection

Don Webster Collection

Aerofax, Inc. collection

U-2C, 56-6707, is seen on final to Davis-Monthan AFB in Arizona. Note slipper tanks, "sugar scoop," and tail warning sensor (on starboard wing trailing edge).

U-2A, 56-6708, in clean configuration. Aircraft is unpainted except for normal Air Force markings and a unit citation on the vertical fin. Note that flaps and ailerons make up the entire wing trailing edge.

U-2A, 56-6714, being prepared for display at airshow. Aircraft is in early Air Force all-black paint scheme.

Balancing the U-2 after touch down and during the low speed portion of the roll-out was no easy task. HASP-configured U-2A 56-6715 is seen with its drag chute deployed.

continuation of the US U-2 overflight program. In exchange for several concessions in US policy in Europe and elsewhere, the Soviets and Cubans agreed to permit the overflights to continue without opposition.

Frequent U-2 flights over Cuba continued into 1963. They were still in progress when President Kennedy, remarking "I must say gentlemen, that you take excellent pictures. . . ." presented on November 26, 1962, an Outstanding Unit Award to the 4080th Wing during their duty in Florida. This was, in fact, the second such award received by the unit, which had first been honored in March of 1960.

On July 12, 1963, the last U-2 left Laughlin AFB for the 4080th's new home in the desert at Davis-Monthan AFB, near Tucson, Arizona. In spite of numerous training and operational accidents that had destroyed at least a dozen aircraft and ten pilots, unit strength remained at some twenty U-2's. HASP missions continued to keep the unit busy and interspersed among them were a number of highly classified sensor system missions that usually demanded the 4080th's services at a distant OL while utilizing only one or two aircraft.

At the very end of 1963, a new chapter for the 4080th began when President Johnson approved Air Force U-2 reconnaissance flights in Vietnam. In March of 1964, following the abrupt termination of HASP (the international agreement to discontinue above ground nuclear weapons testing killed the program), all HASP aircraft were reconfigured to accommodate conventional optical and ELINT sensor systems and were then deployed, under the aircraft codename of *Dragon Lady,* to Bien Hoa base near Saigon. Within a matter of days, they had embarked on their first operational sorties. This recce effort would continue for the following twelve years.

In 1964, the Air Force had a limited tactical reconnaissance capability in-theater with its *Able Mable* force of six RF-101C's. Though efficient and effective, the *Able Mable* operation had deficiencies in the type of sensory data it could generate and also in the speed at which it could generate it. The 4080th's U-2's were expected to offset these failings and provide covert surveillance of N. Vietnam's border areas and its Vietcong infiltration routes. Less obviously, but just as importantly, it was also tasked with helping to develop a contingency list of targets inside N. Vietnam itself, should the war be escalated.

Once the 4080th had been committed to the Vietnamese war, it became apparent that the "non-combat" grey and aluminum paint schemes (which actually had been maintained primarily to give the impression of peaceful weather reconnaissance aircraft) worn by Air Force U-2's were significantly more visible than need be. Accordingly, a decision by the Strategic Air Command in October of 1964, under project *Ram Rod One,* was made to paint them over-all flat black (which, incidentally, added no less than 40 pounds to the empty weight of the aircraft), exactly like the aircraft flown by the CIA. In the fall of 1964, the first Air Force aircraft to undergo this color transformation, 56-6680, was ferried by Maj. Ed Smart to Anderson AFB, Guam, with the intention of getting the local logistics crew to undertake the repainting. Unfortunately, the Guam logistics operation was inundated with work and it was virtually impossible for them to accommodate Smart's request. Undaunted, Smart decided to tackle the project himself and after finding a spray gun, he moved 56-6680 into an empty air refueling squadron hangar and went to work. With paint barely dry, he then returned to Bien Hoa and there, promptly laid claim to the first all-black Air Force U-2!

In common with previous wing practice, the Bien Hoa detachment was numbered as an Operating Location (OL-20) and given a code-name: *Lucky Dragon.* The latter lasted only a short while, eventually being changed to *Trojan Horse* and, finally, to *Giant Dragon.*

In the early days of the Vietnam war there were regular high-altitude overflights of N. Vietnam and even a few ad-hoc low-level missions. The threat from surface-to-air missiles soon intensified, however, denying overflight opportunities to the U-2 and underscoring the fact that the aircraft's overflight days were rapidly drawing to a close. As U-2 overflight activity slowly phased out, *Lightning Bugs,* or remotely piloted vehicles (RPV's) consisting primarily of various Teledyne Ryan A- and BQM-34 drones, took over the task. These vehicles were integrated into the 4080th SRW in July of 1963 under the auspices of the 4028th RS. Drone operations, under the codename *Blue Springs*, were then mounted alongside those of the U-2's.

The advent of drone activity created a direct threat to the U-2's Air Force operations. For the first time since the birth of the *Dragon Lady,* a recce vehicle was in service that could match it in both technique and capability. The rivalry between the U-2 and RPV factions of the 4080th grew strong during the Vietnam war years, even resulting, in one case, of clandestine sensor equipment thievery—a *Combat Dawn* RPV payload configuration study was quietly exorcised from one RPV program by a Melpar team and with the help of several Lockheed reps, secretly studied as a U-2 payload. The accidental discovery of this event at Melpar's Falls Church, Virginia, facility by an Air Force RPV representative created quite a stir in the RPV community.

Many war stories were of course generated by U-2 pilots during this period, and what follows, written by Capt. Robert Birkett (now Col. retired), the day after the incident, is just one of hundreds. This particular piece was actually written for the PIF (pilot's information file) to inform pilots of a possible operational problem:

"The mission was normal until the recovery phase. After passing the last checkpoint and turning toward Bien Hoa, I tuned in Bien Hoa radio beacon and Ton Son Nhut VOR. I identified the VOR but was unable to get a positive i.d. or hear Bien Hoa radio beacon, probably due to my distance from the station. The radio compass in this aircraft (56-6953) also had a loud background noise."

"I was unable to establish contact with 'Paris Control' (GCI) on our normal frequency to obtain the current Bien Hoa and Ton Son Nhut weather. While attempting to do so, I was also completing the "green card" (flight log) and "cleaning up" the cockpit. I had not left altitude because of the unknown weather conditions at my destination. About this time, "mobile" called asking my status. I reported that I was inbound to the station with 220 gallons remaining and that I was still at altitude. I then requested the weather. Mobile indicated that a storm was "in progress" at Bien Hoa, and that I was to remain at altitude and to throttle back to "min-e.p.r." (exhaust pressure ratio). Mobile stated that he was going to check the weather and radar scope."

"While mobile was checking the weather, I retuned Bien Hoa radio beacon. I was unable to hear the station i.d. due to noise and static, but the needle was pointing straight ahead, the same as the VOR needle which was correct for my inbound heading. Mobile now called and advised me to begin an immediate descent, that the storm was passing and that another would be moving in in about 20 minutes. He also mentioned that the area northwest looked best for a final approach.

Standard Air Force all-black paint scheme on U-2C, 56-6716. The serial number on the vertical fin is painted in red. Aircraft may have been under the auspices of the Agency at the time the photo was taken.

U-2A, 56-6718, sits on the ramp at RAAF Laverton in September of 1963, during one of several HASP deployments to Australia. Aircraft was painted light grey over-all.

Though configured as a U-2A, 56-6953 was purpose-built as a U-2D. Note tip skids with above-wing extensions to clear aileron counter-balances.

Though configured as a U-2C, 56-6954 (0-66954 in photo) was originally purpose-built as a U-2D. This particular aircraft, however, actually may have been an early U-2A reassigned a U-2D serial number following modifications to the U-2C standard.

43

John Andrews

The last early-variant U-2 to roll from Lockheed's production line was U-2D 56-6955. This aircraft was later lost on August 14, 1964, while being flown by a Nationalist Chinese pilot undergoing training at Davis-Monthan AFB.

René Francillon collection

The first U-2 to be preserved was 56-6714. It now resides as a gate guardian at the main entrance to Beale AFB, California. Significant damage sustained during emergency landing led to its final fate.

Paul Swendrowski

The Air Force Strategic Air Command Museum at Offutt AFB, Nebraska received U-2C 56-6701 in July of 1982. Note missing tail wheel doors.

Dave Menard

The Air Force Museum has been given U-2A (ex-U-2D) 56-6722. This aircraft was reconfigured to give it the appearance of being a single-seat variant. It is perhaps the most authentically painted and restored U-2 on display in any museum.

He told me to go out to a 300- or 320-degree heading and to come in on the 280- or 290-degree radial."

"About this time, the ADF needle swung and I started turning to 300-degrees while establishing a maximum rate descent. I also contacted Saigon approach control who told me their radar was out. They then cleared me to Bien Hoa GCA. Bien Hoa was contacted and I advised them that I was passing through 50,000' and would start a left hand turn at 40,000'. GCA began to attempt establishing radar contact."

"By now I was descending through layers of cirrus clouds and was expecting to become VFR as I got lower. GCA was unable to pick up my transponder or identify me by i.d. turns. The VOR was pointing toward 170- to 180-degrees and the ADF was swinging slowly to the left and becoming a little erratic, indicating that I was getting close to Bien Hoa."

"It now seemed like I had been inbound to the base for a long time. I was leveling off at 7,000' and could occasionally see the ground, but I was in low broken clouds. I was now down to 100 gallons of fuel. GCA requested I squawk 77 and turn to a heading at 100-degrees. Mobile's radio faded out at this time and the GCA's transmissions became broken. GCA had not received my 77 squawk and at this time I realized that I was further northwest of Bien Hoa than expected. I declared an emergency, retracted the gear, and began a slow climb. Mobile then advised me that it was too late to land at Bien Hoa—the second storm had hit."

"I now turned directly toward Ton Son Nhut VOR. The ADF became very erratic and I encountered heavy turbulence with much lightning. I contacted Ton Son Nhut tower and declared my emergency with them and stated that I was north of the VOR and requesting their weather. I was given 3500' broken to 4000' overcast but that the weather was lower to the east and that another storm was moving in. The tower asked if I wanted to contact approach control. I asked if their radar was back in and they replied negative. I said that I would remain on tower frequency and that I was down to 30 gallons. At this time I crossed the VOR at 21,000' in moderate turbulence."

"The aircraft was now let down over the VOR and the landing configuration was established. The stall strips would not extend on the first attempt due to structural icing. VFR conditions were established at 3000' with one end of the runway. The other end of the runway was IFR due to the approaching storm."

"A down wind landing (because of the storm) was completed with a throttle burst required to clear the "BAK-12" arresting cable on the approach end. In total darkness the aircraft was taxied off the runway and the engine shut down with 7 gallons of fuel remaining in the tanks. The pilot sat in the aircraft for an additional 45 minutes

From hangar queen to the Smithsonian Institution's National Air and Space Museum, U-2C 56-6680 has seen it all. This is perhaps the most historically significant preserved U-2, as it was the first to overfly the Soviet Union.

while the rain subsided enough so that tower personnel could verify his arrival visually."

Editor's note: The U-2C flown by Birkett was equipped with ADF (automatic direction finding) and VOR (visual omni-range) navigation aids only. There was no TACAN or ILS (instrument landing system) installed. Southeast Asia was covered by TACANS. The only VOR was a weak and obsolete French VOR located at Saigon. The GCI (ground control intercept) site had been knocked off the air by the thunderstorm shortly after Birkett started his descent.

With the drones taking over overflight duties, the U-2 mission now became one of stand-off surveillance. Improvements in the aircraft also had been introduced by this time, including a new uprated powerplant and a totally new airframe (the U-2R). Both improvements permitted increases in sensor system and countermeasures system payload capability and in the case of the new airframe, a significant improvement in range, pilot accommodations, and flight characteristics.

Birth of the U-2R, essentially a second generation design (some sources indicate that it was at one time referred to as the "WU-2C" and that it began life as the U-2N), had come about, like that of the first-generation U-2's, through a specific requirement within the confines of the Central Intelligence Agency (the original U-2 was engine limited with the J57; introduction of the J75 made the original aircraft airframe limited). This requirement, coupled with a high first-generation aircraft attrition rate, had led to a decision to grant Lockheed a production contract in August of 1966, calling for a totally new aircraft. The latter had been under design development throughout the early and mid-1960's in response to the first-generation's well known failings. Among the latter were marginal controllability at altitude, poor payload capacity (which, with steadily increasing payload weights was beginning to adversely effect performance at altitude), exceptionally poor landing characteristics, marginally sufficient range, marginal structural life (due to the exceptional weight restrictions specified early in the program), and a cockpit that was too small to permit the use of a full-pressure suit (in defense of the first generation aircraft it is only fair to mention that it was not originally designed to be a long-lived multi-mission aircraft, but rather was designed to achieve extremely high altitudes carrying a minimal sensor system payload—while having a fatigue and airframe life that was nominal, at best).

With these problems in mind, the Skunk Works, under the direction of Kelly Johnson and his able assistants Ben Rich and Fred Cavanaugh, forged ahead with a total redesign of the basic U-2 configuration that explored the potential performance improvements that might be gained by using such advances as supercritical airfoil sections for the wings and tail surfaces. The end result was a totally new aircraft offering a 23'

March AFB, in California, has received and placed on display U-2D, 56-6721. This aircraft retains its modified Q-bay crew compartment, but has been repainted in gloss black paint!

Striking view of highly-modified U-2R, 68-10336. This aircraft has a significantly enlarged nose radome to accommodate a very large SLAR unit (possibly ASARS).

Extended nose of U-2R, 68-10336, is readily apparent in this view. Also discernible is external ribbing on horizontal stabilizer to control a buffett induced fatigue problem.

Lockheed-California Company

Low-speed pass by U-2R, 68-10336, presents excellent view of flexible high-aspect-ratio wings. Note that tail configuration indicates nose-up trim has been added to compensate for new nose radar.

Brian Rogers Collection

Transient at the 55th SRW's Offutt AFB, U-2R 68-10337 is prepared for the long cross-country to Beale AFB. The only markings on this aircraft are the red serial numbers.

Brian Rogers collection

COMINT/SIGINT mission is now the most important reserved for the Air Force U-2R fleet. U-2R, 68-10337, is equipped with at least one SLAR pod (possibly ASARS) and a large antenna farm.

USAF via René Francillon

Markings on U-2R and TR-1A aircraft are kept to a minimum. Typical scheme, such as that seen on U-2R, 68-10337, is flat black over-all with red tail numbers.

increase in wingspan (the supercritical airfoil section idea was dropped and the stock NACA 64A airfoil was retained, though proportionally enlarged); some 400 additional sq. feet of wing area; a lower wing structural weight of 3 lbs. per sq. foot; an improved L/D (lift over drag) of 27 to 1; a totally new and enlarged fuselage providing a substantial increase in internal volume for sensor system and electronic countermeasures system payloads (and also permitting the elimination of the drag producing external oil cooler intakes and allowing the length of the empennage to supplant the "sugar scoop" modification for lowering the exhaust infra-red signature); revised and enlarged horizontal and vertical tail surfaces; folding wingtips to permit aircraft carrier accommodation (and stressed in appropriate areas to permit the attachment of an arrester hook); hydraulically actuated roll (outboard) and lift (inboard) spoilers on the top surfaces of each wing; a zero/zero ejection seat; larger retractable leading edge stall strips; accommodations for large wing-mounted sensor pods (referred to as "super pods"); and beefier landing gear to accommodate the resultant weight increases. The powerplant remained unchanged from that of the earlier U-2C as it was sufficiently powerful to accommodate the needs of the new design at altitude. Additionally, and perhaps most importantly, the experience base with the J75 had resulted, by this time, in an engine that was very dependable.

Initial operational use of the U-2R followed close on the heels of its first flight on August 28, 1967, (with Lockheed test pilot Bill Park in the cockpit), from North Base at Edwards AFB, California, and the completion of an extensive flight test program. Service introduction, occuring in late 1968, was under the auspices of the Agency and the work conducted at that time was primarily related to U-2R operations conducted by the Nationalist Chinese. Edwards North Base, as a point of interest, became the primary base of operations for Agency U-2R activities. It also served as a training base for new Air Force pilots (the first two to fly the U-2R were Jack Fenimore and Robert Birkett) and four of the six U-2R's operated by the Agency were based there. While two of these aircraft were assigned, in 1968, to the first U-2R OL at McCoy AFB in Florida, two others departed North Base for Taiwan.

In 1966, the U-2 operating units had been involved in an orgy of renumbering undertaken by SAC in order to preserve some of its more famous unit designators which were threatened with extinction because of the B-47's imminent phase-out. In consequence, the 4080th was redesignated the 100th Strategic Reconnaissance Wing and the 4028th became the 349th Strategic Reconnaissance Squadron. As the wing celebrated its tenth birthday, they calculated that a modest fifty manhours had been consumed in support of each 6 hour (average length) U-2 mission.

In 1968, OL-20 completed 1,000 missions; in 1970, it achieved full squadron status as the 99th SRS around the time that the operation was moved, on July 11, 1970, to U-Tapao in Thailand.

During the intensive *Linebacker II* aerial bombardment of North Vietnam in the closing months of 1972, U-2 flights were codenamed *Olympic Torch* and with the aforementioned RPV's, took part in pre- and post-strike reconnaissance activity.

For its work in 1972, the 100th SRW was awarded SAC's Paul T. Cullen Memorial Trophy and the Gen. John A Desportes trophy for Best Reconnaissance Wing in the 15th Air Force. In January of 1973, the 99th SRS achieved a record 500 hours of flying time. This monthly total had never previously been attained by any U-2 squadron.

By now, a lot of 99th SRS flying time was devoted to the *Senior Book* program which, with the help of the RPV's, collected COMINT from mainland China while remaining at high altitude outside Chinese airspace. *Senior Book* U-2's were modified to "minimally-manned" configurations. The pilot's role was confined to handling the aircraft controls while the payload was exercised remotely. Signals intercepted by the aircraft's receiving sensors were transmitted in real time from a transponder in the U-2 over a data link feature in the Air Force's UPQ-3 microwave command guidance system. The U-2's were tracked continuously by the command guidance system at line-of-sight ranges up to 400 miles from a ground or airborne station. The range could be extended by using an airborne station as a relay. With the "minimally-manned" configurations, the Air Force was able to track the U-2 accurately throughout its flight profile and to correlate the precise target positional information with realtime surveillance data relayed from the aircraft.

The accident-free record and reliability of the U-2R permitted the 99th a new monthly total flying hours record of 600 in December of 1974. *Senior Book* and associated sensor system missions occupied the unit steadily during the remainder of the war and in April of 1976, the unit was finally withdrawn from Thailand and dispersed to other OL's around the world.

In late 1972, and early 1973, the Navy began to explore the U-2's operational possibilities by borrowing from the Agency two U-2R's (including 68-10339) in order to test the viability of its proposed EP-X (electronics patrol-experimental) mission. The actual modified aircraft were initially delivered to North Base at Edwards AFB in the spring of 1973. The program ran for the following year with the majority of the test missions being flown off the southern California coast. The experimental Navy-funded effort sought to verify the effectiveness of several sensors including a highly modified RCA X-band radar, a United Technology Laboratories AN/ALQ-110 electronic intelligence receiver, and a forward looking infrared system. All three were used in real-time monitoring of maritime and naval ship movements from high altitudes. Additionally, a modified Texas-instruments AN/APS-116 forward looking radar was mounted in the nose of 68-10339 (for submarine snorkel and periscope detection). Antennas for the AN/ALQ-110 and X-band radar were mounted, on at least one aircraft, on a common pedestal in the Q-bay area and slung underneath the aircraft in a faired radome that hung down nearly 3' from the bottom of the fuselage. The forward looking infra-red system was carried in special wing pods developed specifically for the EP-X aircraft. The U-2 EP-X study also led to exploratory work by Lockheed calling for the abil-

Roger Freeman via Chris Pocock

U-2R, 68-10338, is seen with Snoopy cartoon on its tail being pushed into hangar at RAF Mildenhall. U-2R's and TR-1's are now permanently based in England at RAF Alconbury.

George Cockle

Transient at Offutt AFB, Nebraska, U-2R 68-10338 is towed into hangar for overnight keeping. Note antennas on fuselage spine.

George Cockle

Departing Offutt AFB, U-2R 68-10338 initiates gear retraction sequence. Both the main landing gear and the tail wheel retract forward.

USAF via René Francillon

U-2R's were used extensively in Vietnam. A U-2R is seen taxiing out for takeoff on a mission from U-Tapao RTNAF, Thailand in November of 1975.

Chris Pocock

Mounting SLAR pods and several ELINT antennas, U-2R 68-10339 is seen taxiing out on a mission from RAF Mildenhall. Note "sag" to wing, indicating full fuel load.

Lockheed-California company via Robert Lawson

The U.S. Navy acquired two U-2R's on temporary loan for use in their U-2 EP-X program. U-2R, 68-10339, is the only aircraft that has been definitely identified as being configured for the EP-X mission.

U.S. Navy

The U-2 EP-X mounted two unusual slipper type pods with each configured to contain a different sensor. The port pod is thought to have contained a forward looking infra-red sensor system.

Bob Birkett collection

U-2R's have been seen carrying a wide variety of ELINT-type sensors. U-2R, 68-10339, is seen mounting at least one SLAR pod on the starboard wing.

ity of the aircraft to carry the electro-optically-guided *Condor* anti-ship missile.

In 1974, Air Force operations with the older U-2 models began to phase down as ex-Agency U-2R's were absorbed. The new model permitted significant improvements in every facet of the program, including deployability and support of the reconnaissance objectives of the Joint Chiefs of Staff. It remained constantly in use.

In August of 1970, two aircraft were sent to monitor an uneasy cease-fire in the Mid-East. Flights were initially mounted every two or three days but were suspended during the first week in November following Egyptian objections. In mid-December, the aircraft returned home. Two years later, following the October 1973 war, the Mid-East surveillance operation was activated once again with the approval of both warring sides. The war's aftermath had resulted in a peace-preserving buffer zone and it was requested that U-2's be used to safeguard against unwarranted activity therein. The monitoring 100th SRW U-2 detachment was based at RAF Akrotiri, from where it also proved convenient in 1975 to monitor the Soviet military build up in Somalia.

In 1973, the first dual control U-2CT trainer, 56-6692 (nicknamed the *White Whale*), was delivered to Davis-Monthan AFB. This aircraft had started life as a conventional single-seat U-2A, and later had been updated to the U-2C configuration. An accident in late-1972 led to a decision to utilize its airframe for the first two-seat trainer modification project. The aircraft was then moved to Lockheed's Palmdale facility and there modified to accommodate an elevated second seat and a second set of controls in what had formerly been the Q-bay area behind the forward cockpit. On February 13, 1973, Lockheed test pilot Bill Park piloted the aircraft on its first flight, from the Palmdale facility. Funding for a second trainer modification was eventually allocated, this

Chris Pocock collection

U.S. Navy via René Francillon

Carrying what must be one of the most extensive antenna farms ever mounted on a single seat aircraft, U-2R, 68-10339, is seen on final to RAF Mildenhall.

The Navy's U-2 EP-X configuration involved significant sensor system modifications but no major changes to the airframe (with the exception of the revised nose radome).

resulting in U-2D, 56-6953, being reconfigured also to accommodate an elevated rear seat and associated controls.

By 1973, the Air Force U-2C fleet, consisting primarily of U-2A's that earlier had been uprated by Lockheed through the incorporation of a more powerful engine, had been reduced through attrition to a skeleton collection of approximately six aircraft. A small number of J57-powered U-2A's were also extant, but it was painfully obvious that replacement aircraft were sorely needed. The majority of the losses were directly attributable to training accidents. The aircraft was unlike any other then operational in the Air Force and its zero-track landing gear arrangement demanded landing skills that were antithetical to everything conventional military pilots had been taught. Stall/spin accidents during final approach were particularly numerous—and, unfortunately, also particularly dangerous. Additionally, the aircraft was sensitive to porpoising after touchdown and more than a few serious accidents were attributed to this phenomenon.

In 1975, six of the surviving U-2C's were deployed to Europe in order to test a prototype target location system called *Pave Onyx*. The system had been developed for use in Southeast Asia, but had never been deployed. *Pave Onyx* and the follow-on *Pave Nickel* were designed to accurately locate Warsaw Pact emitters along and behind the Iron Curtain by a type of triangulation method. The time taken for hostile signals to be received by each of three U-2's cruising in friendly airspace at precisely known distances could then be measured and compared; the minute differences in the time of arrival of the emitter signal at each U-2 could then be relayed to a ground terminal which would then compute a precise geographic fix for the emitter.

Despite being repainted from "sinister black" to a more innocuous two-tone grey camouflage (known as the "Sabre Scheme") at the specific request of the British government, the presence of U-2's in force attracted some adverse comment and publicity, especially when one piloted by Capt. Robert Rendelman crashed on May 29th, 1975, in West Germany. Rendleman was unharmed, but the now-scarce U-2C was totalled. The *Pave Onyx* deployment continued into early August, at which time the remaining aircraft were ferried back to Davis-Monthan AFB.

By the time its twentieth anniversary arrived in 1976, the 100th SRW and its predecessor, the 4080th SRW, had notched up six Outstanding Unit Awards. This enviable record went with the unit in March as it moved once again, this time to Beale AFB, near Sacramento, California (the first U-2 to land at Beale as part of this move was U-2CT 56-6692). As part of a lengthy series of post-Vietnam budget cuts, the Air Force had elected to consolidate its unique stable of U-2 and SR-71 strategic reconnaissance aircraft at Beale under the 9th Strategic Reconnaissance Wing. The old wing and squadron numbers (100th and 349th/350th respectively) were now assigned to KC-135 units already at Beale. The 99th would become the designator for the relocated U-2 squadron. This activity was officially completed in October of 1976.

Not all Air Force U-2 missions during the 1970's were military in nature. During this period, SAC received and executed various requests from the Forestry Service and the Department of Agriculture, and on numerous occasions participated indirectly in similar non-military high-altitude sensor system-dependent programs such as geothermal energy monitoring, flood control, hurricane monitoring, and tornado damage assessment. Many of these requests were accommodated within normal training flights.

Michael Grove

The first U-2CT modification was 56-6692. It was built-up at Lockheed's Palmdale facility from the remains of several seriously damaged U-2A's and U-2C's.

Michael Grove

Second U-2CT, 56-6953, is seen on final approach to Davis-Monthan AFB. Like the first U-2CT, this aircraft was also built up from the surviving parts of damaged U-2's.

Lockheed-California Company

U-2CT, 56-6953, is seen during a training flight over Davis-Monthan AFB. Note that the tipskids on this aircraft have the above-wing extensions associated with a revised aileron mass balancing system.

Bob Birkett collection

As takeoff speed is reached, the lift being created by the wings of U-2CT, 56-6953, can be seen causing stress wrinkles on the fuselage underside. Note that the main gear tires have just cleared the runway.

Prior to its official roll-out ceremonies, the first TR-1A, 80-1066, was pulled onto the Palmdale ramp for photos. There are no discernible changes between the U-2R and the TR-1A, with the possible exception of a revised dorsal antenna support blade.

Another pre-roll-out ceremony view of TR-1A, 80-1066. Like the U-2R, There are no markings on the aircraft except for the red serial numbers on the tail.

The second TR-1A, 80-1067, is seen during a pre-delivery test flight over southern California. The mismatch in paint on the starboard wingtip is interesting, as is the fact that the aircraft is carrying a lower Q-bay hatch for optical sensors.

On February the 8th and 13th, 1976, for instance, two extended flights each of ten-and-a-half hours were flown from Davis-Monthan AFB to photograph the effects of an earthquake on Guatemala. These missions had been requested by the US Agency for International Development and they provided photo imagery for damage assessment and rebuilding requirements.

Again in 1976, in yet another example of peace-time U-2 operations, a U-2's cameras literally saved the life of a sunken ketch's adrift passenger. Bruce Collins had survived in a liferaft in the Pacific Ocean for some three weeks following the ketch's accidental sinking on September 27th. He and four other people had been en route from Hawaii to San Francisco when the sinking occurred. By October 18th, only two passengers had been safely rescued. Maj. David Hahn, of the 99th SRS at Beale AFB, was assigned the search and rescue mission on October 22nd. After ascending to 60,000 feet, Hahn proceded to photo an assigned 600 sq. mi. area in the Pacific Ocean where it was thought the survivors would most likely be. When the U-2 and its payload returned to Beale, the color film was quickly processed and analyzed. Miraculously, though his yellow liferaft was only a spec on a negative, Collins was spotted. A rescue effort was then successfully undertaken some 780 miles west of San Francisco by the Coast Guard vessel *Campbell*.

Now that the U-2 squadron was established at Beale AFB alongside that for the SR-71, it became easier to identify which missions were best allocated to each of the two thoroughly dissimilar aircraft—which were nevertheless in the same over-all business. As the Air Force was now losing interest in the complex and expensive *Compass Cope* RPV program, the prospects for increased U-2 employment rose.

Interestingly, at this time, Lockheed proposed to the Air Force a U-2R RPV that, it was presumed, could compete with Teledyne Ryan's and Boeing's forthcoming *Compass Cope* submissions. Primarily because it was based on an aircraft that was already in production, Lockheed argued that the U-2R RPV could be built for substantially less money than either of its competitors and yet accomplish all the specified mission objectives.

Compass Cope died a seemingly premature death, and along with it went any hope that a U-2R RPV might be built.

In August of 1976, the 99th SRS began detaching U-2's to RAF Mildenhall in Eastern England with increasing regularity. The detachment became permanent in 1979, with at least two U-2R's (and two SR-71A's) on station at all times. These aircraft, usually seen configured for ELINT, SIGINT, and/or COMINT surveillance, flew missions from Mildenhall at very regular intervals. Many of the missions spanned in excess of ten hours and involved peripheral flight work along the borders of the various European Communist block countries and the Soviet Union.

In Early 1978, a year after it had been proposed to the Air Force, the first details of the new TR-1A program were released. The TR-1A, simply a new-production U-2R with minor changes in secondary internal systems, would be adapted to carry a Hughes Advanced Synthetic Aperture Radar System (ASARS) and a UPD-X side-looking airborne radar, with a range of nearly 50 miles, for use in the European theater. This system, offering excellent high-resolution radar-generated imagery, would be used to provide battlefield commanders with detailed tactical intelligence.

In July of 1977, Lockheed won a full-scale four year development contract for the passive Precision Emitter Location Strike System (PLSS). Tested in prototype form aboard several of the U-2R's operating in and out of Mildenhall during the period from 1977 thru 1980 (these aircraft *may* have been operating as TR-1's and not TR-1A's), PLSS was a direct descendent of the earlier *Pave Onyx* and *Pave Nickel* programs offering tremendous increases in overall speed and accuracy. Additionally, due to advances in solid-state micro-electronics, it was a substan-

Sans super pods and other appurtenances, the second TR-1A, 80-1067, cruises serenely over southern California during a pre-delivery test flight. This aircraft is now assigned to RAF Alconbury in England.

Prior to its delivery flight to England, TR-1A, 80-1067, is seen on the ramp at Beale AFB. Note wing supports required to stabilize the aircraft in a static position.

Rear view of TR-1A, 80-1067, gives a good impression of the split flap configuration distinctive to this U-2 model and appropriately modified U-2R's. The gap in the flaps accommodates the aft portions of the large super pods.

Front view of TR-1A, 80-1067, emphasizes again the split flap arrangement found on this variant. Note, too, the wide stance of the pogos—necessitating SAC-type runways for operation.

TR-1A, 80-1069, taxies out for test mission out of Beale AFB. This aircraft has now joined several other TR-1A's to form the 17th SRW, 95th SRS at RAF Alconbury. This unit is expected to be permanently located at RAF Alconbury and, though remaining under SAC control, will operate in close cooperation with TAC and USAFE.

Another view of Static TR-1A, 80-1067. Aircraft is equipped with both ailerons and spoilers. The latter are utilized more for lift dumping than for roll control.

tially lighter system than its predecessors and therefore less burdensome to its carrier aircraft. In service, PLSS would require the services of several TR-1A's orbiting over friendly territory as they gathered hostile emissions and transmissions. Using a conventional but sophisticated triangulation method, PLSS would permit the precise location and identification of the emitting system and then direct allied aircraft to it for an attack. A portion of the PLSS operation would involve the services of a ground station which would provide direct data link communications with three aircraft at one time.

As the Iranian crisis deepened in 1979 and the US began to expand its military presence in the Indian Ocean, a U-2R was detached to Diego

The first TR-1 two-seat trainer, TR-1B, 80-1064, was delivered to Beale AFB from Lockheed's Palmdale facility in early 1983. The second aircraft, 80-1064, now also has been delivered. Both bear the standard all-white paint scheme chosen by the Air Force for training versions of the U-2.

Garcia, and there utilized in the Iranian and Indian Ocean surveillance role. Direct overflights of a number of sensitive areas followed and the information gathered proved of inestimable value in making decisions of both tactical and strategic importance.

On November 16, 1979, after nearly a twelve year production lapse, the U-2 was reinstated as a production aircraft by the Air Force. The initial contract award to Lockheed, for $10.2 million, called for the refurbishment of Lockheed's Palmdale, California (Air Force Plant #42) facility of old U-2R production tooling that had been in storage at Norton AFB in California since 1969, and the creation of whatever new tooling might be required. The actual production contract, for $42.4 million, calling for an initial batch of two TR-1A's for the Air Force and a single ER-2 for the NASA, was announced less than a month later. This was followed by the news that the Air Force intended to buy ten TR-1 aircraft in 1982, four in 1983, and five in 1984, with a total requirement for 35 (25 TR-1's and possibly 10 U-2R's) by the time production ended. Not widely publicized at the time, but equally important, was the fact that production contracts for the TR-1A/B would be complemented by a small contract for additional U-2R's. These latter aircraft would be utilized to offset attrition that had been suffered since the U-2R's Agency and Air Force introduction in the late 1960's, and also to accommodate the needs of several non-indigenous intelligence forces (i.e., the Nationalist Chinese and, rumor has it, the British, the West Germans, and the Israelis).

Having learned from its past experience with early model U-2's, the Air Force also elected to provide two dual-control training versions of the TR-1 to the 9th SRW for flight training. These aircraft, designated TR-1B, were to join the two U-2CT's for what was originally to have been the 5th Strategic Reconnaissance Training Squadron after the old SAC 9th Wing unit. This unit designator was waived, however, when it was decided to revive the 4029th number from 4080th SRW days. At a later date, the name *The Dragon Tamers* was chosen for the new 4029th SRTS.

Following roll-out from Lockheed's Palmdale, California facility (which employs some 200 personnel) in July of 1981, the first prototype TR-1A (81-1066) took to the air for the first time on August 1st, with Lockheed test pilot Ken Weir at the controls. Pilot introductory work using the first two aircraft was undertaken later that year and by April of 1982, six TR-1A's had been deliverd to Beale. The first TR-1B was completed at Palmdale in January of 1983, and following preliminary ground checks, made its first flight on February 23rd, with Lockheed test pilot Art Peterson at the controls.

At the end of March, 1981, the British government announced that a TR-1 squadron would be based at RAF Alconbury in England from 1983. The support structure for the new outfit, in the form of the 17th Reconnaissance Wing and the 95th Reconnaissance Squadron, had officially come into being on October 1, 1981. Plans as of mid-1983 call for ten of the eighteen TR-1A's eventually expected to be assigned to the Alconbury operation to be equipped with PLSS. The final TR-1A delivery to Alconbury is expected to take place in 1986.

In 1982, with the knowledge that renewed production of the U-2R was assured, the Air Force elected to decommission its remaining U-2C's. These aircraft, by 1982, had logged an extraordinary number of flight hours and in some cases were approaching their theoretical fatigue lives. Following this decision, aircraft picked for permanent preservation were delivered to the Air Force Museum at Wright-Patterson AFB, near Dayton, Ohio, the SAC Museum next to Offutt

AFB near Omaha, Nebraska, the March AFB Museum near Riverside, California, and the National Air & Space Museum in Washington, D.C. Additionally, a damaged U-2C, sometime before the decision to ground the rest of the fleet, had been refurbished following an accident and placed on a pedestal as a gate guardian at Beale AFB (see Appendix "A" for specific aircraft details).

In February of 1983, the first two European-based TR-1A's, 80-1068 and 80-1070, were flown in two-segment non-stop hops from Beale AFB to RAF Alconbury in England—logging nearly 14 hours of flying time and almost 6,000 miles enroute. These aircraft, joining several U-2R's already on station (including the landing accident-damaged 68-10337 — which subsequently was repaired), though operating in Europe and therefore normally falling under the jurisdiction of USAFE, nonetheless remained SAC controlled. It is interesting to note that U-2R's and TR-1's have, on occasion, flown nonstop from Beale AFB to RAF Alconbury—a very revealing feat of extraordinary single-engine aircraft performance and pilot endurance. The 5,600+ miles involved normally takes over 13½ hours to traverse.

TR-1 and U-2R activity continues at a high rate as of the date of this writing. Virtually every military event worldwide of any importance is monitored by these aircraft while operating from any one of some twenty or so OL's. In March of 1982, for instance, the US government revealed that U-2's had photographed an extensive military build-up in Nicaragua. This information was used politically to underscore the Reagan Administration's claims against the Sandanista regime there, and also to back statements concerning the Soviet Union's extensive backing of Sandanista military activities.

The only major change differentiating the TR-1B from the TR-1A is the elevated rear cockpit. The TR-1B maintains most of the combat capabilities of the single-seat version.

The second TR-1B, 80-1065, has only recently been delivered to Beale AFB. This aircraft is identical to the first TR-1B.

Lockheed-California Company

Peter Lewis via Rene Francillon

The 6512th Test Group operating out of Edwards AFB North Base utilized a number of different U-2's including U-2A, 56-6682. Note optical sensor port in lower Q-bay hatch.

Mounting a communications antenna fairing above its rear cockpit, U-2D, 56-6954, is moved into airshow display position at Edwards AFB. This aircraft was attached to the 6512th TG.

Now residing at March AFB as a museum piece, U-2A, 56-6721, configured as a U-2D, is seen during its more active period at Edwards AFB. At the time, it was part of the 6512th TG.

EDWARDS OPS

In the late 1950's, while Gary Powers and other Agency operatives were flying U-2's across the Iron Curtain on their secret missions to gather intelligence data on Soviet military installations, another group of U-2 pilots nearly ten-thousand miles away were helping to perfect reconnaissance systems of the future in the California desert. They worked for the 6512th Test Group of the Air Force's Air Research and Development Command (ARDC) and their specially-modified U-2's flew from Edwards AFB in California on a variety of recce-satellite related support missions.

These programs had been redirected and expanded in 1958 in response to fears that the Soviets were opening up a significant lead in space. The Soviets had successfully orbited the *Sputnik 1* two months ahead of America's *Explorer 1*, and the SS-6 missile used to launch the *Sputnik* satellites was obviously powerful enough to lift significantly heavier and potentially more useful payloads.

At this time, Lockheed was in the forefront of the rapidly accelerating US effort to gain a foothold in space. They were prime contractors on the *Agena* second-stage rocket used to propel satellites into precisely defined orbits, and they also led the team of contractors responsible for developing some of the earliest US recce and early warning satellites including *Discoverer*, SAMOS, and MIDAS.

Early tasks for the Edwards-based U-2's concerned work directly related to the *Discoverer* satellite's data capsule recovery system. The problems associated with successfully retrieving from orbit a sensor system capsule were enormous and they took many years to overcome.

The services of an entire squadron of Fairchild C-119 (later Lockheed C-130) recovery aircraft were eventually required to support the operational requirement. They were (and the C-130's still are) based primarily on Hawaii, and their sole responsibility was (and the C-130's still is) the recovery of recce satellite sensor system payloads.

U-2A, 56-6721, was often seen and photographed at Edwards AFB and as a result, its various modifications are fairly well documented. Here it is seen with a rotating optical sensor ball mounted ahead of the faired communications antenna.

The Edwards U-2's assisted in perfecting this esoteric art by carrying mock-up capsules to altitudes of approximately 70,000 feet and ejecting them into the atmosphere below. Recovery aircraft, practicing their trade, would attempt to intercept the 300-pound dummy capsules as they passed near by. This activity was often photographed by chase U-2's flying overhead.

When the actual *Discoverer* launches got underway in 1959, U-2's flew at high cruising altitudes in the recovery zone to photograph and track the reentry vehicles as they returned from space. This work proved of vital importance as it not only helped perfect sensor capsule recovery technique, it also permitted the reentry data to be used in the search for suitable *Titan* and *Minuteman* warhead reentry vehicle shapes.

Three Lockheed U-2D's were radically modified to support the MIDAS program in *Project Low Card,* which was later renamed *Project Smokey Joe.* These aircraft carried an airborne optical spectrometer in a special rotating "pickle-barrel" housing atop the fuselage, behind the cockpit. The cylinder-shaped installation contained a forward-facing lens which could be used to scan for missile exhaust plumes. An observer was carried in the reconfigured Q-bay to monitor the obtained infra-red signatures. Two small side windows were added to the Q-bay area to give the observers a limited view of the outside world.

MIDAS (Missile Defense Alarm System) was supposed to provide extended warning from space of a Soviet ICBM launch against the US. Edwards U-2D's were detached to Patrick AFB, Florida and Ramey AFB, Puerto Rico, from where they were used to test the MIDAS sensors against American launches of missiles and satellite boosters from Cape Canaveral. These sensors were designed to be able to determine the type of missile, its thrust rating, its trajectory, and its staging.

The MIDAS sensor system technology, unfortunately, was not easily mastered and despite many hours of development aboard the U-2D's during which general background infra-red measurements were taken for a baseline comparison, the ITT-developed sensors proved incapable of reliably discerning the difference between a genuine missile launch and natural phenomena such as cloud-top reflected sunlight. The ITT system also proved to be overweight, and problems with the *Agena* stage contributed to a launch rate of only three satellites in the year and a half which followed the first attempt in February of 1960. Despite some intensive trouble shooting in 1962, the MIDAS system was effectively dead by the following year.

The SAMOS series, also underway at this time, had faired somewhat better than MIDAS. Some excellent photo-recce results had been obtained, including imagery that verified earlier Soviet missile activity first documented by U-2 overflights.

Interestingly, in 1980, DoD planners began to worry about the vulnerability of early warning satellites such as the TRW Block 647's that had been placed in orbit as early as 1970. There was growing concern that these satellites might prove vulnerable to a pre-emptive strike from rapidly developing Soviet anti-satellite systems. The Air Force weapons laboratory at Wright-Patterson AFB proposed to counter this vulnerability with a fall-back warning system of infra-red sensors mounted on a fleet of U-2's which would be used to patrol at 70,000' the probable ballistic missile approach lanes to North America. This program died, but not before extensive studies verified the system's feasibility (these tests may have eventually resulted in the TRIM testbed aircraft mentioned in Chapter 7).

René Francillon collection

Another view of U-2A, 56-6721, as it taxies out on a mission from Edwards AFB shows the aircraft with a revised antenna fairing and a faired-over sensor system hole.

René Francillon

Being given the guiding wand treatment by his back-seater, the pilot of U-2A, 56-6721, is having little difficulty taxiing. Note photo targets on the top of the wing and the side of the vertical stabilizer.

USAF via René Francillon

An unidentified vertical sensor is visible in this photo of U-2A 56-6721 taken at Hickam AFB, Hawaii in July of 1971. Note also the reconfigured communications antenna fairing.

Michael Grove

U-2A, 56-6721, is seen in what was apparently the last major paint scheme of its career. White over-all and with red striping and red AFFTC logo on its vertical fin, it was a striking aircraft from any angle.

Another 6512th TG aircraft, U-2D, 56-6722, with gear down and flaps extended. Note the "Smokey Joe" cartoon on the vertical fin and the rotating optical sensor mounted just ahead of the faired communications antenna.

U-2D, 56-6722, was used to carry dummy recce satellite reentry capsules to altitude for ejection and recovery practice by aircraft flying far below.

Two of the 6512th's several U-2's, 56-6722 and 56-6701, formate over Edwards AFB for a photo session. "Smokey Joe" is visible on the tail of 56-6722.

Though configured as a U-2A, 56-6722 was in fact purpose-built as a U-2D. It is seen bearing its final paint scheme at Edwards AFB prior to removal from the active Air Force inventory.

Though the U-2 branch of Edwards' 6512th Test Group became known as the *Smokey Joe* detachment for its MIDAS support flights, it also performed many other research tasks, as well. With its now-expanded fleet of five aircraft and eight pilots, the assignments became more diverse and included a variety of projects. Among the many were airborne tests of the SAMOS cameras and tests of NASA's *Tiros* and *Nimbus* weather-reporting satellites. During early *Tiros* development, U-2's flew over and photographed at precisely the same time-track of *Tiros* so that a comparative evaluation of the data being returned from the satellite could be made. A similar photo-comparison project was also set up using the North American X-15 research aircraft.

Project Rough Rider was a thunderstorm research program in which large cumulonimbus clouds were penetrated by test aircraft at various flight levels. *Smokey Joe* U-2's participated in this project by flying above the cloud formations being investigated below by other program aircraft. Late in the project, an instrumentation package developed by the Cambridge Research Laboratories was also carried by the U-2's to measure disturbances of the electrical field caused by such thunderstorms. Data obtained with this sensor package was used to assist in the development of a tornado warning system.

The phenomenon of clear air turbulence (CAT) became quite serious in the early 1960's with the development of aircraft that cruised at high subsonic speeds at marginally high altitudes. A number of catastrophic accidents had been directly attributed to CAT and, accordingly, a comprehensive investigation program was initiated to determine its cause and define its characteristics. In 1963, one of the Edwards U-2's (56-6722) was modified under the HICAT program to carry extremely sensitive CAT measurement equipment. The prime purpose of HICAT was to define statistically the essential characteristics of high-altitude clear air turbulence for the purpose of establishing criteria for the design of airframe

Interesting overhead view of 56-6722 taken over the desert near Edwards AFB. Note flaps in gust position.

structures. A secondary function was to correlate the turbulence measurements with significant geophysical and meteorological factors.

The HICAT instrumentation system comprised two main elements: the sensor-equipped aircraft and the ground station. The U-2 had a long, stiff boom (nicknamed a "barber's pole") extending from the aircraft nose, upon which vanes were mounted to sense vertical and lateral gusts; longitudinal gusts were sensed by a pressure transducer in the aircraft pitot-static airspeed measuring system. Fluctuating air velocities, due to rough air, were detected by the vanes, and the responsive small movements that they made generated proportional electrical signals which were recorded on magnetic tape. In order that a true record of atmospheric conditions be obtained, these signals were corrected by subtracting from the apparent gust velocities the effects of gust-induced movements of the sensor aircraft, as measured by accelerometers and by rate and attitude gyros.

The aircraft contained equipment for making an analog oscillograph (time history) record of the flight. This "quick look" record was processed immediately after a HICAT search flight, and was examined to evaluate the flight from three aspects: 1. Structural safety; 2. Satisfactory measurement of data; and 3. Indication of HICAT encounter. After evaluation, the flight-recorded tape and "quick look" records were transmitted to the ground station at Burbank, California, where the information was processed for use in a computer. The significant portions of the flight-recorder tape were then converted to an edited and modified form; this revised tape was then fed into a computer which detected errors and corrected them, then calibrated and numerically filtered the data.

Corrected gust velocities were next computed and plotted graphically with such other flight parameters as airspeed, Mach number, altitude, temperature, and center-of-gravity acceleration. Because of the apparently random character of atmospheric turbulence, statistical methods of analysis were required. These consisted primarily of peak counts of the gust-velocity time-histories and computations of gust-velocity power spectra. Peak counts were simple classifications of the number of gust velocity peaks within a set of designated velocity intervals. The power spectra concept was somewhat complex but, basically, showed how the average intensity of gust-velocity varied with the turbulence wavelength. Very short wavelengths, of about 60 feet, had little power and did not have any significant effect on most aircraft, whereas the longer wavelengths, of 1000 feet or more, usually had a much more powerful

effect. HICAT gust-velocity peak counts and power-spectra data were computed and plotted from measurements obtained over a wide range of altitude, geographical locations, and meterological conditions.

The HICAT project was conducted over several years and took the uniquely marked all-black aircraft initially to Puerto Rico, Alaska, and Panama. The program was extended in 1965, and with improved instrumentation, the HICAT U-2 visited Fiji, New Zealand, and Australia in October of 1966, and Britain in March of 1967. The British program resulted in a two-month stay with operations taking place at the RAE airfield at Bedford.

The main subject of the latter assignment was wave turbulence generated by the Scottish mountains. Data derived from this assignment was later used in research for the Anglo-French *Concorde* supersonic airliner and the projected American SST.

Although U-2 research flight activities at Edwards were scaled-down in the late-1960's, two aircraft continued to serve the Air Force Flight Test Center in a variety of roles until they were returned to Lockheed in 1978. Interestingly, the surviving Edwards U-2's, at the time of their return to Lockheed, were the last Air Force aircraft still flying powered by Pratt & Whitney J57's.

A decision to use a U-2 as the HICAT sensor system testbed led to this modification to 56-6722. Note the large boom protruding from the underside of nose.

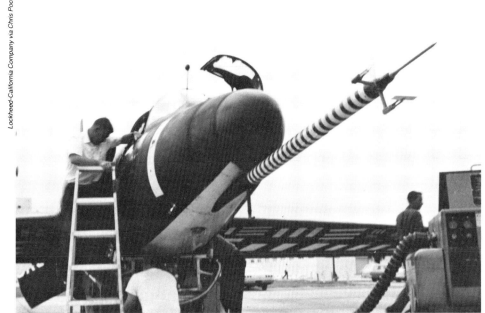

Detail of HICAT sensor boom shows yaw and pitch sensors and paint scheme unique to the HICAT aircraft. Program produced significant data on clear air turbulence.

Following HICAT, 56-6722 remained configured for the mission, though most of the related sensors had been removed. At the time of this photo, the aircraft was painted in a variety of photo markings for ground-based tracking camera calibration tests.

NASA currently flies and maintains two U-2C's, including 56-6681 (NASA 708). These aircraft are used for a wide variety of earth resources related programs and, as of this writing, are the only U-2C's still being flown.

Bearing an early NASA paint scheme, 56-6682 (NASA 709), sits on the main ramp at NASA's Ames, California facility prior to departure on a research mission. Aircraft is identified as being "Earth Survey Aircraft No.5." NASA 708 at the time was referred to as being "Earth Survey Aircraft No.4."

Newest addition to NASA's high-altitude aircraft stable is the ER-2. This aircraft is a demilitarized TR-1A and is, in fact, the first aircraft to roll off the rehabilitated Palmdale, California U-2R/TR-1 production line. The ER-2 has been allocated the 80-1063 Air Force serial number.

Chapt. 6:
THE OPERATIONAL HISTORY— NACA/NASA

As has already been mentioned elsewhere in this book, the first involvement of the NACA in the U-2 story came at an early stage when the Central Intelligence Agency decided that the NACA's fictionalized use of the aircraft would serve as the U-2's cover. The existence of the U-2, in fact, was revealed under just this guise when on May 7, 1956, Dr. Hugh Dryden, then director of the NACA, issued a press release stating that the U-2 was a new NACA research tool developed for the study of turbulence and meteorological conditions. It also stated that the NACA was running the U-2 program with the technical assistance of the Air Force's Air Weather Service.

This first release was followed, on May 22nd, with another which covered the first move to Europe. This announcement took great pains to point out that the operation was a non-military affair that used "civilian planes with civilian pilots." Heavy emphasis was placed on the fact that the aircraft were being used for meteorological studies.

As the U-2 overflight program progressed in Europe, it became more and more difficult for the NACA and, in 1958, the NASA, to maintain the long-transparent cover. In fact, the NASA weather reconnaissance program that did eventually eminate from the original U-2 recce program was undertaken as a by-product of the intelligence flights, rather than a dedicated separate activity.

Gary Powers eventually brought an end to the NACA/NASA cover program and following the loss of his aircraft to the Soviets, a number of NASA releases were provided the media in an effort to explain the Administration's U-2 involvement in more believable terms. After the Powers shoot-down, Dryden told a Senate committee that there had been some 200 flights since 1956 which carried NASA and Air Force Air Weather

Service instrumentation. The flights had logged some 264,000 miles with no less than 90 percent of the flight time being spent at altitudes above 40,000' and 40 percent above 50,000'. Some of the mileage (which was later raised to 315,000) mentioned by Dryden was almost certainly logged totally by the Air Force with no NACA/NASA involvement whatsoever.

Powers' loss also permitted the first close-up media examination of the U-2 when a purported NASA aircraft with the fictitious serial number of 55741 on the vertical fin was placed on display at NASA's Edwards AFB facility on May 6, 1960. This aircraft had, in fact, been operated by the Agency at Groom Lake and Edwards' North Base, and was almost certainly one of the first aircraft built—though information documenting this fact was never released.

NASA's work with the U-2 was strictly a paper exercise for the benefit of the Central Intelligence Agency from 1955 through 1970. However, on April 2, 1971, the NASA was at last permitted actual use when the Air Force, through its Acquisition Logistics Division at Wright-Patterson AFB, agreed to place on permanent loan to the NASA, two U-2C's, 56-6681 and 56-6682, which in fact had originally been assigned to the Agency as N-801X and N-802X (Articles 347 and 348), respectively and earlier used for the aircraft carrier trials conducted in 1963 and 1964. Once assigned to the NASA, they were registered N-708NA and N-709NA and based out of the Ames Research Center at NAS Moffett, California.

It should be noted that the original intent of NASA was to fly these aircraft with U.S. civil registrations only visible. However, when it was discovered that a loophole in the Federal tax laws would permit the aircraft to use fuel without hav-

ing to pay Federal fuel taxes if they bore their official Air Force serial numbers externally, the numbers were duly painted in place. The NASA aircraft continue to wear their Air Force serial numbers to this very day for only this reason.

The NASA U-2's, now called Earth Resources Survey Aircraft, formed the nucleus of what soon became the NASA High Altitude Missions Branch (HAMB) under the auspices of the Ames Astronautics Directorate, and were assigned the responsibility of conducting data collection flights to support a variety of earth resources related projects.

An initial long term assignment for the newly arrived U-2's was the Ames Airborne Instrumentation Research Project (AIRP). This was designed to collect data over various test sites simultaneously with the passes of the Earth Resources and Technology Satellite (ERTS); to support general earth resources programs in conjunction with other government agencies; to conduct observations in astronomy, high-altitude atmospheric physics and geophysics; and to collect data for disaster assessment.

Many missions were eventually flown in support of the ERTS which had been preceded by missions to provide satellite simulation data over a variety of test sites for use by government, university, and industry scientists connected with the ERTS program. Once launch of the satellite was accomplished in July of 1972, the project began to provide "underflight" support data to over 50 ERTS program investigators. At a later date, the project also provided support to the *Skylab* Earth Resources Experiment package launched aboard *Skylab* 1 in May of 1973.

Besides AIRP missions, the NASA U-2's have been used to fly numerous disaster assessment flights. Under an agreement with the State of

Overhead view of a NASA U-2C and its many sensors illustrates the wide variety of cameras and other sensors available to civilian contractors through the NASA. Most of these sensors are described in detail in the sensor system chapter.

Excellent view of 56-6681 on final to NASA Ames. aircraft is equipped with pylon-mounted fuel tanks and a nose sensor boom.

Outfitted for optical sensors, 56-6682 heads for a landing at NASA Ames. Note lower Q-bay hatch with large camera ports. Both NASA aircraft were originally assigned to the Agency.

NASA aircraft bear both NASA numbers and their original Air Force-assigned serial numbers. Note that one man is capable of moving the entire tail section of the aircraft using special dolly.

NASA maintains its U-2C's and ER-2 in a single hangar at Ames research Center. Both types are shown undergoing routine maintenance. Note that NASA 709 is sitting on its special transport dolly.

California, the U-2's help state officials evaluate fire and flood damage. Missions are flown to get the fastest possible aerial photographic coverage of natural disasters. In the case of forest and brush fires, U-2 photos have shown previously unknown access routes on an advancing fire front, have indicated ideal placement of new fire-breaks, and have identified dangerous areas where fire fighters could be trapped. Experience with numerous fires has shown the U-2 data has helped fire fighters contain fires sooner with direct savings of manpower and equipment and valuable resources of forest, watersheds, and wildlife habitat.

In addition to generating photo imagery, a number of sensor system experiments have been conducted and continue to be conducted as of the date of this publication. Studies range from astronomy to stratospheric sampling to earth observation. In deployments to Honolulu, Hawaii; Fairbanks, Alaska; Wallops Island, Virginia; Loring AFB, Maine; and Howard AFB, Panama, NASA U-2's have been used to measure the distribution and extent of ozone, nitric oxide, and aerosol particulates in the atmosphere at altitudes up to 70,000'. These expeditions are part of a semi-global study to aid a national research program concerned with how these gases and particulates may affect the ozone layer over a long period of time.

Prior to the launch of the *Nimbus* G satellite, an Ocean Color Scanner (which is an imaging radiometer), was flown in a NASA U-2 to test the remote sensing of ocean color to identify and map regions of high food productivity, upwelling regions, extent of the tide, sediment concentration off the coast, and coastal zone inventory.

NASA's U-2's were also utilized to fly the Heat Capacity Mapper. This thermal scanner was another breadboard system to simulate *Nimbus* G. Among the studies pursued were: measurement of variations of soil moisture content, thermal pollution in water, and crop production inventories.

NASA U-2's also participated in a study called the Aether Drift Experiment in which Lawrence Lab physicists at Berkeley explored the validity of the "big bang" theory of the universe's origins. Using an upward looking radiometer they located and measured minute variations in cosmic radiation heat intensities.

NASA maintains an inventory of cameras that has been used extensively in earth observation studies—particularly in support of satellite missions. Some camera payloads (or configurations) use four identically pointed 70mm film cameas with filters to simulate the LANDSAT multi-spectral scanner. Higher resolution imagery is obtained by using 9" film with 6", 12", 24" and 36" focal length lenses. Although the 6" and 12" lenses are used with a 9" × 9" image format, the 24" and 39" lenses are frequently used to make a 9" × 18" negative or transparency. The ground coverage and resolution are a function of lens focal length and film format.

A variety of film types is used, depending on the intended use of the imagery. Included, for example, are Panatomic-X Aerial and Plus-X black and white, Infrared Aerographic black and white infrared, Aerochrome (color) Infrared, Aerial Color, and Ektachrome EF Aerographic natural color films. Each frame of imagery is automatically annotated with a 16-digit code indicating the sensor, film type, date, and time of exposure. All imagery is indexed and archived in the NASA U-2 Data Facility.

Most nonphotographic sensors flown on the NASA U-2's are client-supplied and funded. An investigator's equipment can be installed in several areas on the U-2 subject to load factors,

A Lockheed team completes the move of NASA's ER-2 fuselage into the final assembly building at Lockheed's Palmdale facility in March of 1981. The ER-2 was the first aircraft completed on the newly revamped U-2/TR-1 production line and as such, became the prototype for the new TR-1 series.

safety standards, and construction constraints.

The Q-bay on NASA U-2's is quite similar to that found in military and CIA aircraft and is pressurized and heated. It holds a maximum of 750 pounds and has top and bottom hatches that are easily removed by means of external latches. Racks to support or contain electronics or other equipment generally must be made to fit the Q-bay attachment points. In addition to the Q-bay, two wing pods can hold up to 300 pounds (ea.) of sensor equipment at ambient pressures and temperatures. An additional 100 pounds of equipment can be supported in the upper fuselage in the dorsal canoe also at ambient conditions.

NASA has available a high-density M14E magnetic tape data recorder that is available for client use, but it has been noted that most clients prefer to provide their own. Client-supplied sensors that have been carried by NASA U-2's include a heat capacity mapping radiometer; an ocean color scanner (OCS); an HRB-454 thermal scanner; an Ames in situ gas sampler; a cryogenic and whole air sampler; a high-speed Michelson interferometer; an infrared scanning spectrometer; an Ames filter sampler; a water vapor radiometer; an aerosol particle sampler; a resonance fluorescence experiment package; a carbon dioxide collector; and an infrared radiometer.

To complement its U-2 efforts, the NASA has an aircraft support Data Facility located at Ames Research Center that is responsible for maintaining complete flight documentation, a computerized image storage and selection system, copies of all imagery, a microfilm browse file, and a variety of light tables and optical image viewing equipment. If arrangements are made in advance, all imagery is available for viewing by visitors, and photo-copies of imagery may be made with the visitor's own equipment. By established policy, all NASA earth resource imagery, both satellite and aircraft, is in the "public domain."

Flight summary reports are published for each data collection flight. These brief reports list the sensors used and the kinds of data collected. They also contain a track map showing the location of individual data runs. The Data Entry System is used to compile descriptive data for each image in a computerized memory bank with the use of a digitizer tablet and reference maps. The data can then be retrieved through the computerized Image Selection System via a graphics terminal. Available images can be identified according to geographic location, imagery scale, film type, data format, cloud cover, quality, spectral band, etc. Selected scenes can then be viewed quickly and easily with the microfilm

A successful ending to a successful first flight. NASA's new ER-2, still unpainted, comes to a rest on its port wing skid at Palmdale following its first flight on May 11, 1982.

Though the landing gear were cycled during the first flight, this photo shows them in the down and locked position with the aircraft in a cruise attitude. Lockheed test pilot Art Peterson was at the controls.

Lockheed-California Company

On final to Palmdale, Art Peterson prepares for a first landing in the ER-2. Aircraft remained unpainted unti shortly before delivery to the NASA.

Aerofax, Inc. collection

ER-2 went into immediate service at NASA Ames following its arrival and has proved a worthy successor to its two significantly older stablemates. Greatly increased payload capacities have been a boon to researchers.

Michael Grove

Like TR-1's, the ER-2 is equipped to carry large super pods. These are used only for the transport of sensor systems, as the aircraft carries more than sufficient fuel in its wings for any possible mission.

Aerofax, Inc./Jay Miller

Ground handling of the ER-2 is facilitated by folding wingtips. The TR-1A and U-2R also have folding wingtips. Note hatches removed from the Q-bay in this photo.

browse film for final assessment before the actual imagery is retrieved for viewing.

The U-2C's have been used at a rate of approximately 100 flights per year per aircraft since their acquisition. NASA feels that the aircraft offer investigators an opportunity to conduct experiments in flight regimes that would otherwise be impossible to achieve. The NASA's Ames Research Center is prepared to assist prospective investigators in developing flight test procedures. U-2 flight support is initiated through a simple flight request system and approval process. This process integrates all aspects of the test program from aircraft scheduling to data processing.

In June of 1982, NASA's two U-2C's were complemented by the arrival of the ER-2 (80-1063/N-706NA). This aircraft, a "demilitarized" TR-1A, had been a line item in NASA's budget for some time, and some sources claim, had directly led to the virtual termination of high altitude flight test work using the NASA's three General Dynamics RB-57F's (operating, at the time, out of NASA's facility at Ellington AFB, near Houston, Texas). Money that had originally been intended for RB-57F program support was supposedly all but eliminated in order to fund the new ER-2.

NASA's ER-2 had preceded the first TR-1A off the production line (technically becoming the prototype for the TR-1A series), and was delivered (following its first flight at Palmdale, California on May 11, 1981, with Art Peterson at the controls) on June 10th to the high-altitude flight operation at Ames Research Center. The first operational NASA mission took place on June 12th. While development of the ER-2's dedicated sensor "superpods" was being completed, this aircraft was initially used for training missions to familiarize NASA pilots with its performance characteristics.

The ER-2 offers a marked improvement in payload capacity, endurance, and range over that of its two U-2C stablemates, and most importantly, it is also a significantly more comfortable aircraft for pilots. The payload capacity is in excess of 3,000 pounds and the aircraft is capable of carrying this weight over a range in excess of 3,000 n. miles. Available time at altitude is over

There are no major external differences between the ER-2 and the TR-1A. The "demilitarization" process involved in clearing the ER-2 for NASA use concerned removing dedicated internal support systems for certain military sensors.

6 hours and 30 minutes, and maximum altitude capability is in the vicinity of 75,000'. Cubic footage space available is as follows: "superpods," 86 cubic ft. ea.; nose compartment, 47 cubic ft.; data link bay, 1.8 cu. ft.; and Q-bay, approximately 85 cubic ft. The "superpods" are capable of accommodating up to 750 pounds each; the nose can handle 600 pounds; and the Q-bay, 750 pounds (these figures are applicable to the U-2R and TR-1, as well).

The ER-2 has been delivered to NASA capable of accommodating a number of extant sensor systems including the following: high-altitude multispectral scanner; linear array scanner; large format camera systems; real-time data link; multi-component experiments (stratospheric sampling, severe storms/meteorology, shuttle experiment development, and research in astronomy and astrophysics); a Wild-Heerbrugg RC-10 dual camera configuration (9" × 9" format); and an Itek Iris II high resolution panoramic camera (4½" × 58" format). A digital X-band synthetic aperture radar was requested but never funded.

Other stratospheric experiments capable of being transported by the ER-2 include: airborne gas chromatograph; Decibi ozone monitor; cryogenic sampler; stratospheric air sampler (SAS II); INS stratospheric wind experiment; infrared spectrometer; Knollenberg 2d probe; frost point hygrometer; water vapor radiometer; multi-filter sampler; aerosol particulate sampler; and an infrared radiometer.

Both U-2C's and the single ER-2 remain operational with the NASA at this time. The U-2C's are apparently the only examples of this U-2 model still in service as of this writing. It is now assumed to be only a matter of time before the U-2C's are withdrawn from NASA service and replaced by a second ER-2.

NASA's ER-2 taxies in from landing following pre-delivery test flight from Palmdale. Shortly after ER-2 arrival at Ames, super pods were removed for reconfiguring to NASA sensor system specifications.

ER-2 departs Palmdale during pre-delivery test flight. Aircraft was painted in NASA scheme shortly before delivery to Ames.

Photo taken by Agency U-2 during Soviet overflight in 1959 shows Tyuratam missile launch facility. The Type B camera was used.

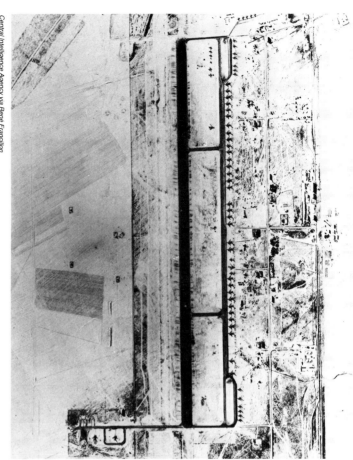

A Type B camera photo of a Soviet airbase illustrating a large number of Mya-4 "Bisons" and Tu-16 "Badgers."

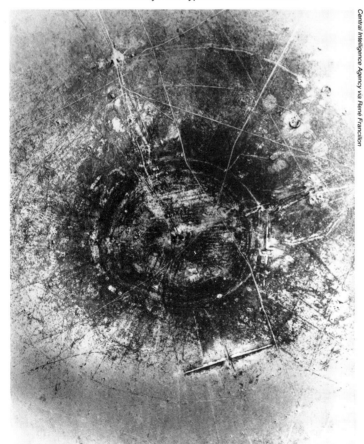

A nuclear weapons test site photographed by a U-2 using a Type B Camera during an overflight of the Soviet Union in 1959.

A view of a Soviet submarine base in the Barents Sea showing "Whiskey" and "Foxtrot" class submarines next to tenders. Taken from a U-2 using a Type B camera.

Chapt. 7:
SENSOR SYSTEMS AND INTERPRETERS

With the birth of the U-2 program in late-1953 came a high priority need for a dedicated photo interpretation unit of the highest caliber. Extraordinary advances in the quality of photo imagery underscored this need, and the end result, in 1953, was the creation of the Central Intelligence Agency's Photographic Intelligence Division. This high-technology unit, which specialized in defining objects of interest gathered on the film of recce aircraft and other photo intelligence gathering devices, was headed by a Richard Bissell-pick, University of Chicago instructor, Art Lundahl. Lundahl, in turn, directed a team of thirteen master photo interpreters who could tell from the shadows cast by an object between the ideal recce times of 10 a.m. and 2 p.m., exactly how tall, long, or wide it was.

Lundahl was no novice at photo interpretation, himself. During World War 2, he had worked with Naval Intelligence and in 1945 had gone to Anacostia with the Navy's division for what was then called "photogrammetry" (the art and science of imagery analysis). Later, after joining the Agency, he played a key role in the creation of a photogrammetric division within the Directorate of Intelligence which, in 1958, was merged with a statistical analysis division from the Office of Current Intelligence to form the Photographic Intelligence Center (PIC). In 1961, after the Powers affair had begun to cool, this was made a "service of common concern" to be utilized by the entire intelligence community and operated by the Agency. It was then renamed the National Photographic Interpretation Center (NPIC).

The PIC, by the late 1950's, had become the core unit for the interpretation and dissemination of photo imagery acquired by clandestine reconnaissance. Film from all over the world was transported to this Washington, D.C. facility for interpretation, and oftentimes, also for processing. The interpretive process was complex, and involved a variety of sciences. It was facilitated, with the advent of the U-2, by the development of highly refined optics, greatly improved films, and an ever expanding interpretive experience base.

Lundahl, after being "brought in" on the U-2 project in December of 1954, agreed to head up the small and very secretive photo interpretation unit. He spent several days trying to locate an inconspicuous spot for his new operation and eventually settled in a room located over an auto repair shop in a slum section of southeast Washington, D.C. Shortly afterwards, he coined the code name *Automat* for the operation and immediately went to work assembling the equipment and personnel required for the job.

There were, in essence, three primary tools required for the U-2 to be successful in its mission. The first was a camera, the second was a high-accuity lens, and third was a special film. Work on all three had been completed by the time the U-2 overflight program had been initiated by the Agency and the resulting fruit were the secret marvels of the photography world.

The camera, known as the "B Camera" (or Model 73B), was a high-technology machine offering extraordinary stability, an articulation technique permitting it to rotate its lens from side to side in order to create overlapping stereoscopic imagery, and a nominal weight of just over 400 pounds. It had the attributes of precise image movement compensation (the ability to accurately

Photo of Davis-Monthan AFB taken from a distance in excess of 75 miles at an altitude of approximately 70,000' using a Type H LOROP camera.

compensate for the movement of the transport aircraft over the ground and the movement of the film during the photography process), automatic lens focusing (in consideration of altitude variations), and automatic exposure control (offering a minimum light seeking ability which enabled the camera to ignore things such as scattered clouds and expose for the shadows). It was the end product of work undertaken by Dr. Edwin Land, the father of Polaroid and a photo genius of unparalleled ability. The Hycon Corporation was the producer of this sophisticated high resolution strip film device and when the U-2 program was funded, a contract was let to Hycon for production of some twenty-five units.

Perhaps the heart of the U-2's photo imagery gathering ability was the "B Camera's" lens. This device was the end product of work done by Dr. James Baker, a respected Harvard University astronomer who had for years struggled with the complex optical mathematics and glass chemistry required to create a lens of the quality demanded by high-altitude recce photography. Baker's end product, a 36" focal length unit, offered resolving power unmatched by any other lens in the world at the time of its debut. Its accuity was rated at nearly 60 lines per millimeter—no less than four times the maximum obtainable from comparable lenses developed less than a decade earlier during World War 2. At 65,000', surface objects less than 2' in diameter were discernible and interpretable.

Extant films in the early 1950's had several major failings when it came to using them in the recce role. For one thing, their film base (the clear

gel-like substance that serves as the carrier base for the light-sensitive emulsions) was disproportionately thick and heavy (thus limiting the amount of film that could be carried), and for another, it was not strong enough for the job. Eastman Kodak tackled these and several other disconcerting problems and created the first of its mylar-base films. This new base, coupled with tremendous improvements in emulsions and their related coating methods, resulted in films offering high speed, fine grain, high accutance, high contrast, and maximum utilization of camera film cartridge space. Particularly important was the ability to place a layer of emulsion no thicker than 5 microns on the thin mylar. This reduced turbidity (the scattering of light rays through the emulsion) and thus greatly improved the sharpness of the final image.

Another important high-altitude photo recce element that was mastered was that of camera bay environmental control. Great pains were taken in the U-2 to control such things as temperature, humidity, and pressurization, and these proved instrumental in providing photo imagery of the highest quality obtainable. Temperature and air pressure were rigorously controlled in the Q-bay where the "B Camera" was mounted, and time was allocated for these two factors to stabilize (known as "cold soaking") as transitions were made from one altitude to another. Temperature changes had a significant effect on the lens as the expansion and contraction factors that came into play could wreak havoc on the fine focusing required for the sharpest images.

In a final improvement to the recce photo imag-

Overhead view of NASA U-2C Q-bay with both upper and lower hatches removed. A large variety of payloads can be accommodated in this bay.

View inside U-2C Q-bay looking aft. Empennage section control cables can be seen running down either side. The Q-bay structure supports the cockpit and nose section.

View inside ER-2 Q-bay looking forward. Round cut-outs on bulkhead are bleed valves for pressurized air from the cockpit. Note the large number of electrical connectors.

ery process, Lundahl and his interpreters became some of the first of a new breed of photo analysis experts who were permitted to actually interpret the film without permitting "field commanders" access to the end product. This change came about as a result of strong and undeniably valid arguments in favor of interpreting directly from the negative, rather than from a printed image. It was difficult for novices to understand, but intelligence data could more easily be gleaned directly from a negative than it could from a print. Paper prints had a contrast range of 100 to 1, whereas the associated negative offered a contrast range of no less than 1000 to 1. This fact, coupled with the higher resolution and lower transfer losses achieved by working directly from the negative, permitted interpreters to extract intelligence data that otherwise would have forever remained undiscovered.

The U-2's ability to gather photo imagery is well documented elsewhere in this book, but suffice it to say that there was a continuing program within the intelligence community to develop better and more sophisticated sensors of all kinds, including those of the optical and other electromagnetic frequencies.

Most of the monitors developed for the gathering of ELINT, unfortunately, remain extremely sensitive as of this writing, but basically, they consist of dedicated (by frequency band) antennas, interpretive electronic filtering systems, and large capacity tape recorders. In most cases, these units are used simply to gather electromagnetic radiation in the form of communications and active radiating systems (such as radar) and this data is then recorded on mylar tape for interpretation after the aircraft returns to base. This is primarily a passive activity with no jamming or communicating ability being involved.

Data gathered using these passive receivers is accumulated in order to develop potential countermeasures and to categorize the various systems. The development of countermeasures is very dependent upon the interpretation of the radiated signals, as their frequency, band widths, pulse, and power are all subject to virtually infinite variability that will drastically affect the design and performance of the countermeasure.

Since the birth of the U-2 as a viable sensor system platform in 1956, a tremendous number of sensors have been utilized aboard the aircraft. It is virtually impossible to list them all and give their capabilities, but the following is a summary based on the best information available at the time of this writing. Wherever possible, data concerning the system's use and user agency, is given.

TYPE H CAMERA:

This unit built by Actron (now the imaging systems group of McDonnell Douglas Corp.) is a folded-optics camera of some 66" focal length. It is considered to be a LOROP (Long Range Oblique Photography) system designed for use at high altitudes and slant ranges approaching 100 miles. This camera was developed for use by the CIA and the Air Force in the U-2 and A-12 in the late 1960's to compensate for the curtailment of direct overflight capability. The first of three operational units was delivered in April of 1965. The camera used a 4.5×4.5 film format, and with Ektachrome 3414 film it provided an image resolution of 65 lines per mm. Control of the Type H camera was maintained from the cockpit and the pilot could aim it using the U-2's driftsight meter to determine target angle. This data was then manually transferred to the camera by a control mounted in the cockpit. The lens indexed through 7 positions (nadir, 3 left oblique and 3 right oblique).

Close-up of HASP configured U-2A, 56-6714. Particulate collectors are located in hard nose and Q-bay.

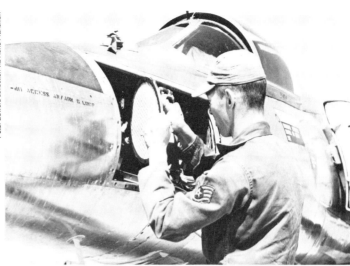

Servicing filters in hard nose section of HASP U-2A. Normal procedures require the wearing of gloves.

KA-102A CAMERA:

This camera, manufactured by Itek under contract to the Atomic Energy Commission and the Air Force, is similar in most respects to the Type H camera and has 66" focal length folded optics. It is considered to be a LOROP system and is designed for use at extremely high altitudes and slant ranges approaching 100 miles. It is thought still to be operational. It uses 4.5×4.5 film format, and with Ektachrome 3414 film, provides an image resolution of 65 lines per mm. The film magazine contains 700 feet of 5" wide film with a capacity of 1,675 frames per roll. Angular coverage is 3-deg. 54'. The lens indexes through 7 positions (nadir, 3 left oblique and 3 right oblique).

TYPE B CAMERA:

This camera, developed primarily for the CIA and described in some detail earlier, was the first of the super-high-resolution cameras to be carried by the U-2. The lens was identified as an HR73B1 of 36" focal length. The angular field of view was 28-deg. The camera imaged onto two 9½" wide frames of film through a single lens, producing an 18" × 18" exposure. The lens indexed through 7 positions (nadir, 3 left oblique and 3 right oblique). Camera operation was mechanically programmed to provide a 50% to 70% overlap.

VINTEN MULTI-SPECTRAL CAMERA SYSTEM:

This consists of four 1¾" focal length, 70mm Vinten framing cameras which can spectrally simulate the Return Beam Vidicon (RBV) aboard LANDSAT. Film/filter combinations may be installed as required by specific mission requirements. Each camera magazine is capable of a 100' film load or approximately 450 exposures. Overlap is controlled by an intervalometer which is variable from 2 to 120 seconds in 1 second intervals. Format size is 2¼" × 2³⁄₁₆"; the lens is a Leitz 1¾" f2.8 with an angular field of view of 64-deg. 30'; ground coverage from 65,000' is 14 × 14 n. miles; ground resolution from 65,000' is 30' to 50'.

RC-10 METRIC CAMERA:

The Wild-Heerbrug RC-10 is a standard 9" × 9" format aerial camera with interchangeable 6" or 12" focal length lens cones. They have been certified for aerial mapping purposes by the U.S. Geological Survey. The film magazine is capable of holding a 400' roll of film providing approximately 450 exposures. The image overlap is controlled by an intervalometer adjustable from 2 to 120 seconds in 1 second intervals. The nominal 60% overlap is 58 seconds for the 6" lens and 29 seconds for the 12". The lens is a Wild-Heerbrug Universal Aviogon II and the angular field of view is 73-deg.45' for the 6" lens and 41-deg. for the 12"; ground coverage from 65,000' is 16 × 16 n. miles for the 6" lens and 8 × 8 n. miles for the 12"; ground resolution from 65,000' is 15' to 25' for the 6" lens and 4' to 15' for the 12".

A-3 CAMERA SYSTEM:

The A-3 consists of three vertically mounted HR-732, 24" focal length cameras. The configuration allows for the cameras to be operated simultaneously, singly, or in combination to allow for either extended data acquisition or multi-emulsion coverage. Image motion compensation (IMC) is provided for by an assembly which rocks all three cameras simultaneously. Camera opera-

Close-up of Q-bay equipped with particulate sampling equipment. Barely visible in particulate sampler intake is valve for controlling airflow. HASP-configured U-2A is 56-6696.

Detail of precedent-setting Type B camera. Folded optics lens and bulk quantity film magazines made this a formidable intelligence instrument. Lens rotated from side to side.

The Vinten multi-spectral camera system consists of four small cameras arranged to spectrally simulate the RBV aboard LANDSAT.

tion is controlled by an intervalometer which is adjustable in 1 second intervals from 2 to 120 seconds. A nominal 60% overlap is provided by a 15 second intervalometer setting. Each camera magazine is capable of holding up to 1,800' of film or approximately 1,200 exposures. Format size of 9" × 18"; the lens is an HR-732 of 24" focal length with an angular field of view of 41-deg. × 21-deg.; ground coverage from an altitude of 65,000' is 4 × 8 n. miles; and ground resolution from 65,000' is 2' to 8'.

A-4 CAMERA SYSTEM:

The A-4 camera configuration consists of two cameras: one RC-10 and one HR-732. This system is used to provide large area coverage and small area, large scale coverage along the same flight path. The RC-10 camera is mounted vertically and is identical to those previously described. The HR-732 camera can be operated in vertical or "rocking" modes. The rocking mode provides sequential vertical, left oblique, and right oblique coverage. Image motion compensation is provided for the HR-732. Camera operation is controlled by an intervalometer and is adjusted in 1 second intervals from 2 to 120 seconds. All other specifications are the same as those listed for the cameras in preceding configurations.

DUAL RC-10 CAMERA SYSTEM:

The dual RC-10 configuration consists of two vertically mounted RC-10 cameras. The system is normally flown to provide multi-emulsion or multi-scale coverage. Camera operation is controlled by an intervalometer which is variable from 2 to 120 seconds in 1 second intervals. All other specifications are the same as those listed for this camera in preceding configurations.

IIS MULTI-SPECTRAL CAMERA:

The IIS (International Imaging Systems) camera consists of a single camera body and four separate lenses to provide for multi-spectral coverage. All lenses image on the same film emulsion, eliminating the chance of roll-to-roll processing variation. Camera operation is controlled by an intervalometer which is variable from 2 to 120 seconds in 1 second intervals. Format size is four 3½" × 3½" images on a 9" × 9" format; the lens is actually four 3.95" lenses with angular fields of view of 47-deg.; ground coverage from an altitude of 65,000' is 9.5 × 9.5 miles; and ground resolution from 65,000' is 20' to 30'.

OPTICAL BAR CAMERA:

The Itek optical bar camera is a high resolution panoramic camera with a 24" focal length Itek KA-80A lens with an angular field of view of 120-deg. The format size is 4½" × 50". The magazine is capable of holding up to 6,500' of film. Ground coverage from an altitude of 65,000' is 85 square miles; ground resolution from 65,000' is 2'.

VINTEN CAMERA (tracker installation):

This is an experimental configuration used in conjunction with the Ocean Color Scanner. It consists of the Vinten Multi-Spectral Camera System as described previously.

HP37 PANORAMIC CAMERA (tracker modification):

This is an experimental configuration using a Hycon HP-307 panoramic camera fitted with a remote intervalometer mounted adjacent to the camera, which can be adjusted to provide various percentages of photo overlap.

T-35 TRACKER CAMERA:

A relatively small camera used in conjunction with client developed experimental sensor payloads.

The Wild-Heerbrug RC-10 metric camera is optimized for aerial mapping purposes.

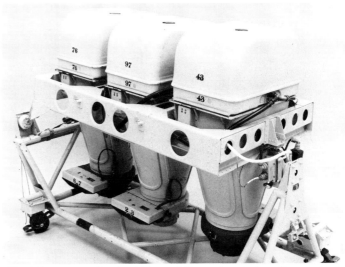

The A-3 camera system is a high-resolution system designed to operate at very high altitudes. Early U-2's often carried this system.

The dual RC-10 metric camera configuration provides either multi-emulsion or multi-scale coverage of a target area.

The Itek optical bar camera is an extremely high resolution sensor designed for panoramic (horizon-to-horizon) coverage of a target area.

Almost all of the above optical sensor systems were originally developed for use by the Central Intelligence Agency and/or the Air Force. With few exceptions, they remain in service in one form or another, many being utilized on a regular basis by the NASA. Known U-2 optical sensor systems that AEROFAX was unable to obtain descriptive information about include the Delta III camera, the A-1 camera, the A-2 camera, and the Perkin-Elmer Model 501 camera.

JOINT SURVEILLANCE TARGET ATTACK RADAR SYSTEM (J-STARS):

An Air Force/Army program under contract to Hughes Aircraft Co., Grumman Aerospace, UTC, and Norden Systems, to develop a common radar that will satisfy the services' needs for a Fixed Target Indicator, Moving Target Indicator, and Synthetic Aperture Radar to detect, track, and direct weapons against stationary and slow-moving ground targets. The system will consist of this radar integrated aboard the TR-1, the Army OV-1, and the C-18, ground stations, weapon guidance units, and sufficient aircraft to support the RDJTF mission all tied together by a common data link with interfaces into the existing C^3 (Command, Communications, and Control) network.

JOINT TACTICAL INFORMATION DISTRIBUTION SYSTEM (JTIDS):

An Air Force program under contract to Hughes Aircraft Co., Singer/Kearfot, IBM, and Federal Systems Division, to develop a high-capacity, reliable, jam-protected, secure, digital information distribution system that will provide a high degree of interoperability among data collec-

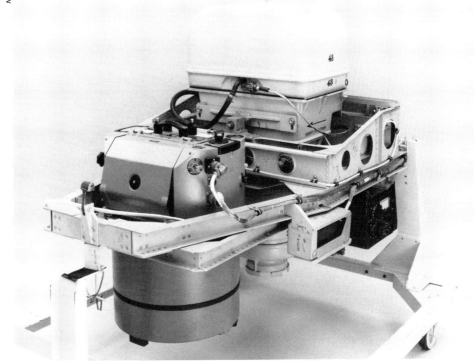

The A-4 camera configuration consists of a single RC-10 metric camera and a single HR-732 camera. It provides both large and small area coverage of targets.

The IIS multi-spectral camera combines four lenses with a single camera body. All lenses image on the same film emulsion.

Filtered samplers can be commanded from the cockpit to pop out of the sides of the aerosol particulate sampler. This unit resembles a wing pylon but is not designed to support other sensors.

tion elements and command and control centers within a military theatre of operations. The TR-1 is expected to be made integral with this system.

Most of the U-2's sensor systems require specialized equipment bay (Q-bay) lower hatches. Accordingly, there are a large number of lower hatch configurations available, including the EAQ80, the F151, the F202, the F210, the F220, the F845, the F921, the 75F177, and the 75F194, with appropriate accommodations for the respective sensor (including the EAQ-1 and EAQ1-500 Universal Racks).

NASA has utilized the U-2 in a wide-ranging set of experiments with heavy emphasis on earth resources. Details of all the many sensors developed for this program are too extensive to list here, but some of the more important systems include the Aether Drift experiment; the Solar Energy Monitor in Space (SEMIS); the CO_2 Collector; The Water Vapor Radiometer (WVR); the Infra-Red Spectrometer (FLO); the Resonance Fluorescence Experiment (REFLEX); the Stratospheric Cryogenic Sampler (SCS); the Stratospheric Air Sampler II (SAS II); the High Speed Interferometer (HSI); the Filter Wheel Infra-Red Radiometer (IRR); the Aerosol Particulate Sampler (APS); the F-2 Air Particulate Sampler; the Ocean Color Scanner (OCS); the Heat Capacity Mapper Radiometer System (HCMR); and the Thermal Infra-Red Scanner (TIRS).

Following the loss of Gary Powers over the Soviet Union, Soviet information sources stated that his aircraft had been equipped with the following sensors: an ELINT system with microwave, decimetric, and metric wavelength receivers by Hewlett-Packard and Huggins Laboratories and a Model 73B camera. There may also have been a Perkins-Elmer Model 501 camera aboard.

There have been many hundreds of modifications to the basic U-2 aircraft over the years, but none was as spectacular as that involving a U-2F for the *TRIM* (Target Radiant Intensity Measurement) program. This extraordinary modification, giving the aircraft the image of a winged camel, was utilized for infra-red spectral measurement of launch vehicle exhaust plumes. TRIM was activated in mid-1972 and ran through 1974.

Finally, it should be mentioned that significant work on new sensor system technology has resulted in the development, by Itek, of a new electronic imaging system that is sometimes

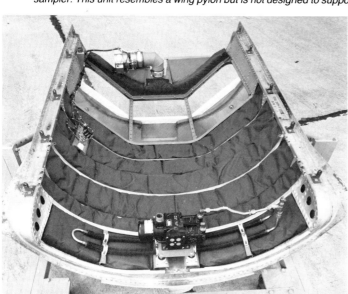

There are a large number of upper and lower Q-bay hatches available for a variety of sensors. This is an EAQ-207-1 hatch.

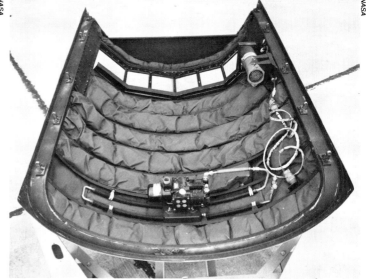

Most of the Q-bay lower hatches, if they are designed to operate with a particular optical sensor, come with defogging heaters and other related accouterments.

referred to as an electronic camera. This high-resolution device is capable of real-time transmission of its acquired imagery to line-of-sight ground receiving and interpretation stations. Attributes of the Itek system include its exceptionally low weight, its versatility, and the quality of its imagery under less-than-ideal lighting conditions. Imagery from the new system is transmitted and processed in digital form and stored on magnetic tape for post-mission analysis and comparison with earlier or subsequent imagery, or for correlation with data from other sensors.

Close-up of an optical bar camera as installed in a NASA U-2C.

Latest TR-1A configuration is capable of carrying nearly 4,000 pounds of sensor equipment in miscellaneous bays, a nose compartment, and its two wing-mounted super pods. Second TR-1A, 80-1067, is shown.

Perhaps the most bizarre U-2 sensor system installation ever to reach the hardware stage was project TRIM. Designed to measure the radiation characteristics of re-entry vehicles for future tracking criteria, it was tested for some two years before being abandoned.

Following completion of the TRIM program in 1974, the TRIM aircraft was demodded and flown with fairings placed over the holes left after the TRIM sensor units were removed. Final disposition of the aircraft is unknown, as is its serial number.

Gary Powers models early style MC-2-type high-altitude partial pressure suit. U-2F, N-800X, is in the background.

Lockheed-California Company via Rene Francillon

Lockheed-California Company

U.S. AI
64X
FOR OFFI

USAF via John Andrews

Early versions of the MC-2 had to be tailored to the individual, as fit was extremely critical. Capt. Don Evans is modeling suit in photo.

The S1010B suit is restricted to use in the U-2R/ER-2/TR-1 series aircraft because of its cockpit dimensional requirements.

Chapt. 8:
PARTIAL AND FULL PRESSURE SUITS

The birth of an aircraft capable of sustained cruising altitudes in excess of 70,000' brought with it myriad human physiological support problems, not the least of which was sustaining a pilot in a near-oxygenless low-pressure atmosphere. Work on pressure suits had been underway for no less than three decades by the early 1950's and the advent of the U-2 and a number of extremely high performance research aircraft finally created a legitimate need for suits that were both efficient and functional.

The need for forced breathing of oxygen and the wearing of pressure suits had become apparent during the late 1920's and early 1930's when aircraft began penetrating into altitude regimes above the levels capable of sustaining life. At 26,000' a man could remain conscious for only three minutes without external support, and at 46,000', this time dropped 10 to 20 seconds.

At altitudes of approximately 50,000' the lack of oxygen problem was compounded by the fact that low atmospheric pressure allowed the waste products of the respiratory system—carbon dioxide and water vapor—to settle in and completely fill the lungs, thus preventing the intake of air or even of pure oxygen under pressure.

At altitudes of 63,000', at what was soon referred to as "Armstrong's Line," it was discovered that the air pressure was so low (roughly 3% that of sea level) that conventional liquids boiled at 98-deg. F. This being normal human body temperature, the concern became not only one of lack of oxygen, but also one of pressure; at 63,000' body fluids including blood, would explode and vaporize if the body was left unprotected.

To complicate things even further, research uncovered the fact that conventional pressurization systems were virtually useless at altitudes in excess of 65,000'. The reason was that most pressurized aircraft derived their cabin pressure differential by sucking in and compressing external air. At 65,000' and above, the air was found to be mixed with heavy concentrations of ozone or triatomic oxygen—gases which were not at all compatible with the human breathing system.

The high-altitude support problem, in general, remained basically unsolved into the early 1950's. With the realization that a number of aircraft were in the mill that would soon be penetrating to altitude levels well in excess of those requiring functional high-altitude pressure suits, the initiative was taken by the Air Research and Development Command to create a solution. A technical program-planning document was assembled in late 1955, entitled, "Airborne Environment Protection and Maintenance of Personnel." This was later released to potential contractors and bids were requested for the production of a high-altitude suit.

The end result of this program was the David Clark Company's T-1 partial-pressure suit (the suit was referred to as being a partial pressure type due to the fact that the feet, which were encased in boots, were left without a pressurized covering; later suits, which will be covered in a moment, included pressurization for the feet and thus were referred to as full pressure) and the Aero Medical Laboratory K-1 full-pressure helmet (with a clear faceplate that had four embedded-wire heating elements to prevent fogging). Derivatives of the suit, the first production flight

Deacon Hall models the MC-2/MC-3 type suit and MA-2 helmet, with a disassembled suit on the ground. Aircraft in background is U-2, 56-6714.

clothing to incorporate the newly invented "capstan principle" (an ingenious combination of inflatable tubes along the sides of the arms, chest, thighs, and legs that pulled the suit's fabric tightly against its wearer's body to apply mechanical counterpressure against the internal expansion of gases and water vapor in the blood vessels and tissues) resulted in the MC-3 partial pressure suit. A derivative of the K-1 helmet was also generated and this became the MA-2 helmet. This combination of suit and helmet became the operational protective clothing worn by the first U-2 pilots during the initial overflight activity in 1956.

With the advent of the suits and the high altitude mission came the development of a method of field operation referred to as physiological support. The aim of this concept was to provide total, integrated support of the crew member by insuring that properly inspected and maintained protective equipment was correctly mated with a physically fit and mentally alert pilot.

Flight surgeons, aviation physiologists, and physiological training officers made up the bulk of the personnel assigned to these physiological support units. Their duties usually consisted of recording pilot blood pressure, pulse rates, and temperatures prior to each mission. Additionally, the pilot's pre-mission weight was recorded, and then recorded again following the mission. Weight losses of from four to six pounds were routine during the course of an average U-2 flight.

Following a high protein meal of steak, eggs, toast, juice, and coffee (this is sometimes referred to as a low-residue meal—its purpose is to avoid activating the gastro-intestinal mechanisms causing defecation—a normal bodily function that could cause serious discomfort during

Deacon Hall collection

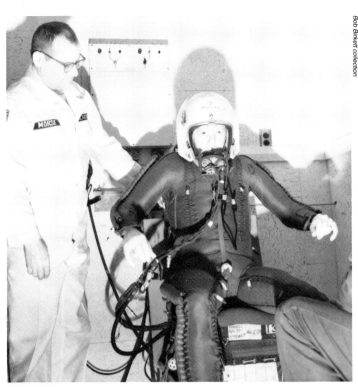

Fully inflated MC-3 was not particularly comfortable, but it would keep a pilot alive at extremely high altitudes.

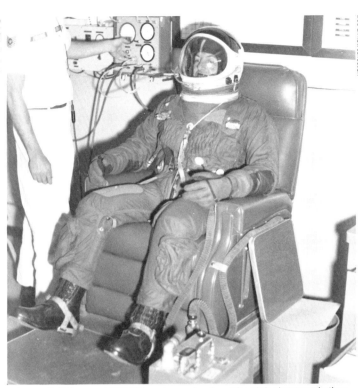

Col. Bob Birkett and S1010B undergo check-out for air leakage and other problems. If suit was ever needed, leaks could not be tolerated.

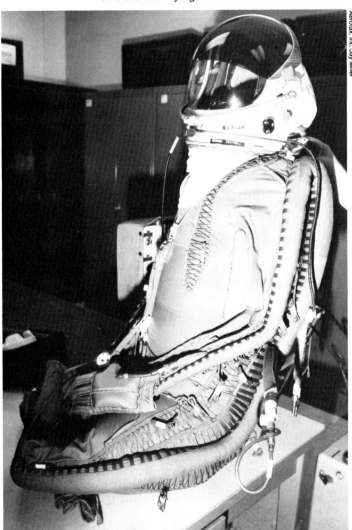

Genious of MC-2/MC-3, and S1010B series suits is the "capstan principle" used to maintain bodily gases and fluids under low pressure conditions.

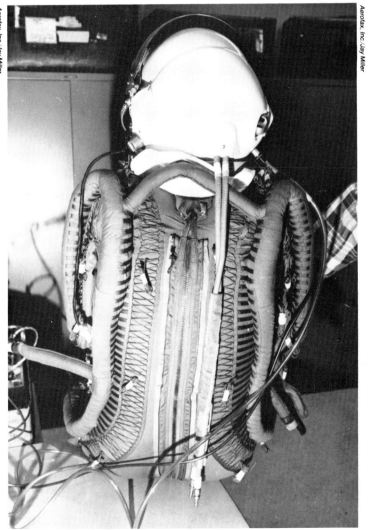

Back side of MC-3 suit and helmet. Lacing is adjustable to accommodate various crew member sizes.

the course of a seven to ten hour mission), suiting out was undertaken along with "pre-breathing." The latter, a process wherein pure oxygen is breathed in order to denitrogenate the blood, was a preventive procedure to curtail an occurance of the "bends"—a physiological phenomenon caused by the separation of nitrogen from other blood gases and the related pain caused by the formation of nitrogen bubbles in the joints and elsewhere. Pre-breathing was normally a 30 or 45 minute process, though some pilots would pre-breathe for up to an hour prior to takeoff.

The suiting out process was somewhat time consuming due to the number and complexity of the garments making up the MC-3 suit. Long white underwear were usually the first items put on—with the seams out. This was followed by entering the suit itself (from the front), and then, if required, an outer garment, or flight suit and finally, helmet, gloves, and boots.

Though the MC-3 suit and helmet were modestly comfortable, there were a number of areas that demanded improvement. The advent of the X-15 research aircraft and *Mercury* manned space capsule gave incentive to develop improved high-altitude garments, and the spin-offs from these programs generated new suits for U-2 pilots.

The ultimate expression of this developmental process became the S1010B—the rear-entry full-pressure suit currently worn by U-2R, TR-1, and ER-2 pilots during high altitude flights. The S1010B is technically referred to as being "a protective assembly" consisting of a helmet, a restraint assembly with exterior cover, and pressurized gloves and boots. The suit components consist of a coverall, a restraint assembly, a bladder assembly, a capstan assembly, an exterior cover, gloves, a helmet, a face barrier, and a take-up assembly. The suit weighs approximately 25 pounds when complete, and provides total protection at any altitude the U-2 is capable of achieving. A survival kit can also be worn externally with the suit.

The S1010B is restricted to use in U-2R variants only, as its bulkiness does not permit it to be worn in the smaller cockpit of early U-2 versions. Each pilot is normally assigned two form-fitted S1010B's at a unit cost of over $10-thousand each. As a point of interest, the S1010B is "classified" by the Air Force and detailed information pertaining to its design and performance is restricted.

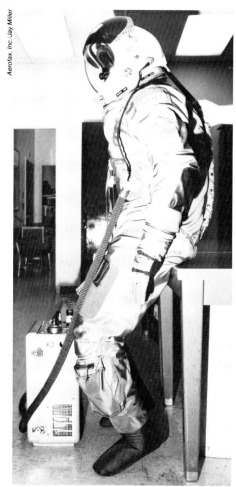

S1010B is a full-pressure suit and includes restraints for the feet.

Small field support unit provides oxygen and air conditioning for S1010B.

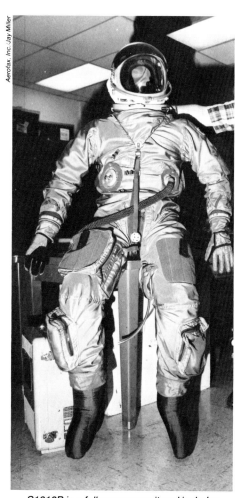

Close-up of S1010B glove and connector detailing special fitting straps.

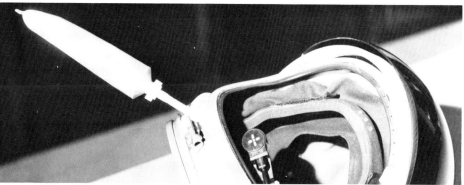

Three views of S1010B high-altitude helmet. Visor is externally mounted and there is accommodation provided for a food tube to be inserted through a special pressurized valve.

75

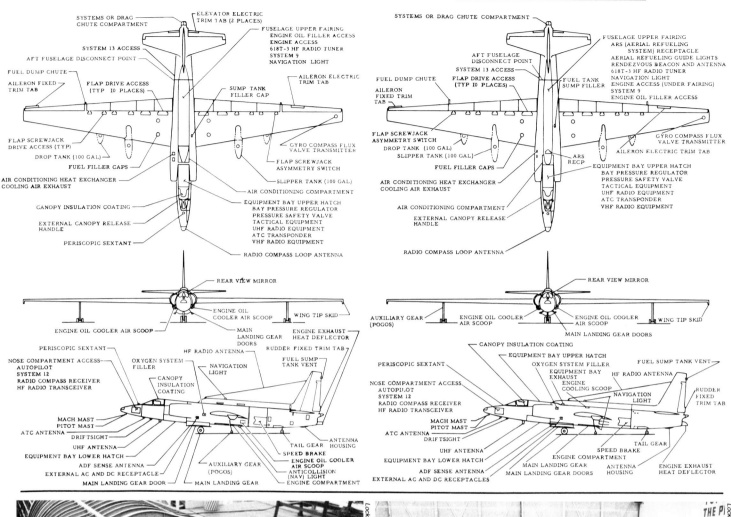

GENERAL CONFIGURATION - MODEL U-2C

SYSTEMS OR DRAG
CHUTE COMPARTMENT
ELEVATOR ELECTRIC
TRIM TAB (2 PLACES)
SYSTEM 13 ACCESS
FUSELAGE UPPER FAIRING
ENGINE OIL FILLER ACCESS
ENGINE ACCESS
618T-3 HF RADIO TUNER
SYSTEM 9
NAVIGATION LIGHT
AFT FUSELAGE DISCONNECT POINT
FUEL DUMP CHUTE
AILERON FIXED TRIM TAB
FLAP DRIVE ACCESS (TYP 10 PLACES)
AILERON ELECTRIC TRIM TAB
SUMP TANK FILLER CAP
FLAP SCREWJACK DRIVE ACCESS (TYP)
DROP TANK (100 GAL)
FUEL FILLER CAPS
GYRO COMPASS FLUX VALVE TRANSMITTER
FLAP SCREWJACK ASYMMETRY SWITCH
AIR CONDITIONING HEAT EXCHANGER COOLING AIR EXHAUST
SLIPPER TANK (100 GAL)
AIR CONDITIONING COMPARTMENT
CANOPY INSULATION COATING
EQUIPMENT BAY UPPER HATCH
BAY PRESSURE REGULATOR
PRESSURE SAFETY VALVE
TACTICAL EQUIPMENT
UHF RADIO EQUIPMENT
ATC TRANSPONDER
VHF RADIO EQUIPMENT
EXTERNAL CANOPY RELEASE HANDLE
PERISCOPIC SEXTANT
RADIO COMPASS LOOP ANTENNA

REAR VIEW MIRROR
ENGINE OIL COOLER AIR SCOOP
WING TIP SKID
ENGINE OIL COOLER AIR SCOOP
MAIN LANDING GEAR DOORS
ENGINE EXHAUST HEAT DEFLECTOR
RUDDER FIXED TRIM TAB
FUEL SUMP TANK VENT

PERISCOPIC SEXTANT
NOSE COMPARTMENT ACCESS
AUTOPILOT
SYSTEM 12
RADIO COMPASS RECEIVER
HF RADIO TRANSCEIVER
OXYGEN SYSTEM FILLER
NAVIGATION LIGHT
HF RADIO ANTENNA
CANOPY INSULATION COATING
MACH MAST
PITOT MAST
ATC ANTENNA
DRIFTSIGHT
UHF ANTENNA
EQUIPMENT BAY LOWER HATCH
ADF SENSE ANTENNA
EXTERNAL AC AND DC RECEPTACLE
MAIN LANDING GEAR DOOR
AUXILIARY GEAR (POGOS)
MAIN LANDING GEAR
TAIL GEAR
ANTENNA HOUSING
SPEED BRAKE
ENGINE OIL COOLER AIR SCOOP
ANTICOLLISION (NAV) LIGHT
ENGINE COMPARTMENT

GENERAL CONFIGURATION - MODEL U-2F

SYSTEMS OR DRAG CHUTE COMPARTMENT
FUSELAGE UPPER FAIRING
ARS (AERIAL REFUELING SYSTEM) RECEPTACLE
AERIAL REFUELING GUIDE LIGHTS
RENDEZVOUS BEACON AND ANTENNA
618T-3 HF RADIO TUNER
NAVIGATION LIGHT
ENGINE ACCESS (UNDER FAIRING)
SYSTEM 9
ENGINE OIL FILLER ACCESS
AFT FUSELAGE DISCONNECT POINT
SYSTEM 13 ACCESS
FUEL DUMP CHUTE
FLAP DRIVE ACCESS (TYP 10 PLACES)
FUEL TANK SUMP FILLER
AILERON FIXED TRIM TAB
FLAP SCREWJACK ASYMMETRY SWITCH
DROP TANK (100 GAL)
SLIPPER TANK (100 GAL)
FUEL FILLER CAPS
GYRO COMPASS FLUX VALVE TRANSMITTER
AILERON ELECTRIC TRIM TAB
ARS RECP
EQUIPMENT BAY UPPER HATCH
BAY PRESSURE REGULATOR
PRESSURE SAFETY VALVE
TACTICAL EQUIPMENT
UHF RADIO EQUIPMENT
ATC TRANSPONDER
VHF RADIO EQUIPMENT
AIR CONDITIONING HEAT EXCHANGER COOLING AIR EXHAUST
AIR CONDITIONING COMPARTMENT
EXTERNAL CANOPY RELEASE HANDLE
RADIO COMPASS LOOP ANTENNA

REAR VIEW MIRROR
AUXILIARY GEAR (POGOS)
ENGINE OIL COOLER AIR SCOOP
ENGINE OIL COOLER AIR SCOOP
WING TIP SKID
MAIN LANDING GEAR DOORS

CANOPY INSULATION COATING
EQUIPMENT BAY UPPER HATCH
OXYGEN SYSTEM FILLER
FUEL SUMP TANK VENT
PERISCOPIC SEXTANT
EQUIPMENT BAY EXHAUST
ENGINE COOLING SCOOP
HF RADIO ANTENNA
NAVIGATION LIGHT
RUDDER FIXED TRIM TAB
NOSE COMPARTMENT ACCESS
AUTOPILOT
SYSTEM 12
RADIO COMPASS RECEIVER
HF RADIO TRANSCEIVER
MACH MAST
PITOT MAST
ATC ANTENNA
DRIFTSIGHT
UHF ANTENNA
EQUIPMENT BAY LOWER HATCH
ADF SENSE ANTENNA
EXTERNAL AC AND DC RECEPTACLES
MAIN LANDING GEAR
MAIN LANDING GEAR DOORS
ENGINE COMPARTMENT
SPEED BRAKE
TAIL GEAR
ANTENNA HOUSING
ENGINE EXHAUST HEAT DEFLECTOR

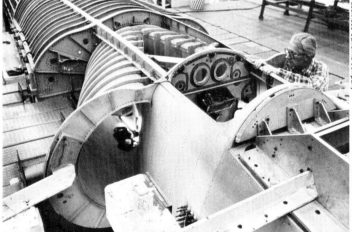

Intake and E-bay section of TR-1A under construction gives good detail of structure.

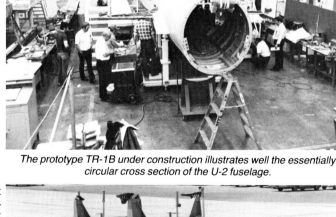

The prototype TR-1B under construction illustrates well the essentially circular cross section of the U-2 fuselage.

Special ground transport dollys have been built for both basic U-2 configurations. Note articulated support arms on U-2A/G dolly.

The ground transport dolly for the U-2R/ER-2/TR-1 series aircraft is substantially more robust than that for early model U-2's.

All major variants of the Lockheed U-2 are single- or two-seat jet powered aircraft designed for extremely high altitude flight over long ranges. General construction is all metal with aluminum being the predominant construction material. Construction technique is generally conventional, with diversions from the norm centering around the extraordinary weight saving measures taken to keep the aircraft empty weight as low as possible. Most variants of the U-2 have maximum g-load capabilities of +3 and −1½ in a clean, lightly loaded configuration and at a speed of 240 knots. This envelope is reduced considerably depending on the weight and configuration of the aircraft, and whether or not the gust control system (which see) is activated.

Two major airframe configurations make up the U-2 family. One, typified by the Lockheed U-2C, represents the original configuration as flown in August of 1955, and the other, typified by the Lockheed U-2R, represents the aircraft as it is flown operationally by the Air Force, today.

Descriptions of the components of these two basic configurations follow:

FUSELAGE: The fuselage of both configurations is an all-metal and semi-monocoque structure of generally circular cross section and .020" thin-gauge aluminum skin. The finess ratio for the U-2C fuselage is approximately 9 to 1, and that for the U-2R is approximately 10 to 1. Both fuselage configurations offer a number of internal bays for the transport of sensor systems, counter-measures systems, communication and navigation equipment, and other mission related gear. The most commodious of the fuselage bays is the pressurized and air-conditioned "Q-bay," which is mounted just behind the cockpit and ahead of the engine compressor face (later model aircraft also have an "E-bay" behind the Q-bay). The Q-bay is primarily the nose section support structure with removable and reconfigurable top and bottom hatches. The number and type of bays vary from model to model, but at least one is located underneath the empennage section, one in the nose, one in what is normally the drag chute compartment, and if so configured, one in the fuselage upper fairing (thus far seen only on early model U-2's, and not the U-2R). There are also, on some aircraft, small accommodations for sensor system equipment located in the wing root sections, just outboard of the fuselage. Additional sensor systems equipment space is available in the form of wing leading edge slipper pods, "super pods" (for some early U-2 configurations and almost all U-2R and later configurations), conventional underwing pods (for most early U-2 configurations), special wingtip pods, and in the U-2R and later configurations, in the forward engine air intake shell (this normally accommodating the aircraft radar homing and warning system).

Continuously welded aluminum sump tanks containing a complex baffling system and a capacity for 95 gallons of fuel are mounted in the fuselage center section, and all wing tank fuel is cycled into the sump tanks before proceding to the engine.

The bifurcated intake is also part of the fuselage structure and is optimized for the critical airflow requirements of operation at 70,000'+ altitudes. The intake walls are meticulously manufactured to avoid airflow anomalies that

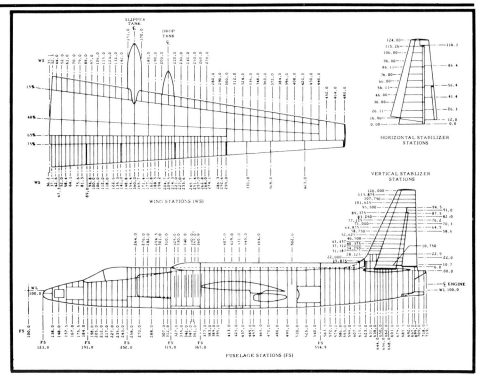

Lockheed-California Company

A U-2R fuselage is hoisted from its jigs and moved into the final assembly area at Lockheed's Palmdale, California facility. Much of the U-2 assembly process is manual, as production quantities do not merit mass production techniques.

Aerofax, Inc./Jay Miller

Internal view toward front of NASA U-2C underscores the simplicity of its fuselage structural design. Note lack of stringers and other forms of structural stiffening.

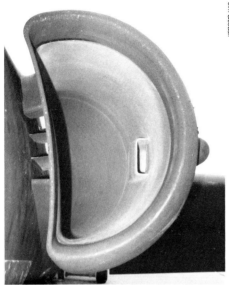

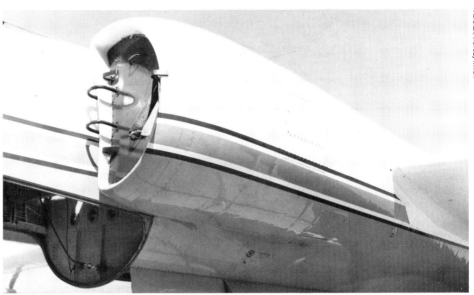

Front view of U-2R intake illustrates its smooth throat walls and the boundary layer bleed between the intake and fuselage.

The ER-2/TR-1 intake configuration provides boundary layer space between the fuselage and intake, internal boundary layer bleed, and a relatively straight throat design.

Detail of standard U-2A nose. Aircraft (56-6696) is equipped for the HASP mission.

Post-flight inspection of U-2R illustrates removable nose paneling and other nose section details. Note "howdah" sun shade.

might be generated by exposed joints or mismatched panels.

Some early U-2 models were modified to accommodate an arrester hook for carrier operations, and all U-2R and later aircraft have this capability. The weight penalty of the arrester hook is estimated to be 150 pounds.

The U-2, in all configurations, is equipped with hydraulically-actuated speed brakes. These are high-drag devices mounted one on each side of the fuselage, several feet behind the wing trailing edge. They are actuated by a three position center-off slide switch on the top of the throttle lever (mounted on the left cockpit console panel). Maximum deployment angle is 50-deg.

COCKPIT: There are numerous differences between the cockpits of the various U-2 configurations, not the least of which is the significant size difference between the cockpits of early model aircraft and those of later models.

In general, the cockpit arrangement for all U-2 models is conventional with minor variations in instrumentation and the inclusion of a Baird Scientific driftsight in the upper center of the panel. The driftsight consists of an optical tracking system using a combination of mirrors and prisms to project a presentation of the local terrain on a scope in the cockpit. This information is used in pinpoint navigation. The system is composed of a scope or viewing screen, a periscope, and a junction box. The driftsight system is operated by a hand control located on the right cockpit panel. This control, depending on the aircraft, is either driven by an electrical servo system or a set of manually driven flexible shafts. The control handle can rotate the scanning head a full 360-deg. in azimuth, and elevate it to an

almost horizontal position. This provides complete coverage under the aircraft. Located next to the control handle is the master switch control which activates the various sensor systems accommodated in the Q-bay, and some of the defensive electronic countermeasures systems located elsewhere.

Integral with the driftsight, but only on early model aircraft, is a conventional bubble type sextant system (later configurations incorporate inertial navigation systems, thus negating the need for a sextant; it has been noted in several publications, however, that Gary Powers' aircraft was equipped with an inertial navigation system developed by the Massachusetts Institute of Technology). This is mounted rigidly to the aircraft, just forward of the windshield. The sextant optical system uses a portion of the driftsight optics and throws its measuring presentation on the face of the driftsight display. The sextant can be adjusted from minus 4-deg. to 90-deg. in elevation, and 360-deg. in heading to give complete coverage of the heavens, except for that part near 180-deg. which is blacked out by the windshield and canopy. The optical system of the sextant is a unit-power telescope with a field of view of 15-deg. The elevation prism is located inside a 5" dia. protective glass dome which projects through the skin of the aircraft.

A rubber cone is provided to attach to the driftsight and sextant display scope. The cone serves two purposes: it keeps out stray light when using the sextant; and its length places the pilot's eyes at the correct distance from the scope when he uses the optical system.

All U-2 aircraft have pressurized cockpits with pressurized air, originating from the engine com-

pressor section, being dumped from the cockpit into the Q-bay through a cockpit pressure regulator valve. The pressurized air, after it leaves the engine compressor, is cooled by a conventional aircraft type refrigeration unit, ducted through a water separator, and directed into the cockpit through five outlets. After being dumped into the Q-bay, the air is exhausted through a second pressure regulator valve into the unpressurized landing gear well. The first two U-2's initially flew without gaseous pressurization, but this system was added once flights above 50,000' were initiated. Cabin pressure remains constant at 3.88 psi, and at maximum altitudes in the vicinity of 70,000, the equivalent cockpit pressure altitude is 28,000. Cockpit heating is also regulated and can be controlled by the pilot.

Though initially flown without ejection seats, all aircraft were eventually reconfigured to accommodate a Lockheed-developed seat of somewhat limited capability. The normal ejection seat for all U-2 models (varying in configuration and capabilities somewhat between the early and late model aircraft) is a simple lightweight design using a "low-g" catapult to minimize the possibility of ejection injury. The seat in early model aircraft has no adjustment provision (late model aircraft do have adjustable seats) and pilot position in the seat is adjustable only by use of wood blocks. A shoulder harness lock-and-release lever is on the left-hand side of the seat. The seat is equipped with an automatic release seat belt. There are no arm rests on early model seats (later models have arm rests) and the ejection sequence is started by pulling up on a D-ring located at the front of the seat between the pilot's legs.

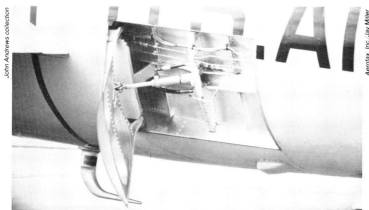

Detail of U-2A airbrake in extended position. Airbrakes are hydraulically actuated.

Detail of ER-2 airbrake in extended position. Though differing in detail, the airbrakes are essentially the same on all U-2 models.

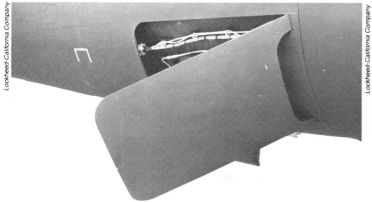

Front view of TR-1A airbrake reveals its simple external design and close hinge tolerances.

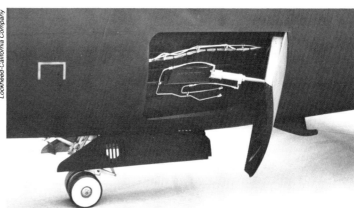

TR-1A airbrake well reveals no major changes from early U-2 variants. U-2 airbrakes are effective only at lower altitudes.

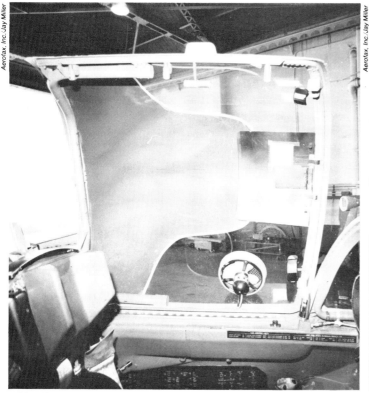

ER-2/TR-1 canopy details. Note rotatable fan for use as defogger. Canopy is manually opened and closed.

U-2C canopy details. Note rotatable fan for use as a defogger. Canopy is manually opened and closed.

Pulling the D-ring (early aircraft only) actuates an M3 initiator which starts the jettison/ejection cycle. The first initiator provides gas pressure to start the canopy sequence and to disconnect the elevator control and stow the wheel forward to clear the pilot's knees and feet (a Kelly Johnson innovation). It also actuates the T-34 initiator which has a 1-second delay before simultaneously locking the shoulder harness, actuating the catapult and another T-34 initiator also with a 1- second time delay to release the seat belt. The catapult imparts a maximum 15-g acceleration to a 350-pound seat/man combination. This is sufficient to clear the vertical fin of early model U-2's by 7' at 260 knots. One safety pin is provided in

COCKPIT DETAILS

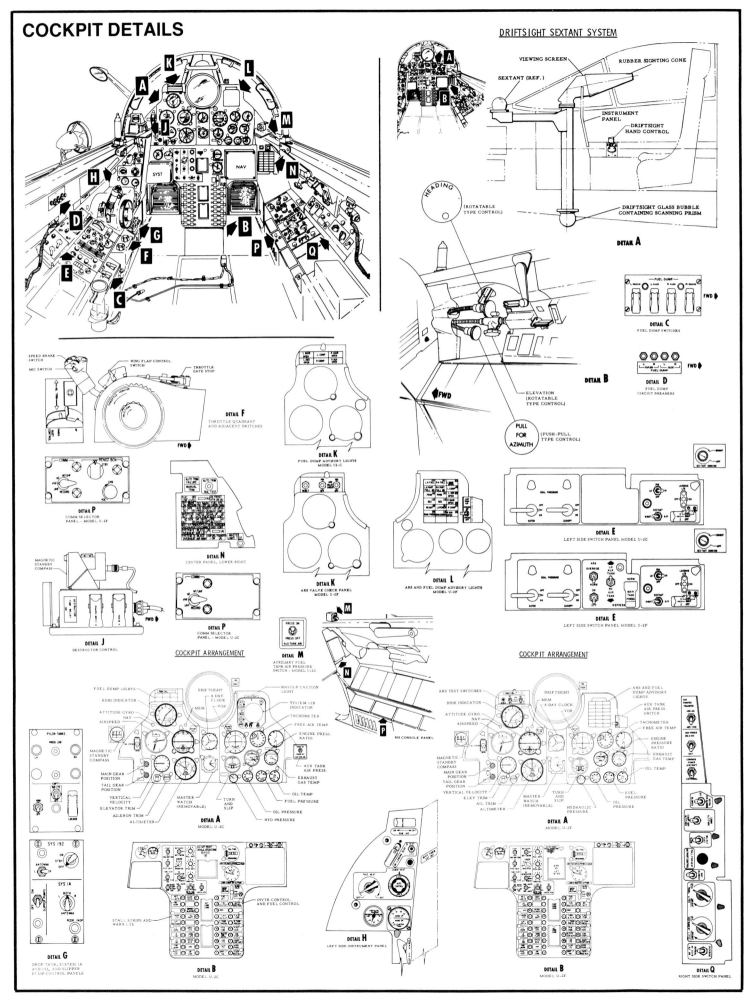

DRIFTSIGHT SEXTANT SYSTEM

VIEWING SCREEN
RUBBER SIGHTING CONE
SEXTANT (REF.)
INSTRUMENT PANEL
DRIFTSIGHT HAND CONTROL
DRIFTSIGHT GLASS BUBBLE CONTAINING SCANNING PRISM

HEADING (ROTATABLE TYPE CONTROL)

DETAIL A

FUEL DUMP
DETAIL C
FUEL DUMP SWITCHES

FWD

FUEL DUMP
DETAIL D
FUEL DUMP CIRCUIT BREAKERS

ELEVATION (ROTATABLE TYPE CONTROL)

DETAIL B

PULL FOR AZIMUTH (PUSH-PULL TYPE CONTROL)

FWD

DETAIL F
THROTTLE QUADRANT AND ADJACENT SWITCHES

SPEED BRAKE SWITCH
MIC SWITCH
WING FLAP CONTROL SWITCH
THROTTLE GATE STOP

DETAIL P
COMM SELECTOR PANEL - MODEL U-2F

DETAIL K
FUEL DUMP ADVISORY LIGHTS MODEL U-2C

DETAIL N
CENTER PANEL, LOWER RIGHT

DETAIL E
LEFT SIDE SWITCH PANEL MODEL U-2C

MAGNETIC STANDBY COMPASS

DETAIL J
DESTRUCTOR CONTROL

DETAIL P
COMM SELECTOR PANEL - MODEL U-2C

DETAIL K
ARS VALVE CHECK PANEL MODEL U-2F

DETAIL L
ARS AND FUEL DUMP ADVISORY LIGHTS MODEL U-2F

DETAIL E
LEFT SIDE SWITCH PANEL MODEL U-2F

DETAIL M
AUXILIARY FUEL TANK AIR PRESSURE SWITCH - MODEL U-2C

RH CONSOLE PANEL

COCKPIT ARRANGEMENT

FUEL DUMP LIGHTS
BDHI INDICATOR
ATTITUDE GYRO
NAV
AIRSPEED
MAGNETIC STANDBY COMPASS
MAIN GEAR POSITION
TAIL GEAR POSITION
VERTICAL VELOCITY
ELEVATOR TRIM
AILERON TRIM
ALTIMETER
MASTER WATCH (REMOVABLE)
TURN AND SLIP
HYD PRESSURE
OIL PRESSURE
FUEL PRESSURE
OIL TEMP
AUX TANK AIR PRESS.
EXHAUST GAS TEMP
ENGINE PRESS. RATIO
FREE AIR TEMP
TACHOMETER
SYSTEM 12B INDICATOR
MASTER CAUTION LIGHT
DRIFTSIGHT
8 DAY CLOCK
MEM
VOR

DETAIL A
MODEL U-2C

COCKPIT ARRANGEMENT

ARS TEST SWITCHES
BDHI INDICATOR
ATTITUDE GYRO
NAV
AIRSPEED
MAGNETIC STANDBY COMPASS
MAIN GEAR POSITION
TAIL GEAR POSITION
VERTICAL VELOCITY
ELEV TRIM
AIL TRIM
ALTIMETER
MASTER WATCH (REMOVABLE)
TURN AND SLIP
HYDRAULIC PRESSURE
OIL PRESSURE
FUEL PRESSURE
OIL TEMP
EXHAUST GAS TEMP
ENGINE PRESSURE RATIO
FREE AIR TEMP
TACHOMETER
AUX TANK AIR PRESS. SWITCH
ARS AND FUEL DUMP ADVISORY LIGHTS
DRIFTSIGHT
8 DAY CLOCK
MEM
VOR

DETAIL A
MODEL U-2F

PYLON TANKS
PRESS LOW

SYS 192
SYS 1A

DETAIL G
DROP TANK, SYSTEM 1A AND 192, AND SLIPPER PUMP CONTROL PANELS

INVTR CONTROL AND FUEL CONTROL
STALL STRIPS AND WARN LTS

DETAIL B
MODEL U-2C

FACE HEAT
CABIN HEAT

DETAIL H
LEFT SIDE INSTRUMENT PANEL

DETAIL B
MODEL U-2F

DETAIL Q
RIGHT SIDE SWITCH PANEL

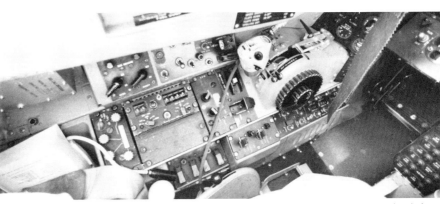

Aerofax, Inc./Jay Miller

The left cockpit console of the U-2C is equipped with a throttle quadrant, a gust control switch, and some navigation gear. Black wheels on throttle quadrant are vernier and friction controls.

Aerofax, Inc./Jay Miller

The U-2C's cockpit is relatively small and equipped with a limited capability ejection seat.

Right cockpit console of the U-2C is equipped with radio equipment, a warning light panel, and the driftsight hand control.

Aerofax, Inc./Jay Miller

Aerofax, Inc./Jay Miller

Following initial problems with seat failures at altitude, penetrator spikes were installed on the seats to facilitate through-canopy ejections.

The U-2R/ER-2/TR-1 ejection seat is considerably more refined and capable than that found in earlier U-2's.

The well-organized ER-2 instrument panel differs only in detail from that of U-2R and TR-1. Driftsight is visible at top of photo. All U-2's utilize a yoke-type control column.

The left console of ER-2 cockpit supports the throttle quadrant and some communications and navigation gear. The gust control switch is located directly below the throttle quadrant.

The ER-2's right console supports communications equipment, sensor system controls, and the driftsight hand control. Barely visible are just a few of the many circuit breakers available.

Detail of dual canopy configuration seen only on two-seat U-2CT and TR-1B trainers. Though there have been other two-seat U-2's built, only the U-2CT and TR-1B have the elevated back seat seen here.

Driftsight optics protrude through the skin of all U-2's just underneath the cockpit. Articulated prisms provide the pilot with a virtually unlimited view of the world underneath.

All U-2's are equipped with an externally-mounted rear-view mirror. Note static pitot sensor.

the M3 initiator on the right-hand side of the seat pan. This must be removed for the seat to fire. Late model U-2's, starting with the U-2R, are equipped with zero-zero capability seats that are capable of extricating the pilot from the cockpit throughout the U-2's envelope.

The first ejection seat installations in U-2's were seriously deficient in capability. One post-accident investigation, for instance, revealed that the seat, which had been designed to eject through the canopy, had failed to penetrate the Plexiglas due to hardening caused by frigid high altitude temperatures. Penetrator spikes were then installed at the top of each seat, and special-canopy ejectors similar to those utilized in the F-104 were incorporated.

Pilot personal equipment normally includes a relief bottle for urine containment, a map case, a seat pack with survival gear and the oxygen regulator, and an emergency oxygen supply. The seat pack has a quick disconnect fitting for emergency egress situations. The emergency oxygen bottle is capable of supplying oxygen for from 15 to 20 minutes.

Communications, navigation, and associated electronic equipment are not yet publicly documented for the late model U-2 configurations, but for the earlier aircraft, they normally consist of microphone and headset connectors; a C-823A/AIC-10 interphone control; a communications selector panel; an AN/ARC-34 UHF transceiver; a 618T-3 control panel; an AN/ARN-59 radio compass; an ARC Type 15F VHF navigation system; an ID453 course indicator; an air traffic control system; an AN/APN-135 rendezvous beacon (U-2F only); an Aircraft Radio Corporation Type 12 VHF transceiver; an AN/ARC-3 VHF radio set; and an AN/APN-153(V) doppler navigation unit with modified AN/ASN-66 dead reckoning navigation computer system. Additionally, some aircraft, depending on their respective missions, were equipped with a B/400 rate meter system (for aircraft used in nuclear test sampling) and the F-2 Foil system control panel (sometimes integrated with the P-3 platform system).

Gary Powers' aircraft is stated also to have had the following equipment onboard when the wreckage was examined by Soviet personnel: an MA-1 compass, a Bendix ARN-6 ADF, and a Magnavox ARC-34 UHF command radio.

The cockpit flight controls for all U-2 models are conventional, consisting of rudder pedals and a wheel mounted on a control column. All surfaces are directly connected to the cockpit controls by cables. No power boost is provided. There are no surface locks except as provided by the ground crew. Electric trim is provided in pitch and roll. There is no directional trim in the cockpit (there's a bendable tab on the rudder) and yaw damping is provided only by the autopilot.

The control wheel has several switches including an elevator trim tab control and an autopilot disengage button on the right hand grip, and a trim tab power switch and radio button on the left hand. A small pointer is mounted on the top center of the control wheel that provides an accurate method of monitoring left or right-wheel displacement which may occur as a result of uneven fuel feeding.

A position indicator below the gear handle gives the pilot a visual reference for trim tab setting. Elevator trim tab position is indicated even though the trim power switch is off.

The rudder pedals on all models of the U-2 are collapsible in order to reduce pilot fatigue by permitting free extension of the pilot's legs. In the collapsed position, the upper portion of each pedal is rotated to the horizontal position. The pedals are returned to their normal position by using a toe or swab stick.

The cockpit canopy on all U-2's is hinged and manually swings open to the left (port) side of the aircraft. It normally has a white, or light color, sun hood painted on the inside. Tinting for protection against ultra-violet radiation is also provided. To prevent pressurization leakage around the canopy (and the upper and lower equipment bay hatches), inflatable seals are provided. Air pressure for the seals is supplied by the engine through a regulator which maintains a system pressure of approximately 17 to 18 psi. The windshield and canopy have primary defrosting systems which are supplied by hot bleed air from the second stage of the air conditioning and pressurization system. Additionally, a small, two-speed, rubber-blade fan mounted on the left side of the canopy constitutes a second defrosting system.

A ground adjustable rearview mirror is also arm-mounted on the left windshield support railing. This permits the pilot to observe contrail production (which usually ceases once the aircraft climbs above the troposphere) and to verify chase activity to the rear of the aircraft. Some early aircraft had this mirror mounted on the center of the windshield support railing.

All U-2's are equipped with gaseous (early model) or liquid (late model) oxygen systems capable of sustaining the pilot throughout any normal mission. In the U-2C, this system consists of three 514 cubic in. cylinders, a filler valve, check valves, two pressure reducers, two shutoff valves, a high pressure gage, two pressure switches, and two warning lights. The high pressure cylinders are located in the left-hand cheek area with the filler on the left side of the fuselage just below the wing leading edge.

In late model U-2's, a food warmer is provided which warms tubes of food that can then be eaten through a hard plastic straw that is inserted through a special leak-proof hole in the helmet. The food tubes look similar to toothpaste tubes and food is extracted in similar fashion to that used to extract toothpaste.

Most CIA and Air Force U-2's, during the course of operational missions into high threat areas, were equipped with a passive warning system and an active countermeasures system. Part of this capability, which in the U-2C and U-2F was identified as being "System 12B," and on some U-2R's as being "System 15," had both visual and aural warning capability and automatically prioritized threats and responded to them accordingly. In an extremely high threat situation, all countermeasure power automatically would be dedicated to the incoming threat with the greatest chance of contact.

Though several different autopilot systems have been utilized on various models of the U-2, the Lear 201 Automatic Flight Control System is representative of one of the most common configurations. The unit provides attitude and heading reference information via a two-gyro, all-attitude platform, and heading information is synchronized to the magnetic flux valve signal. When functioning, which is usually throughout the high-altitude portion of cruising flight, the autopilot effects control of the aircraft through electric servos connected to the aircraft control cable system. It is capable of maintaining pitch axis and Mach hold, automatic pitch trim, roll axis-heading hold, heading select, and aileron and elevator trim indices. Gary Powers' aircraft is reported to have been equipped with a Lear A-10 autopilot.

At least four U-2's have been modified or purpose-built for flight training with accommodations for a second crew member in an elevated rear compartment. Two of these aircraft were early model U-2C/D's and two are TR-1B's. In all four cases, the Q-bay was completely reconfigured, and in fact, virtually eliminated by the placement of flooring and an upper canopy and windscreen shell over the area normally occupied by a hatch. A second ejection seat and a second set of controls was also added, the latter consisting of a control wheel and conventional rudder pedals. An instrument panel with basic instrumentation was mounted conventionally on the reconfigured framework. These aircraft are now considered to be dedicated trainers and do not have a tactical capability.

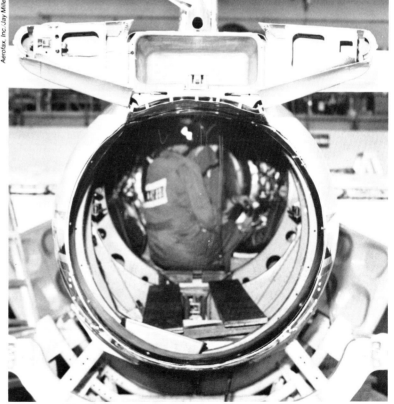

The vertical fin and horizontal tail surfaces of early model U-2's are conventional. All control surfaces, with the exception of the trim tabs, are unboosted.

Aft view of U-2C illustrates drag chute compartment and engine exhaust nozzle accommodations. Drag chute compartment can be used to accommodate ECM systems and other equipment.

Aft view of ER-2 illustrates revised exhaust nozzle configuration of late model aircraft.

U-2R exhaust nozzle, elevators, and tail cone.

TAIL UNIT: The U-2's tail unit consists of conventional horizontal and vertical tail surfaces with a balanced rudder and elevators of all metal construction. Construction is fairly conventional though spot welding is used throughout. Early model U-2 configurations have electric elevator trim tabs with one on each elevator. Late model aircraft have a more sophisticated trim unit consisting of rigidly connected vertical fin and horizontal stabilizer surfaces that are hinged together so that they can be hydraulically pivoted around a point at the base of the fin leading edge. The control surfaces are mechanical and unboosted. Elevator travel is 30-deg. up and 20-deg. down. Rudder travel is 30-deg. left and right. Some late model U-2's are undergoing a modification program wherein external ribbing is being attached to the horizontal tail surfaces to correct a flutter induced fatigue problem that is the result of an airflow anomaly caused by the introduction of the large wing "super pods."

On all early aircraft a 16' drag chute or electronic countermeasures equipment can be carried in a compartment at the base of the vertical tail surfaces above the engine exhaust nozzle.

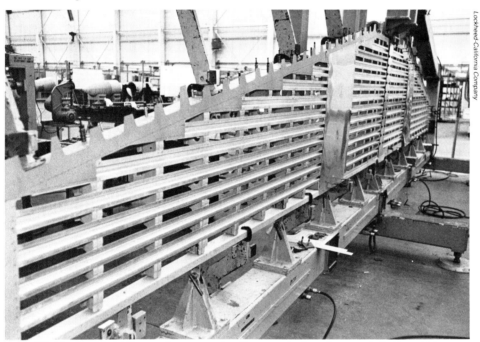

TR-1 horizontal stabilizer under construction. Two-spar design, when coupled with multiple span-wise stiffeners, provides a strong, lightweight structure.

Articulated vertical fin and horizontal tail assembly under construction.

Another view of vertical fin and horizontal tail surfaces under construction. Entire unit is integral and the vertical fin moves with the horizontal stabilizer during trimming.

Detail of the external rib modification now being fitted to select U-2R horizontal tail surfaces. Fatigue problems due to aerodynamic buffeting have brought on the modification.

WINGS: The U-2's all-metal cantilever wing in both basic configurations has remained essentially unchanged both internally and externally. Late model aircraft have greatly enlarged wings with increased wingspans and commensurately increased areas, but in general, the basic configuration is the same as that first envisioned by Kelly Johnson in 1954 with the CL-282 proposal. The airfoil section, a Lockheed-modified NACA/ NASA 64A series, has proven efficient and docile under most high altitude flight conditions, and Lockheed has continued to use it throughout the program.

The wings are not high dynamic load structures and are, in fact, rather fragile. Both basic aircraft configurations incorporate internal fuel tanks, and late model aircraft have true wet wings wherein the skin of the wings serves to contain the fuel. Almost the entire internal fuel capacity of all U-2 configurations is located in the wings and, in the case of late model aircraft, all but the outer, foldable, 6' tip panels serve as a fuel tank (folding is done manually after four bolts are removed). Fuel leakage is prevented through the use of specially developed rubberized caulking compounds which seal the joints where skin contacts the internal supporting structure. Fuel emergency jettison nozzles are located on the trailing edge of each wing between the outer flap segment and the aileron. In early aircraft the fuel is jettisoned by gravity flow, and on late model aircraft by small electric pumps.

The wing tips support downward canted end plates which serve as tip skids during landing. These skids are of all metal construction and have multiple, abradible skid pads attached to their contact edge surface. On approximately five aircraft, the skids extend above the upper surface of the wing tip. This is to cover a revised aileron counterweight configuration developed following a series of landing accidents leading to counterweight damage. The modification was relatively unsuccessful and discontinued, accordingly.

Each wing has three main skin panels top and bottom, machined from extrusions complete with spanwise stiffeners. The skins contain no access panels in consideration of their fuel tank requirement and they are attached with mechanical fasteners and are removable for maintenance. The leading edge is spot welded to the nose rib structures. The wing is a three-spar design with multiple attachment points and an unusual ribbing structure consisting of lattices of lightweight aluminum tubing. Each lattice member is attached to machined fittings with Hi-Lock fasteners having driving heads which shear when tightened to a pre-determined torque. In late model aircraft the spot welded construction ailerons, each equipped with an electrically actuated trim tab, are mechanically actuated, mass balanced, and unboosted. In early models, there is only one electric aileron trim tab and it is on the left (port) surface. A fixed trim tab is located on the right (starboard) surface. Aileron travel is 16-deg. up and 14-deg. down.

The flap system on both basic models makes up nearly 70% of the total trailing edge surface area of each wing. The flaps are segmented (into four sections on each wing) in consideration of the wing's tremendous flex (up to two vertical feet at the tips) and actuation to a maximum of 35-deg. is via two hydraulic motors interconnected by a flexible sychronization shaft.

Integral with the flap system is the U-2's unique gust control system. This device makes it possible to simultaneously shift both ailerons and wing flaps to an up, or gust, position. The ailerons are shifted 10-deg. and the flaps are shifted 4-deg. This has the dual purpose of reducing both wing and tail structural loads by moving the center of pressure forward. The gust control is used to shift

Wing jig for U-2R/TR-1 wing is a large assembly in order to accommodate 51' section. Besides providing lift, the wing also serves as the main fuel tank for the U-2.

Retractable stall strips are located on the leading edge of each wing. When extended, they protrude approximately one-half-inch beyond the leading edge. The stall strip is retracted in photo.

The wing fold on the U-2R/ER-2/TR-1 series aircraft is manual. The folded portion of the wing is the only portion of the wing is the only portion that does not contain fuel. The wing fold facilitates ground handling.

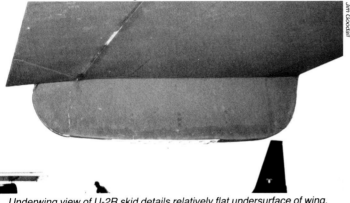

John Andrews collection

A variety of tip skid configurations can be found on the various U-2 models. Standard skid for U-2A is illustrated (kangaroo represents TDY assignment to Australia)

Aerofax, Inc: Jay Miller

Updated skid found on U-2C incorporates abradable skid buttons on bottom. Night light seen on this skid is not found on all aircraft.

Jim Goodall

Underwing view of U-2R skid details relatively flat undersurface of wing, abradable skid buttons, and angular fairing.

Jim Goodall

Hemispherical warning systems are installed in wingtip skid fairings. These function similarly to other radar homing and warning equipment systems.

Lockheed-California Company

Advanced version of RHAW gear found on earlier U-2R's is now found on TR-1 series aircraft. The fairing is much more refined and sensor capabilities have been somewhat improved. Hemispherical coverage is considered to be outstanding.

Hal McCormack

Split flap of TR-1A is one of the few externally distinguishing features of this version. Split is to permit accommodation of super pod. Note the fuel dump tube just outboard of tail warning sensor.

John Andrews

The U-2R's four-segment flap in its fully extended position. Segmenting is necessary to accommodate wing flex.

the surfaces up when flying in turbulent air or when flying at higher speeds in smooth air. The aileron motion is effected by an electric shifting mechanism located under the cockpit floor. The gust control switch is on the left console aft of the throttle.

All models of the U-2 have retractable stall strips on the leading edges of both wings. These are manually operated devices located one-third of the way out from the fuselage between the wing root and the wing tip. They provide improved stalling characteristics at low altitude (i.e., during landing) and they protrude approximately 1/2" when extended and are flush with the wing leading edge when retracted. Late model U-2's are equipped with two small hydraulically actuated plate-type roll/lift spoilers on each wing, forward of the outboard flap segments.

Both large and small sensor system pods are capable of being accommodated on the majority of the basic U-2 configurations. The smaller pods, normally used in droppable fuel tank form, are pylon mounted underneath each wing about mid-span. These can be used to transport extra fuel, or specialized sensors. The large, "super pods" are also mountable on early or late model aircraft, though the payload weight is substantially less when carried by the former. When utilized in conjunction with late model aircraft, these 27' long pods are capable of transporting up to 1,200 pounds of sensors. Only the drop tank-type pods are jettisonable.

LANDING GEAR: The titanium landing gear is a lightweight forward retracting (hydraulically actuated) zero-track bicycle type with twin main wheels and twin tailwheels. Outrigger, or balancer units (also called pogos) are located one under each wing, approximately at mid-span and are free to swivel 360 deg. These each have a pair of wheels and are normally gravity-pull jettisoned shortly after the wings begin to generate lift (though they can be fixed in place through the use of retaining pins). Though the high pressure (300 psi in late model aircraft) main gear tires are conventional, the tail wheel tires and outrigger wheel tires (8" dia. in late model aircraft and slightly smaller in early models) are hard rubber with no inflation capability. The tailwheel is steerable 6 deg. to each side through a system of cables interconnecting it with the rudder and rudder pedals and provides the aircraft with an approximate turning radius of 300'. Hydraulic spot and disc type brakes are attached to each main gear wheel. Emergency deployment of the landing gear is free fall by gravitational pull and aerodynamic download. The gear is locked in place by a spring-loaded downlock mechanism.

ELECTRICAL SYSTEM: The U-2 has both DC and AC electrical systems. The DC system, for most models, is a regulated 28-volt, single conductor type which utilizes the airframe structure for the ground return. DC power is furnished by one 400 amp, 28-volt, engine driven generator, which in this installation is derated to 225 amps.A 35-amp/hour, nickel-cadmium battery is installed to supply emergency power to the DC system.

The AC system, for most models, is furnished by a 750-VA inverter for the normal system. A backup 750-VA inverter is also provided. In addition, a 100-VA emergency inverter and a 10-KVA engine driven AC generator are provided. The inverters are rated at 115-volt, 400-cycle, three-phase output, with an input of 26 volts DC. The AC generator is rated at 120/208 volts, 320-450 cycle, three-phase AC.

In late model aircraft, there is a single AC/DC generator backed up by an AC alternator driven from the hydraulic system. This powers all essential equipment if the main generator fails. There is no backup system in early model aircraft.

Extended spoilers (right) and detail of aileron trim tab are not often seen. Note also fuel dump tube extending beyond wing trailing edge.

External pylon mounted wing pods have been developed for early model aircraft to increase either their fuel capacity or their sensor system payloads. As fuel tanks they can carry up to 100 usable gallons each.

Super pod construction uses conventional aircraft construction techniques. The large number of stiffener rings is reminiscent of construction found in conventional aircraft fuselages.

The super pod is attached directly to the wing and does not require any noticeable aerodynamic fairings. Capacity of each super pod includes up to 1,250 pounds of sensors.

The U-2C's main gear retracts forward and is equipped with dual disc brakes on each wheel. The landing lights are rigidly mounted to the upper portion of the main gear strut.

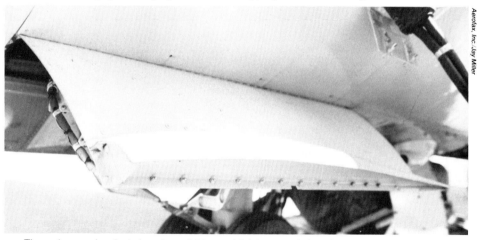

The main gear door includes a large fairing and tightly-spaced piano hinging. A stiffened internal structure prevents flutter problems at high extension speeds.

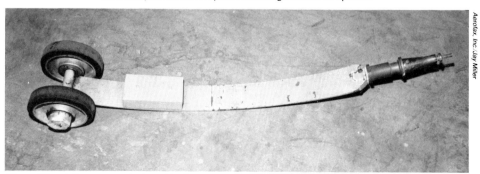

The solid metal pogos are designed for long term reuse and are equipped with lead weights to facilitate their gravity release from the U-2. The tires are hard rubber, and the complete assembly is free-castoring under the wing.

HYDRAULIC SYSTEMS: The hydraulic system operates the landing gear, the speed brakes, the wing flaps, the fuel boost pump drive motor, and on the U-2F, the latch and receptacle mechanism of the air refueling system (ARS), and on the late model aircraft, the pitch trim, and the spoilers. There is a hydraulic quick disconnected receptacle for use with a hydraulic ground cart when operating the hydraulic system on the ground. All U-2 hydraulic systems, though differing somewhat in detail from model to model, are basically the same. The system is a constant 3,000 psi pressure type, incorporating an accumulator and self-regulating engine-driven pump. The air charged accumulator stores pressures for peak demands and thus reduces fluctuations in pump loading. The system relief valve serves as a safety device to bypass oil back to the tank and prevent excessive system pressure. The hydraulic oil is cooled as it circulates through a heat exchanger in the engine oil ram air cooling scoop on the lower right side of the fuselage (early model aircraft only—on late model aircraft, cooling is accommodated within the confines of the fuselage). Engine compressor bleed air is used to pressurize the hydraulic fluid reservoir to reduce foaming and increase pump efficiency at high altitude.

EXTERNAL AND INTERNAL LIGHTING SYSTEM: The aircraft lighting system consists of: warning lights on the instrument panel; instrument panel lighting (small post-type red lights); panel lights (edge lighting type); utility spotlights (on each side of the cockpit for added illumination or map reading); and external navigation lights (consisting of two red rotating beacon lights, one located on the top of the fuselage, and the other located below—many aircraft also now have conventional wingtip navigation lights, as well).

Main gear retraction is hydraulically actuated with drag links pulling the gear well doors closed as the gear moves up.

Small door on wing underside covers hole for pogo attachment pin.

U-2R/ER-2/TR-1 main gear differs significantly from that of early U-2 variants. Brakes are most noticeable change.

Rear view of ER-2 main gear. Note conventional disc brake arrangement.

ER-2 main gear, gear well door, and E-bay lower hatch are located to the rear of the Q-bay. Main gear well occupies space between bifurcated intake tunnel. Small E-bay can be used to accommodate some sensors, if required.

Main gear wheel and high-pressure tire of NASA ER-2.

A special four wheel tow bar has been developed for late model U-2's. It has a hydro-mechanical lift system for raising the tail wheel and is significantly easier to use than the dolly-type ground transporter.

Detail of U-2R tailwheel assembly.

Additional U-2R tailwheel assembly detail reveals hot air vents in gear well doors. The tailwheels are solid rubber and the suspension system is non-shock-absorbing.

Tailwheel assembly of the U-2C is simple and rugged. Tailwheel is steerable and does not have any shock absorption system.

Rear view of ER-2 tailwheel assembly emphasizes its simplicity and illustrates steering mechanism.

Front view of TR-1 tailwheel assembly shows fully extended oleo strut and hard rubber tires to advantage.

SPECIFICATIONS:

	U-2A/B/C/CT/ D/E/F/G	U-2R/EP-X/ER-2/ TR-1A/TR-1B
Length	49' 8.6"	62.9' (est. 62.0' for EP-X)
Wingspan	80' 2"	103.0'
Wing area (gross)	600 sq. '	1,000 sq. '
Wing aspect ratio	10.6 to 1 (approx.)	10.6 to 1 (approx.)
Avg. wing loading	39.9 lbs. sq. '	34.75 lbs. sq.'
Height	15' 2"	16'0"
Power loading	1.3 lbs. per lb. th.	2.0 lbs. per lb. th.
Empty weight	12,000 lbs. U-2A	15,101 lbs. U-2R
	13,000 lbs. U-2B	15,500 lbs. U-2EP-X
	13,870 lbs. U-2C	14,500 lbs. ER-2
	14,200 lbs. U-2D	15,500 lbs. TR-1A
	14,000 lbs. U-2E	15,750 lbs. TR-1B
	14,170 lbs. U-2F	
	14,375 lbs. U-2G	
Gross takeoff weight	22,100 lbs. U-2A	41,000 lbs. U-2R
	23,100 lbs. U-2B	41,300 lbs. U-2EP-X
	23,970 lbs. U-2C	40,300 lbs. ER-2
	24,300 lbs. U-2D	41,300 lbs. TR-1A
	24,100 lbs. U-2E	41,550 lbs. TR-1B
	24,270 lbs. U-2F	
	24,475 lbs. U-2G	
Center of gravity limitations	25.5% to 26.5% MAC, gear down.	?

PERFORMANCE: Few aircraft have maintained the mystery of their performance capability better or longer than the enigmatic U-2. Because of its Central Intelligence Agency origins and the purpose for which it was built, a decision was made early in the program to keep its performance capabilities a tightly held secret.

In many cases, this secret has been well maintained and remains a stalwart reminder to authors and historians that this is no ordinary aircraft. This author worked for many months in what was eventually a successful attempt to acquire the long sought-after performance data for the U-2, and what follows is, with very few exceptions, a verifiable account of how high, how far, and how fast the U-2 can actually fly:

First of all, it must be understood by the reader that U-2 performance is dictated by many variables, not the least of which is aircraft model, aircraft configuration, atmospheric variables such as air temperature and humidity, and most importantly, aircraft weight.

It must also be understood that, to all intents and purposes, the U-2 represents the ultimate high altitude subsonic aircraft. It cruises at the absolute physical limit of altitude attainable without compressing, via supersonic flight, the air molecules available in the upper troposphere and lower stratosphere. There simply isn't enough air density to permit the U-2, or any other subsonic aircraft, to fly higher.

During the course of many interviews with more than a few U-2 pilots, several performance facts became apparent that should not be overlooked. The first of these was that the original U-2A configurations as designed for and used by the Central Intelligence Agency, because of their extraordinary light weight, had the best high altitude performance of all U-2 models—even though they were equipped with the least powerful J57 powerplant; the second was that the late model U-2's, generally speaking, offered very little, if any, improvement in maximum altitude capability over their predecessors but did offer

substantial improvements in range and payload carrying ability; and the third is that many of the published altitude performance figures for the U-2 have been surprisingly accurate.

The maximum altitude capability for the U-2C/F as illustrated by the accompanying chart, is 75,100'. This can be considered an average maximum performance indicator for the entire U-2 family with a 5% improvement in capability for the early lightweight aircraft (thus giving a maximum altitude for the latter of 78,855') and U-2R and later aircraft. The latter, because of their greatly increased payload capability, actually tend to perform more routinely at the 75,000' altitude level.

It should be emphasized that the above figures are accurate only in consideration of assumed weights and configurations, and that they will vary somewhat from aircraft to aircraft and also depending on atmospheric conditions. An example of all these factors is a flight made by one of the Air Force pilots interviewed who stated that

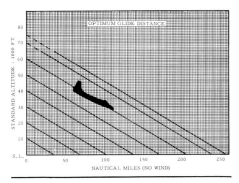

CLEAN CONFIGURATION ONLY

MAXIMUM ALTITUDE CRUISE PROFILE

WITHOUT SLIPPER TANKS

ZFW - 14100 LB
TAKEOFF FUEL 1320 GAL

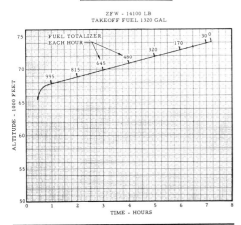

NAUTICAL MILES PER GALLON OF FUEL ALTITUDE 60,000 FEET

WITHOUT
SLIPPER TANKS

STALL AND MACH BUFFET BOUNDARIES

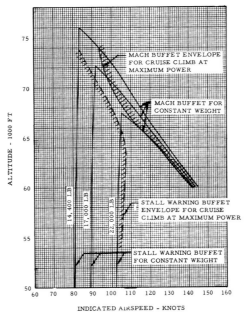

81,000'—while the aircraft was still indicating a slow, modest rate of climb.

Maximum range is obtained by flying the U-2 at a constant engine pressure ratio (EPR), constant Mach .72 cruise climb starting at 59,000' without slipper or drop tanks, or, in early aircraft, 57,000' with slipper or drop tanks, or 56,000' with both slipper and drop tanks. The initial climb is made to 56,000', 57,000' or 59,000' where power is reduced to 2.30 EPR and Mach .72 speed set up per a given speed schedule. This EPR and Mach is then held constant and as fuel is burned and the weight reduces, the aircraft will cruise climb.

Large variations in outside air temperature are common at altitudes between 55,000' and 60,000' and can affect the performance noticeably. This can be caused by changes in temperatures with increasing altitude or can be due to flying into geographical areas of hotter or colder temperatures. The aircraft will cruise climb more rapidly when flying into areas with colder temperatures. When flying into warmer temperatures the aircraft will climb slower, may not climb at all, or may actually descend if the temperature increases enough. A temperature increase of 10-deg. C may cause the aircraft to fly at constant altitude or descend slightly. Then, when colder temperatures are encountered, the aircraft will climb until it is back on the fuel-altitude curve. The warmer temperatures will also incease the fuel consumption rate, but this is partially offset by the faster true airspeed as the temperature increases.

In terms of actual range capability, the early model U-2's with maximum fuel could stay airborne for up to 10 hours 45 minutes under ideal circumstances. Normal missions were held to just under ten hours, however, and absolute maximum range was approximately 4,750 miles. Late model U-2's have the same maximum 3.75 miles per gallon capability as their predecessors, but have the distinct advantage of being able to carry just over 3,000 gallons of fuel internally. This indicates a maximum range of some 6,250 miles, which, when given the fact that non-stop missions flown by U-2R's and TR-1A's from Beale AFB to RAF Alconbury near Cambridge, England encompass nearly 5,600 miles, is almost certainly an accurate figure.

The U-2 is not a speed-oriented aircraft. It's high-aspect-ratio wings and low-q structure limit the maximum Mach number of all models to .80

or 240 knots, whichever is less. Landing and takeoff speeds also vary, though they are dependent more on weight and configuration than other factors. The aircraft accelerates rapidly once the throttle is advanced and takeoff distances are usually very short. Takeoff speeds are generally 115% of the stall speeds. At maximum takeoff weights, the takeoff indicated airspeed is 112 knots. At minimum takeoff weights the indicated airspeed is approximately 80 knots. Normal takeoffs require a nose-down trim to avoid over-rotation during the takeoff process and the maximum allowable cross wind component for a conventional landing is 15 knots.

Once airborne, the aircraft normally takes approximately 35 minutes and 105 miles to reach 65,000'. Again, these figures can vary greatly depending on configuration and weight.

Once at cruising altitude, the U-2 is statically stable, but at high altitude is subject to normal Mach number effects which result in "tuck" or an increase of nose down pitch moment with speed. Generally, when the aircraft is trimmed at a given speed, a push force is required to increase speed, and a pull force is required to decrease speed. The force is usually less than 10 to 15 pounds. At or near placard speeds, attention should not be diverted from flying the aircraft since control force changes with speed are small. The speed may increase beyond limits due to inattention or outside upset before the pilot becomes aware of it. At lower altitudes, the static stability is satisfactory. At high altitude and heavy weight, the aircraft is operating close to the limit of its capabilities. Under these conditions, the aircraft is flying at very high wing lift coefficients, and during manual flights, requires the pilot's full attention.

If the aircraft is flown hands off and the autopilot is not engaged, an attitude upset can cause a long period of motion which may be either stable or unstable. Below 60,000' the aircraft will generally oscillate slowly from a speed above trim. Above 60,000', if upset and left hands off, the aircraft will go into a climb or dive and the airspeed will continue to decrease or increase until the pilot corrects the situation.

The U-2, in all configurations, has a moderate stall with a normal stall warning buffet. Small sharp edged spoilers (retractable) located on the wing leading edge near the fuselage cause turbulence at high angles of attack which impinges on the horizontal tail surfaces and provides the stall warning. Stalls are avoided at high altitude because recovery is extremely difficult due to the narrow range between high speed buffet and low speed stall.

When the air no longer follows the wing contour, separation occurs. A separation is usually unstable and the resulting turbulent airflow which shakes the airframe is called wing buffet. Separation will occur at low Mach numbers as a result of angle of attack alone, and a fully developed separation is called a stall. The localized separation which precedes wing stall results in wing stall warning buffet, and is a warning of impending stall. Separation will occur at high Mach numbers at specific combinations of Mach number and angle of attack which are characteristic of the particular wing. This separation results in wing Mach buffet.

The usable combination of angle of attack and Mach number are bounded by the wing stall buffet boundary and wing Mach buffet boundary. The intersection of the stall buffet and the Mach buffet boundary forms a "corner," nicknamed the "coffin corner," in which the normal wing low speed stall is identical to its high speed Mach buffet limit. An aircraft such as the U-2 can maintain level flight at the stall buffet or the Mach buffet boundary if sufficient power is available.

on a routine return leg to Laughlin AFB, while flying a HASP mission over the continental US, he decided to explore the maximum altitude potential of the aircraft. He was aware that the environmental conditions were near perfect, that the aircraft was performing well and was very lightly loaded (the fuel was minimal and the sensor system package was relatively light), and that all systems onboard the aircraft were functioning normally. He began his ascent while cruising at an altitude in excess of 70,000'. He leveled off and began his descent shortly after exceeding

The descent in the high altitude area from 75,000' down to 70,000' is slow. The engine power, even at minimum flow, with bleed valves open, is still considerable at this altitude and available drag producing items do not produce much drag at indicated airspeeds of 90 to 100 knots. A descent with the gust control faired will probably encounter buffet, rolloff and sharp tucking tendencies at speeds faster than the standard climb speed schedule. Elevator stick forces will be high.

After a descent is established with gear down, speed brakes out, and on descent speed schedule, the gust control is placed in gust. The descent should be limited to the speed for light to moderate buffet. The buffet is normally heavier and will start at lower Mach numbers at higher altitudes and/or heavier gross weights. At medium and lower altitudes a descent speed of 150 knots is used if turbulence is present or anticipated. If the air is smooth, the rate of descent can be considerably increased by descending at 200 knots indicated airspeed.

Landing distances tend to be 2,500' to 3,500' because the aircraft is very clean aerodynamically and engine idle thrust is appreciable. The idle thrust and low drag affect both the float distance and the stopping distance. Although it is generally desirable to leave the engine running during the landing approach, the landing distance will be appreciably shorter if the engine is shut off at the runway threshold. The speed brake drag is not high at landing speed. However, extending the speed brakes does shorten the distance somewhat. The drag chute (available on early models) is the most effective means of reducing both float distance and stopping distance. Stall speeds vary as a function of weight, but their limits for early aircraft configurations are: at a gross weight of 14,000 lbs. and with 35-deg. flaps, 69 knots; at a gross weight of 16,500 lbs. (nominal) and with 35-deg. flaps, 77 knots; at a gross weight of 23,000 lbs. and with 35-deg. flaps, 89 knots.

Early model U-2's have the following information placarded on the inside of the cockpit for pilot reference:

CLEAN

Rough air	150 kts. i.a.s.
Smooth air	220 kts. i.a.s.
Mach no.	.80

GUST CONTROL ON

Rough air	170 kts. i.a.s.
Smooth air	260 kts. i.a.s.
Mach no.	.80
Gear down	260 kts. i.a.s.
Speed brakes	260 kts. i.a.s.
Flaps 0-deg./25-deg.	130 kts. i.a.s.

United Technologies via Hal Keiner/Harvey Lippincott

Pratt & Whitney's rugged and dependable J57-P-31 was the primary powerplant choice among the various early contenders for what eventually became the U-2 program. Several specialized variants of the J57 engine, including the J57-P-31 were built specifically for use in the U-2.

United Technologies via Hal Keiner

The U-2 proved adaptable to Pratt & Whitney's second generation high-performance turbojet engine, the J75. Special high-altitude versions of the J75 were developed specifically for use in the U-2, including the J75-P-13, shown.

Chapt. 10:
POWERPLANTS, FUEL SYSTEMS, AND FUELS

The development of the special engines that have been utilized to power the various U-2 configurations over the years is one of the least heralded, yet most important aspects of the program. In 1954, when the Agency and the Air Force began looking at powerplants for a high altitude recce aircraft, they quickly narrowed their choices to three state-of-the-art turbojets, the J65, the J73, and the J57, which offered the greatest potential for meeting the performance and reliability requirements. Eventually, the decision to work with the J57 was based on its production record, its service reliability record, and its estimated performance at altitude.

The basic J57 engine had been born as a two-spool axial flow turbojet in 1948. Continuous development work spanned the following two years and by 1949, the first production configuration, known as the J57-P-1 (JT3A) had been finalized. Actual full-scale production began in February of 1953. The J57 went on to become one of the more ubiquitous turbojet engines of all time, with some 21,000 being built by Pratt & Whitney before production ceased in 1965. In civil guise, the engine was known as the JT3C.

What follows is a technical description of the basic J57 powerplant and a brief overview of the configurations used in all early model U-2 aircraft:

The basic JT3/J57 nonafterburning powerplant is an axial flow dual compressor turbojet with a compressor pressure ratio of about 10 to 1 at sea level static military rating. The axial flow dual compressor has a nine stage low pressure unit and a seven stage high pressure unit. The dual compressor supplies air to the can annular combustion chamber where fuel is introduced and burned. The gas stream from the combustion section enters the turbine section giving up energy to the split turbines to drive the dual compressor. The first turbine stage drives the high pressure compressor by a hollow shaft. The second and third turbine stages drive the low pressure compressor by a concentric shaft through the hollow high pressure compressor shaft. A gearbox at the bottom of the engine provides external drive pads for the starter, tachometer, fuel pump and fuel control unit, and includes the engine oil pressure and scavenge pumps. The gearbox is driven from the high pressure compressor shaft. The low pressure rotor has three tachometer drive pads at the bottom of the air inlet case. The rotor may have a 10" drive pad at the front of the engine. The engine has two automatically activated overboard bleed valves located between the low and high compressors to facilitate starting, to improve acceleration, and to prevent surge by ducting low pressure air overboard during low power operation. High pressure compressor bleed air is also available to the airframe manufacturer in quantities stated in the engine specification for driving aircraft accessories or cabin pressurization.

The combustion section contains eight combustion chambers commonly called burner cans. Fuel is sprayed into the burner cans through dual-orifice nozzles mounted in clusters of six at the inlet of each burner can (U-2 dedicated J57's have special nozzles to accommodate the special JP-TS fuel). The fuel is ignited by two spark igniters located in burner cans #4 and #5, and the flame is propagated to the other burner cans by connecting flame tubes. The continuous com-

Lockheed-California Company

Specially baffled stainless steel fuel sump tanks located in the U-2's (in this case, the TR-1's) fuselage are designed to conform to the powerplant mounted above them.

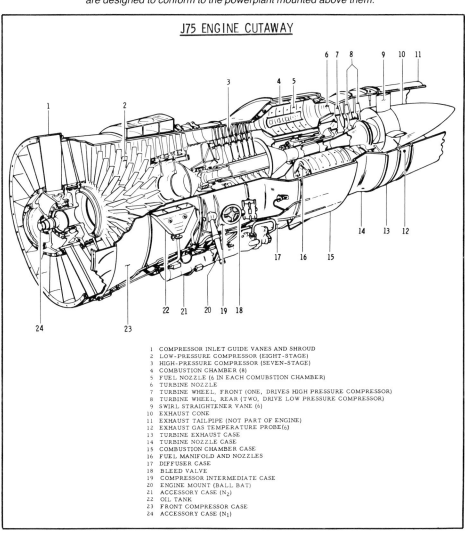

J75 ENGINE CUTAWAY

1 COMPRESSOR INLET GUIDE VANES AND SHROUD
2 LOW-PRESSURE COMPRESSOR (EIGHT-STAGE)
3 HIGH-PRESSURE COMPRESSOR (SEVEN-STAGE)
4 COMBUSTION CHAMBER (8)
5 FUEL NOZZLE (6 IN EACH COMUBSTION CHAMBER)
6 TURBINE NOZZLE
7 TURBINE WHEEL, FRONT (ONE, DRIVES HIGH PRESSURE COMPRESSOR)
8 TURBINE WHEEL, REAR (TWO, DRIVE LOW PRESSURE COMPRESSOR)
9 SWIRL STRAIGHTENER VANE (6)
10 EXHAUST CONE
11 EXHAUST TAILPIPE (NOT PART OF ENGINE)
12 EXHAUST GAS TEMPERATURE PROBE(6)
13 TURBINE EXHAUST CASE
14 TURBINE NOZZLE CASE
15 COMBUSTION CHAMBER CASE
16 FUEL MANIFOLD AND NOZZLES
17 DIFFUSER CASE
18 BLEED VALVE
19 COMPRESSOR INTERMEDIATE CASE
20 ENGINE MOUNT (BALL BAT)
21 ACCESSORY CASE (N$_2$)
22 OIL TANK
23 FRONT COMPRESSOR CASE
24 ACCESSORY CASE (N$_1$)

External differences between stock J75's and the engines (J75-P-13B shown) specifically configured for use in the U-2 were almost non-existant.

Aft view of J75-P-13B shows long exhaust pipe and exhaust bullet. Additional exhaust pipe extensions are built into the empennage section of the U-2.

bustion supplies the heat for expanding the compressor air increasing the velocity of the gas flow to the turbine as described above. The turbine high velocity gases are discharged through a fixed area exhaust nozzle. The engine is furnished with a flange at the exhaust duct to which the aircraft manufacturer may attach a tail pipe.

J57 major component specifications are:

Rotor assembly: dual rotors, each composed of a multistage axial flow compressor driven by split turbine stages.

Direction of rotation: clockwise, viewed from the aft end.

Compressor type: axial flow, two spool.

Compressor stages (total): 16 (7 low pressure and 9 high pressure).

Turbine type: split axial flow.

Turbine stages (total): 3 (low pressure compressor drive in second and third stage and high pressure compressor drive in the first stage).

Combustion chamber type: can-annular with eight burner cans.

Combustion chamber number: eight burner cans, numbered clockwise viewed from the rear (#1 in the 1 o'clock position).

Standard equipment: fuel pump, fuel control, engine ignition system without power service exhaust thermocouples and pressure probes.

Suspension: two plane (in front at the intermediate compressor case and in the rear at the flange of the turbine rear bearing support case).

Several different versions of the basic J57 have been used in the early models of the U-2 since the type first took to the air in 1955. These include the J57-P-37 (standard production engine, used primarily for initial test flight work as it ws not a dedicated high-altitude engine; it was notorious for causing smoke problems in the cockpit), the J57-P-37A (basically the same as the J57-P-37), the YJ57-P-31 (special hand-built J57 high-altitude engine used to replace the J57-P-37A), and the J57-P-31A (the standard production high-altitude engine for the U-2A). In general, these engines were stock in terms of basic configura-

Compressor face view of J75-P-13B verifies that compressor section blade changes from the stock engine, if any, are small.

Exhaust section view of J75-P-13B also reveals lack of major changes in overall configuration of standard engine. Most changes relate to tolerances, and the fuel and oil systems.

tion and accessories, but in the case of the YJ57-P-31 and the J57-P-31A, they differed in being lightened through closer machining of major and minor subassemblies, and in being built to significantly closer tolerances. In fact, the latter was particularly significant in terms of the compressor section where leaks in the turbine casing causing pressure losses and turbine inefficiency simply were not tolerated.

J57 specifications were:

	J57-P-37	J57-P-37A	YJ57-P-31/31A
Takeoff thrust	10,500 lbs.	10,500 lbs.	11,200 lbs.
Military thrust	10,500 lbs.	10,500 lbs.	11,200 lbs.
Normal cruise thrust	8,100 lbs.	8,100 lbs.	9,500 lbs.
Dry weight	4,170 lbs.	4,170 lbs.	3,820 lbs.
Jet nozzle type	fixed	fixed	fixed
Fuel control model	HSD JFC12-5	HSD JFC12-TA	HSD JFC12-8
Diameter	39.81"	39.81"	40"
Length	163.37"	163.37"	157"

In 1958 a decision was made by Lockheed and the Agency to uprate the propulsion system in the U-2 in order to offset performance failings that were the end result of constantly increasing sensor system payload weights. Basically, it had been discovered that every additional pound of weight cost the aircraft one foot in maximum altitude performance. With some of the payloads approaching nearly a thousand pounds, the performance price was proving to be too high for some missions to be conducted safely.

A number of powerplants were studied before the Pratt & Whitney J75 was picked, but like its predecessor it was virtually an uncontested decision. The J75 was a proven, powerful, and exceptionally rugged engine that could be accommodated (though not without difficulty), inside the confines of the standard U-2 fuselage. Of great importance to Lockheed was the fact that no major modifications were involved and production line changes could be kept to a minimum. Additionally, and very importantly, the twenty-five or so U-2A's that had already been built by late 1958 could be easily modified to accommodate the J75.

U-2A's serving with the Agency were the first aircraft to be retrofitted (initially with the J75-P-13 which was a stock engine incorporating high altitude modifications), and these were updated (and redesignated U-2B) while production line aircraft were reconfigured prior to completion. Still newer aircraft were given the new powerplant without having ever had accommodations for the J57.

Historically, the J75 (civil designation is JT4) had been developed from the JT3/J57 engine with similar component arrangements but entirely new design features with emphasis placed on weight control. Production models in both non-afterburning and afterburning versions were manufactured and all had the same number of compressor and turbine stages and all non-afterburning models had fixed area exhaust nozzles. All "B" series engine compressors were redesigned for improved high altitude performance.

What follows is a technical description of the basic J75 powerplant and a brief overview of the configurations used in all U-2 models excepting the U-2A, some U-2D's, some U-2E's, and some U-2F's:

The JT4/J75 engine has an axial flow dual compressor with fifteen stages, eight can-annular combustion chambers, and a split three-stage turbine. The dual compressor consists of an eight stage low pressure unit and a seven stage high pressure unit. The low pressure compressor is connected by a through shaft to the second and third stage turbine wheels. The high pressure compressor is connected independently by a hollow concentric shaft to the first stage turbine wheel. A low pressure overboard bleed valve is provided on each side of the high pressure compressor case. The rpm of the high pressure rotor is governed by the engine fuel control but the rpm of the low pressure rotor is independent of any direct governing devices. The low pressure rotor rpm is a function of the pressure drop across its turbines. The compressor delivers air to the combustion chambers at a pressure ratio of about 12 to 1 for sea level takeoff rating. Both high and low pressure airbleed are available to the airframe manufacturer for various aircraft services.

The eight can-annular combustion chambers in the burner section are supplied with fuel through dual orifice nozzles mounted in clusters of six at the inlet of each combustion chamber (in dedicated J75's for use in the U-2, the nozzles are modified to accommodate the use of the special JP-TS fuel). Dual high-energy ignition units (of the capacitor-discharge 20-joule type) and two spark igniters located in #4 and #5 chambers are used to start combustion. Cross-over tubes propagate combustion to the other combustion chambers in the burner section.

A gearbox from and located beneath the high pressure compressor provides three 5" diameter bolt-circle accessory drive pads for starter (an air turbine starter is provided for ground starts using a GPU nicknamed a "huffer"), generator, and fluid pump. A 10" diameter power takeoff drive is provided at the front of the low pressure compressor and driven at the required speed.

The engine lubrication system provides the pressure lubricant to the main engine bearings and accessory drives and a scavenge system (consisting of five engine driven pumps) which returns the oil from the bearing compartments and accessory gearboxes to the oil tank. A breather system, interconnecting the various bearing compartments, accessory gearbox, and oil tank with a pressurizing valve to maintain above ambient pressure on the system at altitude. Oil cooling is furnished by an airframe supplied 14" air/oil cooler, and a 9" air/oil cooler, connected in series with the engine fuel/oil cooler in the oil supply line from the oil tank to the engine.

The fuel system consists of a two-stage gear type pump; a Hamilton Standard hydromechanical fuel control, a fuel manifold, pressurizing and dump valve to drain the fuel manifold on shut-down, and forty-eight dual-orifice fuel nozzles (specially modified on U-2's to facilitate the use of JP/TS fuel).

Engine exhaust gas temperature limitations for the J75 as used in various models of the U-2 are 630-deg. C. maximum from takeoff to 40,000'; 485-deg. C. maximum from 40,000' to 60,000'; and 665-deg. C. maximum from 60,000' to maximum altitude capability.

J75 major component specifications are:

Rotor assembly: dual rotors, each composed of a multistage axial flow compressor driven by split turbine stages.

Direction of rotation: clockwise, viewed from the aft end.

Compressor type: axial flow, two spool.

Compressor stages (total): 15 (8 low pressure and 7 high pressure).

Turbine type: 3 stage, split.

Turbine stages (total): 3 (low pressure compressor drive in second and third stage and high pressure compressor drive in the first stage).

Combustion chamber type: can-annular with eight burner cans.

Combustion chamber number: eight burner cans, numbered clockwise viewed from the rear (#1 in the 1 o'clock position).

Standard equipment: fuel pump, fuel control, engine ignition system without power service exhaust thermocouples and pressure probes.

Suspension: two plane (in front at the intermediate compressor case and in the rear at the flange of the turbine rear bearing support case).

Several different variants of the basic J75 have been used in the early models of the U-2 since the first conversions in 1958. These include the J75-P-13 (a stock engine coverted to high-altitude specs), the J75-P-13A (designation applied to both production and coverted engines), and the J75-P-13B (designation applied to both production and converted engines). In general, these engines were stock in terms of configuration and accoutrements, but differed from standard production line engines in being lightened through closer machining of major and minor subassemblies, and in being built to significantly closer tolerances. In fact, the latter was particularly significant in terms of the compressor section where leaks in the turbine casing causing pressure losses and turbine inefficiency simply were not tolerated.

Early production J75-P-13 is shown at Pratt & Whitney's Florida plant shortly before delivery to Lockheed. The change to the J75 improved the U-2's payload carrying ability considerably.

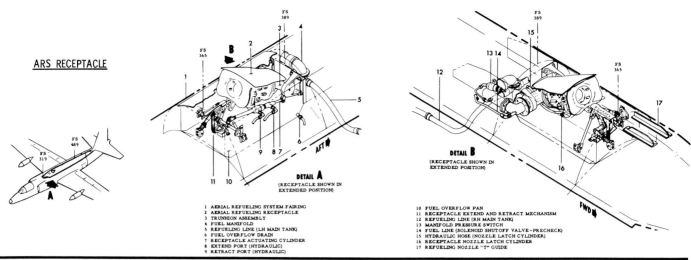

ARS RECEPTACLE

DETAIL A
(RECEPTACLE SHOWN IN
EXTENDED POSITION)

DETAIL B
(RECEPTACLE SHOWN IN
EXTENDED POSITION)

1 AERIAL REFUELING SYSTEM FAIRING
2 AERIAL REFUELING RECEPTACLE
3 TRUNNION ASSEMBLY
4 FUEL MANIFOLD
5 REFUELING LINE (LH MAIN TANK)
6 FUEL OVERFLOW DRAIN
7 RECEPTACLE ACTUATING CYLINDER
8 EXTEND PORT (HYDRAULIC)
9 RETRACT PORT (HYDRAULIC)

10 FUEL OVERFLOW PAN
11 RECEPTACLE EXTEND AND RETRACT MECHANISM
12 REFUELING LINE (RH MAIN TANK)
13 MANIFOLD PRESSURE SWITCH
14 FUEL LINE (SOLENOID SHUTOFF VALVE - PRECHECK)
15 HYDRAULIC HOSE (NOZZLE LATCH CYLINDER)
16 RECEPTACLE NOZZLE LATCH CYLINDER
17 REFUELING NOZZLE "T" GUIDE

J75 specifications were:

	YJ75-P-13/13A	J75-P-13B
Takeoff thrust	15,800 lbs.	17,000 lbs.
Military thrust	15,800 lbs.	17,000 lbs.
Normal cruise thrust	13,900 lbs.	15,100 lbs.
Dry weight	4,900 lbs.	4,900 lbs.
Jet nozzle type	fixed	fixed
Fuel control model	HSD JFC25-15	HSD JFC25-15
Diameter	43"	43"
Length	240"	240"
Spool-up time from idle to Mil-power	approx. 8 sec.	approx. 8 sec.

Throughout the history of the U-2 program, all J57 and J75 powerplants used in the aircraft have been meticulously maintained by Pratt & Whitney.

The fuel used in all models of the U-2 is a special low-volatility, low vapor-pressure kerosene type designated MIL-F-25524A or MIL-F-25524B and is often referred to as JP-TS (Thermally Stable), JP-7, or LF-1A. Though the U-2 can be flown using standard JP-4 or JP-5, this is not recommended because of high altitude performance restrictions and an adverse short-term effect on the powerplant fuel nozzles.

MIL-F-25524A/B provides optimal performance for the U-2 and permits safe operation at extremely high altitudes. It has a very high flash-point of 110-deg. F., a smoke point of 25 mm, a viscosity of 10 centistokes at –40-deg. F., and specific gravity of .850. Standard fuel weight is 6.58 lbs. per gallon at a temperature of 15-deg. C. Because a fuel-oil heat exchanger heats the U-2's fuel, an increase in internal volume of about 3% is realized. It is often delivered to U-2 OL's in 42 gallon barrels.

It should be mentioned that for years there have been rumors that some early model U-2's were equipped with a special system that injected liquid hydrogen into the engine to "improve oxidation of fuel." To date, the author has not uncovered any information verifying this, though the rumors persist.

The U-2's fuel system, like many of its other components, varies somewhat from model to model. In general, it is very simple and requires little attention from the pilot other than monitoring the boost pump fuel pressure, the fuel quantity indicator (because of the tremendous flex in the U-2's wings where virtually all internal fuel is carried, a conventional fuel quantity monitoring system was initially impractical; accordingly, a counter-type or positive displacement type fuel flow meter was utilized that was set to indicate the fuel actually in the tanks; as fuel was burned in flight the gallons were subtracted from the original figure down to zero; more recent early model aircraft had conventional fuel gauges that

read in gallons; and late model aircraft have conventional gauges that read in pounds of fuel consumed per hour), and the fuel warning lights.

All U-2's have four integral wing fuel tanks (the early model U-2's had an inboard wing section tank in each wing and a leading edge section tank that stretched into each outer panel; the late model U-2's have totally wet wings with each wing divided into two tanks; only the outer six feet of the wing tip panel is non-tank area), a fuselage sump tank, and provisions in early aircraft for slipper and drop tanks. All tanks feed by gravity and/or pressure into the fuselage sump tank which then provides fuel to the powerplant through a 200-mesh strainer. Fuel is furnished to the engine via a hydraulically-driven boost pump that operates at a regulated pressure of 14 to 25 psi. An auxiliary boost pump is submerged in the right side of the sump tank. At a normal cruise rpm of 90%, the U-2 in all J75-powered variants consumes fuel at approximately 160 gallons per hour.

Engine compressor bleed air is regulated to 2 psi to pressurize the main, auxiliary, and slipper tanks. The sump tank is not pressurized. The main wing tanks feed into the right-hand side of the sump, and the auxiliary tanks feed into the left-hand side of the sump.

The slipper tanks for early aircraft are external pods that slip on over the leading edge of the wing approximately 10 feet from the fuselage. Fuel from the slipper tanks is forced by air pressure into the auxiliary (aft) wing tanks. From there it feeds into the sump tank through the normal auxiliary tank transfer system. A small electric pump is installed in each slipper tank to ensure complete utilization of available fuel.

Provisions are made for drop tanks with integral pylons which attach on the lower wing surface outboard of the slipper tanks. These tanks are not used unless they are to be dropped when their fuel is expended, as retention of the dry tanks has an adverse effect on range. Fuel from the drop tanks is forced by air pressure into the left hand sump tank by way of the auxiliary tank transfer lines.

In order to provide a means of correcting wing heaviness due to uneven fuel feeding, a small 5-gallon-per-minute electric fuel pump is installed. The reversible pump is controlled by a three-position switch on the lower left instrument sub-panel. It transfers fuel from either main wing tank to the other.

Late model U-2's have a maximum internal fuel capacity of approximately 1,875 gallons. Early model aircraft had a maximum internal capacity of 1,320 gallons and could add 200 more gallons through the installation of either the drop tanks or the slipper tanks. The tank capacities of the vari-

ous early model U-2's were as follows: sump, 95 gal.; main wing, 925 gal.; auxiliary wing, 300 gal.; slippers, 200 gal.; and drop tanks, 200 gal.

All U-2's are equipped with an emergency fuel dump system that allows a rapid reduction in aircraft weight so that landings can be made in emergency situations. The system consists of a dump valve and float switch in each of the four wing tanks and an overboard line on the trailing edge of each wing between the flap and aileron. Each dump valve is controlled independently. As mentioned earlier, both gravity and electric pump emergency dump systems have been used in various U-2 models.

All wing tanks are vented into the sump tank through combination type suction and pressure relief valves. The top of the sump tank is vented to the outside air at the top trailing edge of the vertical fin—in consideration of the high ascent angles often encountered by the U-2 during climb to cruising altitudes.

Due to requirements stemming from the effect of payload on high altitude performance, a number of U-2C's were modified under an Agency program to incorporate an inflight refueling capability into their refueling system. These aircraft were redesignated U-2F following this modification which entailed a change in the fuel usage sequence, the rerouting of several fuel lines, and the addition of the air refueling system (ARS).

The ARS allowed the U-2F to receive as much as 925 gallons of fuel in the main tanks during flight. It was composed of the following items:

1. A retractable receptacle located in a fairing on the top of the fuselage aft of the equipment bay.

2. A pressure switch in the fuel manifold downstream of the receptacle.

3. A dual shutoff valve located at the inboard end of each main tank.

4. A dual float operated pilot valve located near the outboard end of each main tank.

5. Four solenoid operated fuel valves for checking the pilot valves and their control panel on the instrument panel.

6. A part full float switch located inboard in each main tank.

7. A full float switch located outboard in each main tank.

8. A pressure switch in the main tank inboard vent line.

9. A motor operated bypass valve installed between the main tank outboard vent line and the overboard vent.

10. An amplifier system for automatic operation of the ARS.

11. An override system for manual operation of the ARS.

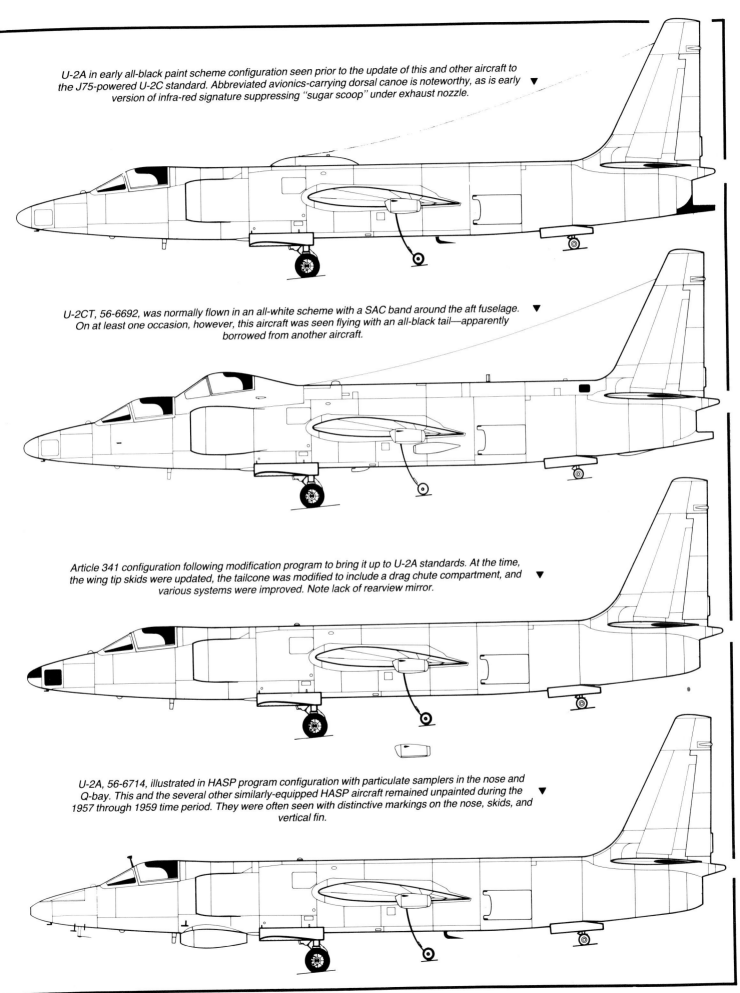

U-2A in early all-black paint scheme configuration seen prior to the update of this and other aircraft to the J75-powered U-2C standard. Abbreviated avionics-carrying dorsal canoe is noteworthy, as is early version of infra-red signature suppressing "sugar scoop" under exhaust nozzle. ▼

U-2CT, 56-6692, was normally flown in an all-white scheme with a SAC band around the aft fuselage. On at least one occasion, however, this aircraft was seen flying with an all-black tail—apparently borrowed from another aircraft. ▼

Article 341 configuration following modification program to bring it up to U-2A standards. At the time, the wing tip skids were updated, the tailcone was modified to include a drag chute compartment, and various systems were improved. Note lack of rearview mirror. ▼

U-2A, 56-6714, illustrated in HASP program configuration with particulate samplers in the nose and Q-bay. This and the several other similarly-equipped HASP aircraft remained unpainted during the 1957 through 1959 time period. They were often seen with distinctive markings on the nose, skids, and vertical fin. ▼

U-2R, 68-10337:

This aircraft (or at least aircraft bearing this serial number) has been seen in various countries and the United States carrying a wide variety of SIGINT and COMINT sensors including SLAR pods and dense fuselage and pod-mounted antenna farms. The paint scheme is standard for the series—flat black with red serial numbers on the vertical fin.

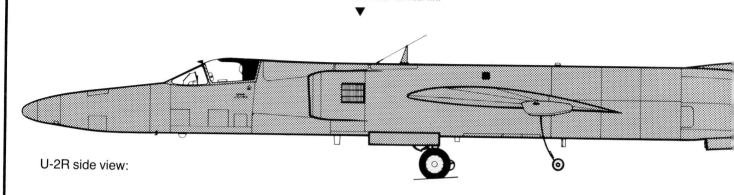

U-2R side view:

U-2A, 56-6708:

This aircraft had a lengthy Agency and Air Force history and was one of a half-dozen or so aircraft to participate regularly in the Cuban overflight program. When last seen, it was painted in the standard flat black color scheme seen on most Agency and Air Force U-2 aircraft during the 1960's period. As illustrated, the aircraft is shown as it was flown by the Air Force in the late 1950's and early 1960's in a natural aluminum finish. Please note that the sunshield, for illustration purposes, is painted black in the drawing whereas it was actually painted white when the aircraft was being flown without paint.

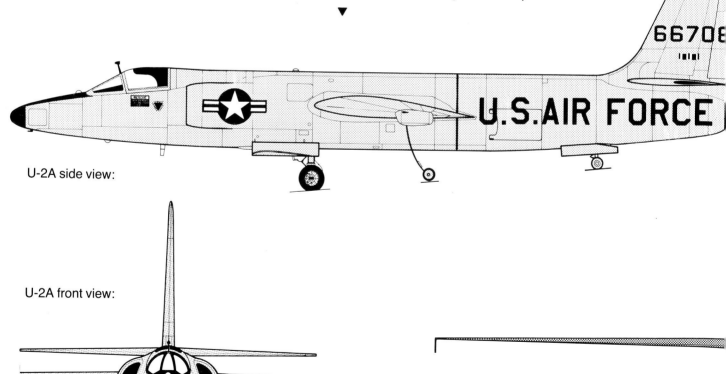

U-2A side view:

U-2A front view:

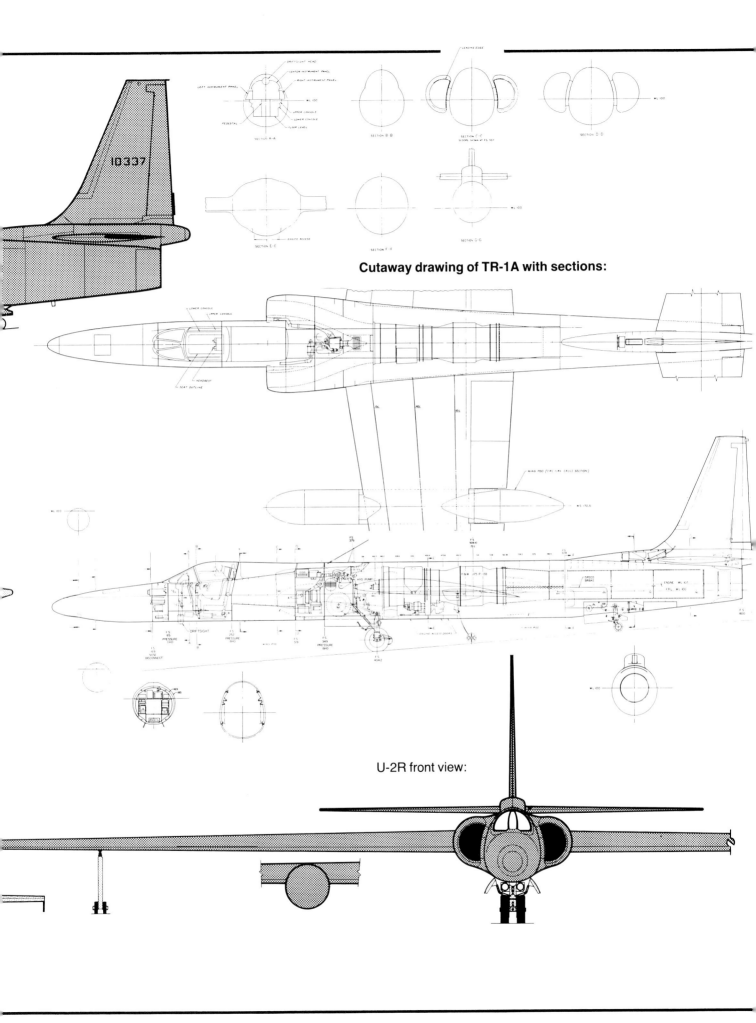

Cutaway drawing of TR-1A with sections:

U-2R front view:

Select Variants:

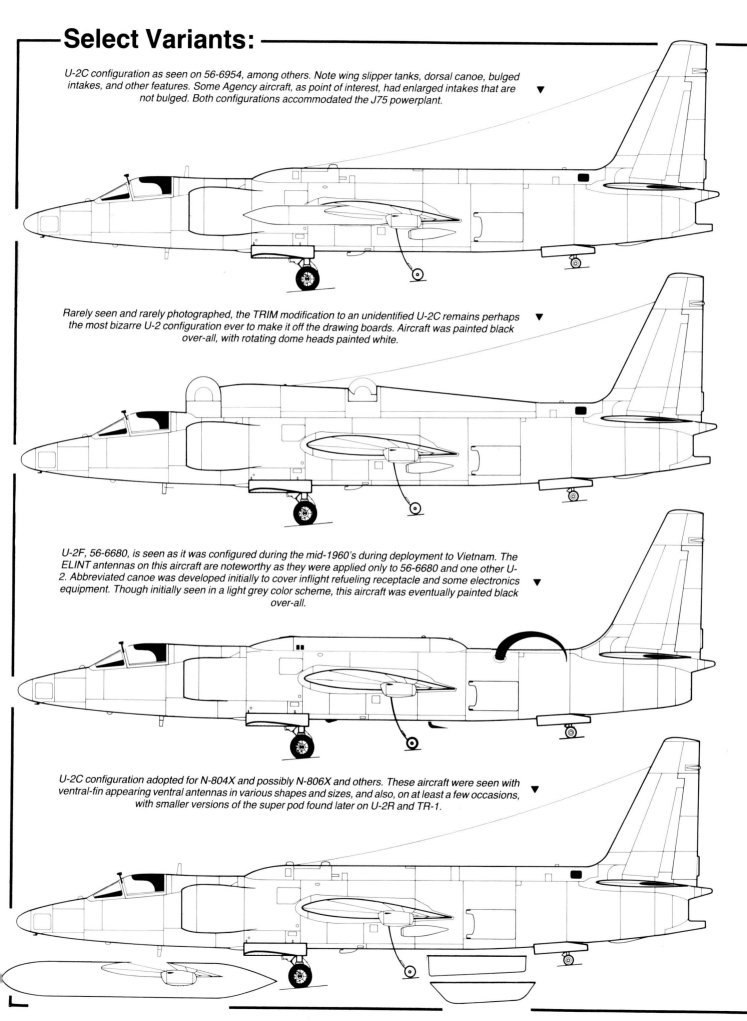

U-2C configuration as seen on 56-6954, among others. Note wing slipper tanks, dorsal canoe, bulged intakes, and other features. Some Agency aircraft, as point of interest, had enlarged intakes that are not bulged. Both configurations accommodated the J75 powerplant. ▼

Rarely seen and rarely photographed, the TRIM modification to an unidentified U-2C remains perhaps the most bizarre U-2 configuration ever to make it off the drawing boards. Aircraft was painted black over-all, with rotating dome heads painted white. ▼

U-2F, 56-6680, is seen as it was configured during the mid-1960's during deployment to Vietnam. The ELINT antennas on this aircraft are noteworthy as they were applied only to 56-6680 and one other U-2. Abbreviated canoe was developed initially to cover inflight refueling receptacle and some electronics equipment. Though initially seen in a light grey color scheme, this aircraft was eventually painted black over-all. ▼

U-2C configuration adopted for N-804X and possibly N-806X and others. These aircraft were seen with ventral-fin appearing ventral antennas in various shapes and sizes, and also, on at least a few occasions, with smaller versions of the super pod found later on U-2R and TR-1. ▼

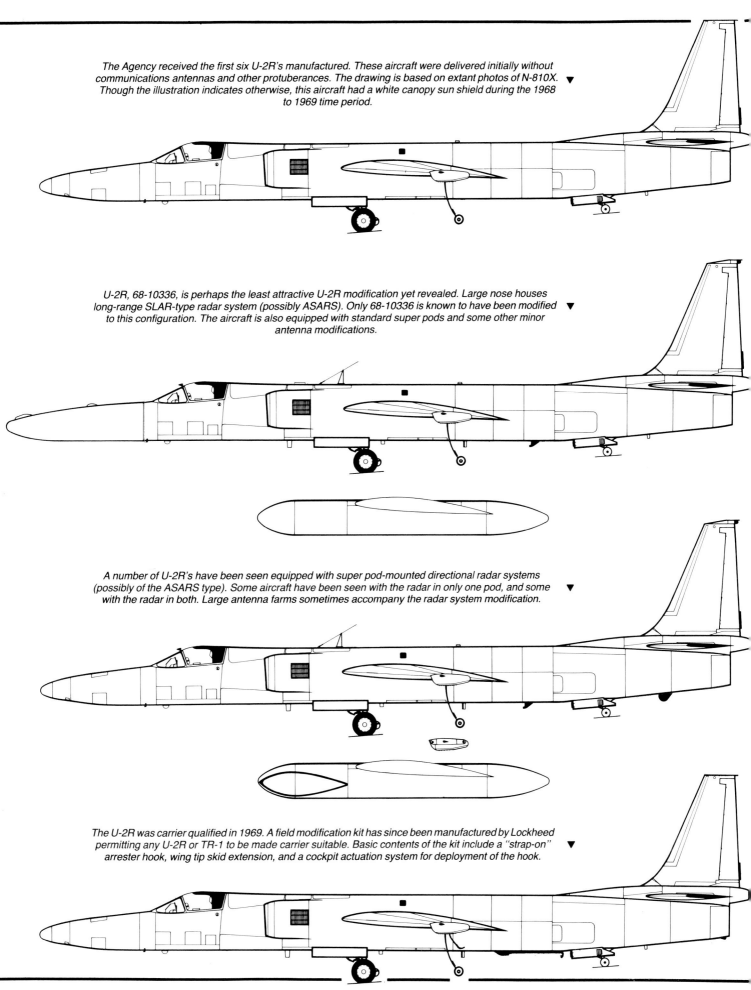

The Agency received the first six U-2R's manufactured. These aircraft were delivered initially without communications antennas and other protuberances. The drawing is based on extant photos of N-810X. Though the illustration indicates otherwise, this aircraft had a white canopy sun shield during the 1968 to 1969 time period. ▼

U-2R, 68-10336, is perhaps the least attractive U-2R modification yet revealed. Large nose houses long-range SLAR-type radar system (possibly ASARS). Only 68-10336 is known to have been modified ▼ to this configuration. The aircraft is also equipped with standard super pods and some other minor antenna modifications.

A number of U-2R's have been seen equipped with super pod-mounted directional radar systems (possibly of the ASARS type). Some aircraft have been seen with the radar in only one pod, and some ▼ with the radar in both. Large antenna farms sometimes accompany the radar system modification.

The U-2R was carrier qualified in 1969. A field modification kit has since been manufactured by Lockheed permitting any U-2R or TR-1 to be made carrier suitable. Basic contents of the kit include a "strap-on" ▼ arrester hook, wing tip skid extension, and a cockpit actuation system for deployment of the hook.

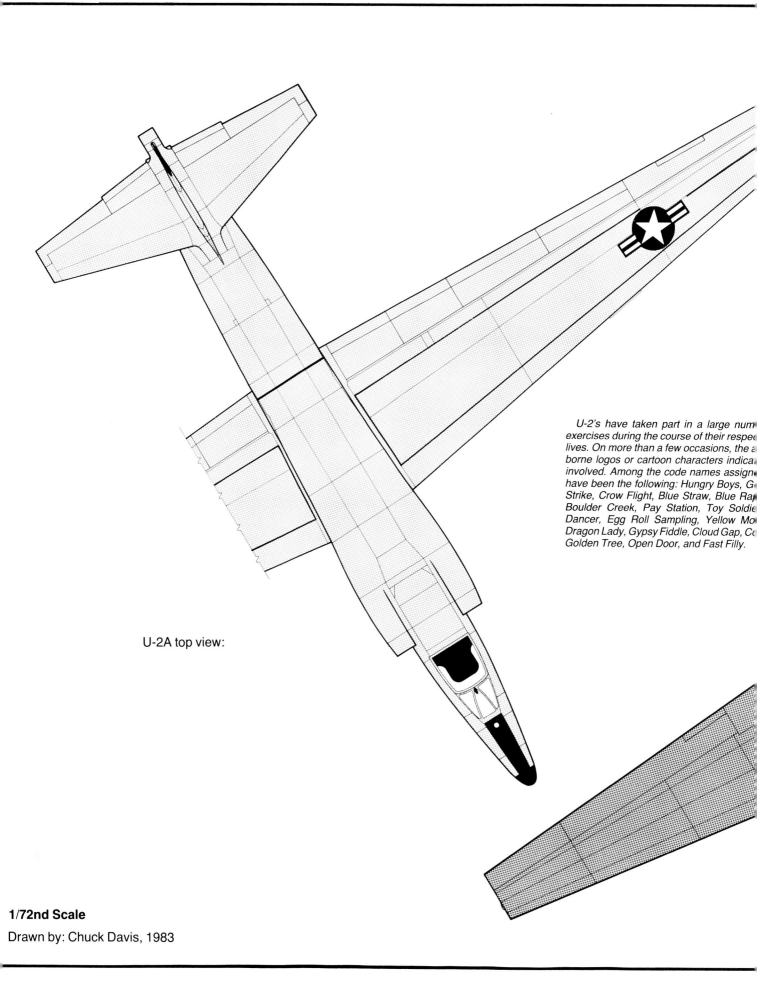

U-2A top view:

U-2's have taken part in a large num
exercises during the course of their respec
lives. On more than a few occasions, the a
borne logos or cartoon characters indica
involved. Among the code names assign
have been the following: Hungry Boys, G
Strike, Crow Flight, Blue Straw, Blue Ra
Boulder Creek, Pay Station, Toy Soldie
Dancer, Egg Roll Sampling, Yellow Mo
Dragon Lady, Gypsy Fiddle, Cloud Gap, C
Golden Tree, Open Door, and Fast Filly.

1/72nd Scale

Drawn by: Chuck Davis, 1983

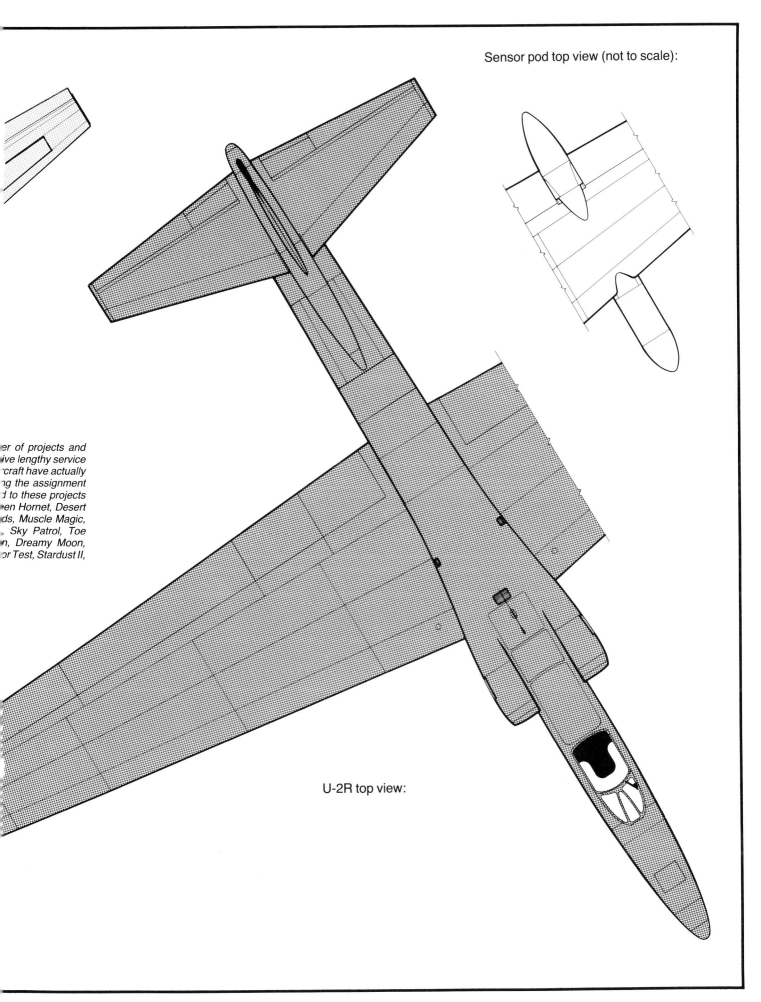

Sensor pod top view (not to scale):

...er of projects and
...ive lengthy service
...rcraft have actually
...g the assignment
...d to these projects
...en Hornet, Desert
...ds, Muscle Magic,
..., Sky Patrol, Toe
...n, Dreamy Moon,
...or Test, Stardust II,

U-2R top view:

Select Variants:

U-2R's in their original configurations were rather plain aircraft with few appurtenances. Standard markings were confined to Air Force serial numbers (in red) or Agency civil registrations (in red or white) on the vertical fin. The over-all color scheme was flat black (excepting the initially unpainted first prototype). The initial batch of aircraft for the Agency had white canopy sun shields. A variety of wing tip skid pods have been seen on the U-2R. ▼

The U-2R is still relatively new and variations on the basic theme are few. The standard aircraft comes equipped with super pods and the updated wing tip skid pods illustrated. Only other noticeable difference between the TR-1A and the U-2R is the rectangular, rather than pointed communications antenna support blade. ▼

The latest member of the U-2 family is the TR-1B with an elevated second (instructor's) seat in the space normally allocated the Q-bay. As is the case with other trainer variants of the U-2, the two TR-1B's that have been built have been painted white over-all. ▼

The Navy's EP-X program resulted in the U-2 EP-X modification with a shortened and slightly reconfigured nose radome, the addition of special wing pods (port pod shown), and miscellaneou antenna modifications. The over-all paint scheme was black with Navy painted in white on both fuselage sides behind the wing. The serial number remained in red on the ventral fin. ▼

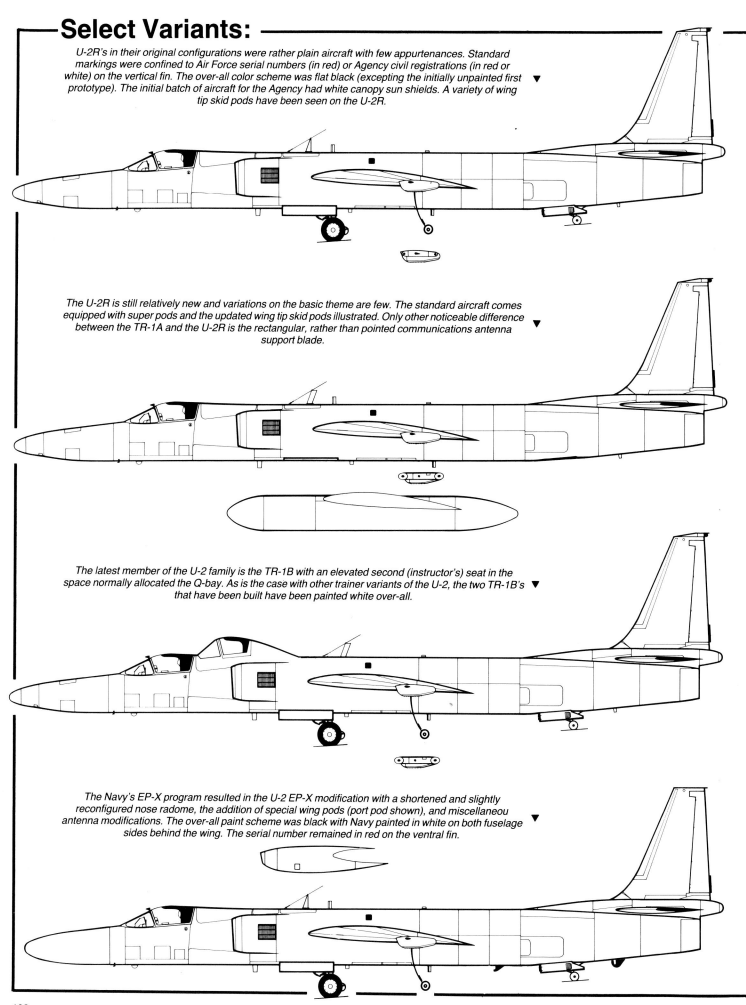

APPENDIX

APPENDIX A.
U-2/ER-2/TR-1 MODELS, SERIAL NUMBERS AND CIVIL REGISTRATIONS:

Of all the many great mysteries that have surrounded the U-2 over the years since its first unveiling, perhaps the most persistent has been that of just exactly how many aircraft were built, and what registrations they were each allocated. A large number of sources and references were examined in order to assemble a listing for this book, and what follows is probably the most accurate and complete coverage of the subject published to date outside the Air Force, Agency, and Skunk Works files:

There have been at least seven model letters officially assigned to the early configuration aircraft and there is strong evidence that others have gone into effect as well. Known designators and information pertaining to them are as follows:

U-2/U-2A—This is the first true production version of the U-2 and was preceded on the "production" line by a single "pre-production" aircraft. The initial order for 20 production U-2A's is thought not to have included the first pre-production sample. The initial designator was simply U-2, though later all aircraft with this designator marked on the aircraft data panel were remarked as U-2A. All aircraft in this series were powered by J57 engines and utilized construction techniques and tolerances not found in later aircraft. Because of this, they were significantly lighter and more sensitive to unusual dynamic loads than later aircraft. Some of these aircraft were later designated WU-2A when flown in the HASP sampling program. All U-2A's were initially delivered to the Central Intelligence Agency, and later, to the Air Force. Most, at a later date, became U-2C's, U-2D's, U-2E's, and/or U-2F's.

U-2B—These aircraft, of which there were approximately 7, were all U-2A's modified to incorporate the J75-P-13 powerplant and a strengthened structure. The U-2B was significantly heavier than the U-2A but was capable of carrying a heavier payload and had a slightly increased range. Additionally, its fatique life was improved over that of its predecessor. Most, if not all, of the 7 or so U-2B's built were eventually transferred to the Nationalist Chinese before the first U-2R's were delivered. Problems with the J75-P-13 led to introduction of the J75-P-13B and the birth of the U-2C.

U-2C—This designation was applied to a mixed bag of old and new airframes. A number of U-2A and U-2B configurations were updated to U-2C standards through the installation of enlarged intakes (the first two aircraft apparently did not initially have the enlarged intakes when first flown), a J75-P-13B powerplant, a slightly extended nose with improved internal accommodations for sensors, increased internal fuel tankage, and the addition of a dorsal canoe (where necessary—some U-2B's had already been so modified). An additional number of totally new airframes were purpose-built as U-2C's. One U-2C, as mentioned earlier in this book, was modified to become a two-seat trainer and following this modification, became the first U-2CT.

U-2D—This designation was applied to an initial batch of five U-2A-type aircraft with specially configured Q-bays capable of accommodating a second crew position and/or specialized sensors. At least one other U-2D was created by "field modifying" a U-2A, and one U-2D was modified into a two-seat U-2CT.

U-2E—This designation was applied to approximately 18 updated and improved U-2A's and possibly several U-2B's assigned to the Central Intelligence Agency. They differed from their predecessor configurations primarily in having advanced electronic countermeasures systems installed in the fuselage empennage section. They were heavier than their predecessor configurations and had a slight performance degradation as a result.

U-2F—This designation was applied to at least four U-2A's with inflight refueling capability. These aircraft were initially assigned to the Agency, and later, to the Air Force. The modification was subtle, but visible. The receptacle was mounted on the top of the dorsal spine approximately a foot from its front. All U-2F's were eventually reconfigured as U-2C's.

U-2G—This designation was applied to two U-2C's modified to incorporate "strap-on" arrester hooks, revised wingtip skids, large lift-dumping spoilers, and minor landing gear strut modifications to permit operations on and off aircraft carriers. These aircraft, as U-2C's, were later assigned to the NASA and are now the only U-2C's known still to be operational.

U-2J—This remains an unverified designator, but there are strong indications that it was applied to "production" U-2G's—or aircraft that were field modified to be capable of operation from aircraft carriers. These aircraft were almost certainly used only by the Agency.

At least five designators have been assigned to late model configurations of the U-2. These are:

U-2R—This was the first production configuration of the most recent (and probably last) major airframe change. Though only twelve aircraft were supposedly built, serial numbers for a total of twenty-five aircraft were allocated.

U-2 EP-X—Designation assigned to two U-2R's placed on short term loan to the Navy to test the Electronics Patrol Experimental program hardware generated by the Navy to explore this mission.

ER-2—Technically, the first prototype for the new TR-1 production program. This aircraft, however, was purpose-built for the NASA and is basically a demilitarized version of the TR-1—which, in turn, is a U-2R with updated secondary systems.

TR-1A—The latest production U-2 model, which is in actuality simply a U-2R with updated secondary systems. As the TR-1A, the new airframe is optimized for high altitude loitering. There is some indication that a number of U-2R's were updated in the late 1970's and early 1980's to accommodate the dedicated TR-1A sensors and redesignated TR-1 (not TR-1A), accordingly.

TR-1B—Two purpose-built training versions of the TR-1A have been ordered built for use by the Air Force. These aircraft have now been delivered. They differ from the single seat aircraft in having a Q-bay area that has been converted to accommodate a second ejection seat and a complete instrument panel and control complement.

There is no great rhyme or reason to the serial number and civil registration systems that have been used by the Agency and the Air Force in marking the individual U-2 aircraft over the past 28 years. The reason for this is that serial numbers were not assigned until the Air Force began getting its own aircraft in June of 1957, nearly a year after the Agency. During that year, the aircraft were referred to only by their Lockheed and Agency-assigned "Article" numbers. With the introduction of the Air Force into the actual operational program, it was determined that a retroactive serial number assignment process should take into account all the U-2's built, including the aircraft built for the Agency (the only known exception to this was Article 341—the first prototype aircraft, which was apparently destroyed before serial numbers were allocated).

Interestingly, serial number assignments were initially made in sequence with the article numbers, but a decision to reassign numbers from destroyed aircraft to aircraft going through depot maintenance or through a major configuration change, led to a purposeful confusion. Additionally, when a decision was made to assign serial numbers, the assignment list took in aircraft that were no longer extant. To complicate things even further, individual U-2's, on occasion, had their serial numbers eradicated in the field and replaced with a different one; and it has been confirmed that at least five new aircraft were built-up from spare parts in an effort to fill the void left by various destroyed aircraft. These latter machines were apparently assigned serial numbers belonging to aircraft that simply no longer existed.

It should also be noted that many U-2's vacillated back and forth between Agency assignments and Air Force. When this happened, the "registration" of the aircraft changed from military to civilian and the individual aircraft records went to the agency in charge. It is therefore not uncommon to identify these same aircraft in both civil and military guise.

U-2's were apparently never allocated name plates. This was done in case of a loss of an aircraft over unfriendly territory—and was another attempt to mask the aircraft and prevent its country of origin from being determined.

The Air Force lists the following serial number groups as being those officially allocated to U-2 aircraft:

56-6675/6722	48 aircraft (U-2A/B/C)
56-6951/6955	5 aircraft (U-2D)
68-10329/10353	25 aircraft (U-2R)
80-1063/1068 +	35 aircraft (ER-2/TR-1)

Lockheed, under an agreement with the Federal Aviation Administration, was given a block of ten N-numbers to use as necessary during U-2 repair and modification programs (and in some cases, operational programs, as well). These numbers, running from N-800X to N-809X, were painted on the aircraft to identify them during these refurbishment and clandestine operational programs (including the aircraft carrier trials mentioned earlier in this book). As the aircraft, at that time, were owned and operated by the Agency and not the Air Force, this was considered the most expedient means of identification.

Still, taken from Lockheed U-2 history film, shows the Article number of 344 on the tail of this aircraft as it begins its takeoff roll at Groom Lake.

Lockheed-California Company

There are individual U-2 record files extant, but they remain inaccessible to researchers at this time. Lockheed, for years, and apparently at the insistence of the Agency, has maintained a listing of "Article" numbers which accurately details all of the aircraft that have been manufactured, and their respective histories. It has been stated that this list will be declassified in 2011.

Wherever possible, a correlation between the Article number and the effective Air Force serial number has been made in the individual aircraft listing given below:

Article 341 / 001 / NACA 320(?): U-2A—After many months researching the problem, the author has verified that this is the official identifier for the prototype aircraft. Underscoring the author's research is a letter written to associate John Andrews on August 22, 1974, by Mr. Angus MacLean Thuermer, the Assistant to the Director, the Central Intelligence Agency, that had the following statement in it, "The first production model U-2 was Article No. 341, Air Force Serial No. 56-6674, and was first flown 1 August 1955." It has since been verified by official sources that Thuermer made a mistake when he stated that 56-6674 was the allocated serial number (it actually belongs to a Sikorsky H-19B) as there was no serial number assigned to this prototype aircraft. It was destroyed in April of 1957 (killing pilot Robert Sieker), some two months before official Air Force serial numbers were allocated.

56-6675 / Article 342(?): U-2A—No other information except that the aircraft was assigned to the Agency and originally tested at Groom Lake. Could possibly have been the mysterious "55741" that was placed on display for the media shortly after the Powers incident in 1960.

56-6676 / Article 343(?): U-2A—no information except that the aircraft was assigned to the Agency.

56-6677 / Article 344(?): U-2A—no information except that the aircraft was assigned to the Agency. A Lockheed film outlining the history of the U-2 shows this aircraft taking off on a test flight at Groom Lake.

56-6678 / Article 345(?): U-2A—no information except that the aircraft was assigned to the Agency.

56-6679 / Article 346(?): U-2A—poss. conv. to U-2B—no information except that the aircraft was assigned to the Agency.

56-6680 / Article 347(?): U-2A—delivered on February 9, 1956, and poss. conv. to U-2B and definitely converted to U-2F at Van Nuys Airport. Following service with the Agency, transferred to the 4080th in 1958. Special multi-frequency scimitar jamming antenna (sometimes referred to as "rams horn antenna") mod added in early 1964 during service in Vietnam. Antennas later replaced by smaller blade antennas and aircraft painted black in the fall of 1964 (first all-black Air Force aircraft). Aircraft converted to U-2C prior to service with 100th SRW. Had logged some 5,000 hours of flying time by January of 1968, at which time it was based out of Bien Hoa. Repainted in two-tone grey for European deployment in 1975. At Beale with the 9th SRW until retirement in 1980 to Lockheed Palmdale. The aircraft has since been placed on permanent loan to the National Air & Space Museum in Washington, D.C. This aircraft was the first U-2 to overfly the Soviet Union; and possibly the aircraft used by Steve Heyser during his famous overflight of Cuba.

56-6681 / Article 348(?) / N-801X / N-708NA: U-2A—poss. conv. to U-2B, then to U-2G, and later to U-2C—used during 4080th HASP program and deployed to RAF Upper Heyford in 1962. One of two aircraft used during 1964 Agency carrier trials documented elsewhere in this book. Transferred from Agency directly to the NASA in April of 1971.

56-6682 / Article 349(?) / N-802X / N-709NA: U-2A / WU-2A—poss. conv. to U-2B, then to U-2G, and later to U-2C—one of two aircraft used during 1964 Agency carrier trials documented elsewhere in this book. Transferred from Agency directly to the NASA in April of 1971.

56-6683 / Article 350(?) / N-803X: U-2A—poss. conv. to U-2B—no information except that the aircraft was assigned to the Agency.

56-6684 / Article 351(?) / N-804X: U-2A—poss. conv. to U-2B—no information except that the aircraft was assigned to the Agency.

56-6685 / Article 352(?) / N-805X: U-2A—poss. conv. to U-2B—no information except that the aircraft was assigned to the Agency and was at one time equipped with short blade antennas at the 10 and 2 o'clock positions on top of the aft fuselage section. These are thought to have been later versions of the original "rams horn" configuration used in Vietnam.

56-6686 / Article 353(?) / N-806X: U-2A—poss. conv. to U-2B—no information except that the aircraft was assigned to the Agency.

56-6687 / Article 354(?) / N-807X: U-2A—poss. conv. to U-2B, and definitely converted to U-2F at Van Nuys Airport—no information except that the aircraft was assigned to the Agency.

56-6688 / Article 355(?) / N-808X: U-2A—poss. conv. to U-2B, and definitely converted to U-2F at Van Nuys Airport—no information except that the aircraft was assigned to the Agency.

56-6689 / Article 356(?) / N-809X: U-2A—poss. conv. to U-2B—no information except that the aircraft was assigned to the Agency.

56-6690 / Article 357(?): U-2A / WU-2A—poss. conv. to U-2B then to U-2C—aircraft assigned to the 4080th in 1958 in 1958/59 following initial work with Agency. Seen at Davis-Monthan AFB in 1963 and crashed during service in Vietnam on October 8, 1966.

56-6691 / Article 358(?): U-2A—poss. conv. to U-2B and then to U-2C—no information except that the aircraft was assigned to the Agency.

56-6692 / Article 359(?): U-2A—poss. conv. to U-2B then to U-2C and finally to U-2CT—conversion to U-2CT took place in 1976. Aircraft served with 9th SRW until retirement in 1982.

56-6693 / Article 360(?) / NASA 360—Thought to be first purpose-built U-2B and also aircraft seriously damaged during emergency landing at Fugisawa Airfield near Atsugi Airport near Tokyo, Japan, on September 24, 1959. Most importantly, this is also the aircraft Gary Powers claimed was his mount when he was shot down over Sverdlovsk on May 1, 1960.

56-6694 / Article 361(?): U-2A—poss. conv. to U-2B and then to U-2C—no information except that the aircraft was assigned to the Agency.

56-6695 / Article 362(?): U-2A—poss. conv. to U-2B and then to U-2C—used for overflight work during Cuban missile crisis. No other information except that the aircraft was assigned to the Agency.

56-6696 / Article 363(?): U-2A/WU-2A—poss. conv. to a U-2B before being converted to a U-2C—assigned to 4080th SRW and was first aircraft delivered to Laughlin AFB from Groom Lake in 1957. Became WU-2A for HASP work in Australia during deployments in 1962 and 1963. Used for overflight work during Cuban missile crisis. Repainted black and last noted in 1966.

56-6697 / Article 364(?): U-2A—poss. conv. to U-2B and then to U-2C—no information except that the aircraft was assigned to the Agency.

56-6698 / Article 365(?): U-2A—poss. conv. to U-2B and then to U-2C—aircraft was assigned to the 4080th in 1958 or 1959, following initial service with the Agency.

56-6699 / Article 366(?): U-2A—aircraft was assigned to the 4080th and written off following an accident in 1957.

56-6700 / Article 367(?): U-2A—converted to U-2C—assigned to the 4080th SRW and deployed to Australia during HASP experiments in 1961. Converted to U-2C and repainted black for the 100th SRW. Used for overflight work during Cuban missile crisis. Repainted to two-tone grey for European deployment in 1975. Written off near Winterberg, West Germany on May 29, 1975.

56-6701 / Article 368(?): U-2A—converted to U-2B and then to U-2C—initially assigned to the Air Force Systems Command following work with Agency. Converted to U-2C for 100th SRW in 1968 when it was their last aircraft in natural metal finish. Repainted black in 1970, and two-tone grey in 1975 for European deployment. Repainted black again by 1979 when serving with the 9th SRW. Aircraft was at one time *The Saint* during AFCRL thunderstorm research program. Flown in Vietnam at which time it was equipped with dorsal fin antenna. Aircraft now on permanent display at the SAC Museum at Offutt AFB, Omaha, Nebraska.

56-6702 / Article 369(?): U-2B—poss. last purpose-built U-2B, poss. converted to U-2C. No other information except that the aircraft was assigned to the Agency and later, possibly to the Nationalist Chinese. Based on available information, the author is presuming that this aircraft has been destroyed.

56-6703 / Article 370(?): U-2A—assigned to 4080th SRW in early 1960's following deployment with Agency. Seen with cartoon figure on tail, possibly for *Operation Toy Soldier*. Thought to have been converted to U-2C configuration. At one time was configured as a U-2F. Used for overflight work during Cuban missile crisis.

56-6704 / Article 317(?): U-2A—later converted to U-2C.

56-6705 / Article 372(?): U-2A/WU-2A—assigned to 4080th and deployed to Australia on HASP during 1960 and 1962. Aircraft used during Don Webster's flight over North Pole on August 15, 1962. Thought later to have been converted to U-2C.

56-6706 / Article 373(?): U-2A—used for overflight work during Cuban missile crisis. Seen in black paint while flying with the 4080th in 1966. Thought later to have been converted to U-2C.

56-6707 / Article 374(?): U-2A—seen in black paint with 4080th SRW at Bien Hoa in 1964 or 1965 and with "rams horn" antennas. Though to have been converted to U-2F at one time. Converted to U-2C with 100th SRW by 1968. Repainted two-tone grey for European deployment in 1975. With the 9th SRW at Beale until retired in 1980 to Lockheed's Palmdale facility.

56-6708 / Article 375(?): U-2A—initially assigned to the 4080th following service with the Agency. Seen with the 4080th during 1960 to 1965 time period. Used for overflight work during Cuban missile crisis. Repainted black when last noted at Lockheed's Palmdale facility. Possibly converted to U-2B or U-2C configuration.

56-6709 / Article 376(?): U-2A—Assigned to the 4080th SRW following assignment to Agency. Possibly converted to U-2B or U-2C.

56-6710 / Article 377(?):—Poss. U-2A destroyed before conversion to U-2C.

56-6711 / Article 378(?):—Poss. U-2A destroyed before conversion to U-2C.

56-6712 / Article 379(?): U-2A / WU-2A—used for overflight work during Cuban missile crisis. Assigned to 4080th SRW on HASP program and deployed to RAF Upper Heyford in 1962. Last noted in 1964. Possibly converted to U-2B or U-2C configuration.

56-6713 / Article 380(?):—No information though possibly U-2A destroyed before conversion to U-2C.

56-6714 / Article 381(?): U-2A / WU-2A—assigned to the 4080th SRW on HASP deployments to Argentina during 1958 and 1960, Australia during 1960 and 1964, and Panama in 1963. Repainted black and converted to U-2C with 100th SRW by 1968. Repainted two-tone grey for European deployment in 1975. Repainted black again with 9th SRW by 1979. Following accident due to fuel starvation, aircraft was repaired by Beale personnel and placed on permanent display as base gate guardian.

56-6715 / Article 382(?): U-2A / WU-2A—assigned to the 4080th SRW following initial assignment with the Agency. Used during HASP deployment to Alaska and Australia in 1960, and to Panama in 1963.

56-6716 / Article 383(?): U-2A / WU-2A—assigned to 4080th and used during HASP deployment to Argentina during 1958 and 1960, and Australia in 1961. Repainted black and converted to U-2C with 100th SRW by 1972. Repainted two-tone grey for European deployment in 1975. Repainted black again with 9th

Aerofax, Inc. collection

Agency U-2F, N-807X, begins its takeoff roll as a pogo, barely visible under the starboard pylon-mounted fuel tank, falls to the runway.

Aerofax, Inc. collection

NASA 708 (56-6681) sits on the ramp at Ames during an open house. This is the current paint scheme utilized on NASA's two U-2C's.

Lockheed-California Company

Many early U-2A's, such as 56-6701, were updated to other U-2 configurations during the course of their service lives. Some became U-2C's, some U-2E's, and a few were converted to U-2B, U-2D and U-2F configurations.

Early all-black scheme for Air Force U-2's, such as U-2A 56-6714, included a white canopy sun shade. Paint eventually changed from the dull semigloss shown, to a full matte finish.

The British public's opposition to U-2 operations out of RAF Mildenhall and other British bases led to a decision to apply this unobtrusive paint scheme to British-based U-2C's (such as 56-6714).

SRW by 1979. Retired in 1980 to Lockheed's Palmdale facility.

56-6717 / Article 384(?): U-2A / WU-2A—assigned to the 4080th and utilized in HASP program deployment to Guam in 1962.

56-6718 / Article 385(?): U-2A / WU-2A—assigned to the 4080th and utilized in HASP program deployment to Australia in 1961 (named *City of Sale* during open house), 1962, and 1963.

56-6719 / Article 386(?): U-2C—operated with 4080th at Davis-Monthan AFB.

56-6720 / Article 387(?):—Poss. U-2A destroyed before conversion to U-2C.

56-6721 / Article 388(?): U-2A—aircraft later converted to U-2D configuration and operated for many years out of Edwards AFB. At one time flown with *Smokey Joe* tail cartoon. Well known for "pickle barrel" infrared optical sensor modification. The "pickle barrel" was replaced by an unidentified sensor system by May of 1966, when the aircraft was seen flying with two photo resolution circles on the tail. The modification was removed by May of 1967. At Hickam AFB in 1971, the aircraft had yet another sensor modification installed in the Q-bay area, and was now painted black overall. There was also an HF aerial housing added. Multiple photo-resolution patches were added in 1972 and retained when the large white USAF marks were deleted in 1973. Repainted into red and white Air Force Flight Test colors by October of 1975. The aircraft was still active until November of 1980, but has since been retired and is now on permanent display at March AFB in California.

56-6722 / Article 389(?): U-2D—aircraft seen at Air Force Flight Test Center with AFFTC tail flash plus badge and *Smokey Joe* tail cartoon. "Pickle barrel" modification also noted a this time. Returned to single-seat configuration for HICAT, and repainted black overall. "Pickle barrel" fairing retained for a while following reconfiguration to

Unit citations on the tails of Air Force U-2's, such as the one seen on the tail of 56-6708, were a common sight in the early 1960's. Once the Air Force decided to go to the less attractive all-black paint scheme, however, the citations, along with most other distinctive markings, disappeared.

single seat. White photo-resolution patches added in late 1960's (possibly for program running concurrent with HICAT). "Barber's Pole" nose sensor boom removed by October of 1974. Used to transport reentry vehicle dummies during satellite sensor system recovery practice at Edwards. Aircraft was then in red and white AFFTC colors with a U-2C-type dorsal canoe added. Aircraft was back in Lockheed custody by 1978 and has since been turned over to the Air Force Museum at Wright-Patterson AFB, Ohio, for permanent display.

56-6951 / Article 390(?):—Purpose built as U-2D—used for overflight work during Cuban missile crisis.

56-6952 / Article 391(?):—Purpose built as a U-2D—configured as a U-2A when assigned to the 4080th in 1963. Painted black and converted to U-2C with 100th SRW by 1968 or 1969. Used for overflight work during Cuban missile crisis. Last noted in 1970.

56-6953 / Article 392(?):—Purpose built as a U-2D—configured as a U-2A / WU-2A. Assigned to the 4080th SRW on HASP deployment to RAF Upper Heyford in 1962. Repainted black and converted to U-2C for 100th SRW by 1968. Converted to U-2CT in 1972 and with 100th SRW, and later 9th SRW, to date.

56-6954 / Article 393(?): U-2D—initially assigned to Air Force Systems Command. Also assigned to the Air Force Flight Test Center and decorated with tail flash plus badge and *Smokey Joe* tail cartoon. Also equipped with "pickle barrel" modification. Photo resolution circles added by 1964. "Pickle barrel" removed later. Converted to U-2C configuration then painted black and possibly with 100th SRW when last seen in the late 1960's.

56-6955 / Article 394(?):—Purpose built as a U-2D—configured as a U-2A. Assigned to 4080th SRW when written off near Boise, Idaho on

In service, 56-6680 was known for being somewhat of a hangar queen. Somewhat surprisingly, it was this very aircraft that was chosen to fly the first overflight of the Soviet Union.

Early semi-gloss all-black scheme used on Air Force U-2A's is readily apparent in this photo of 56-6953— which though appearing otherwise, is actually a purpose-built U-2D. Tail numbers were in red.

Another formation shot of 56-6701 (background) and 56-6722. Both aircraft were based out of Edwards AFB with the 6512th Test Group. Note "Smokey Joe" cartoon on vertical fin of 56-6722.

Lockheed-California Company

Jim Goodall

SLAR (ASARS?) equipped 68-10336 takes off on test mission from Palmdale. Aircraft mounts what must be the most bizarre nose modification of the entire U-2 program.

Interesting photo of NASA 708 undergoing major overhaul at NASA Ames. Totally disassembled wing is rarely seen. Note conventional three-spar construction.

August 14, 1964, while piloted by Nationalist Chinese pilot Capt. Sheng Shi Hi. Used for overflight work during Cuban missile crisis.

68-10329: U-2R—first noted in 1970 while serving with the 100th SRW. Aircraft equipped with extremely sensitive ELINT system in early 1970's. Later served as a development aircraft with Lockheed.

68-10330: U-2R—first noted in 1968 while serving with the 100th SRW. Later assigned to the 9th SRW from 1976, and written off at Akrotiri on December 7, 1977.

68-10331: U-2R—first noted in 1969 while serving with the 100th SRW. Later assigned to the 9th SRW from 1976.

68-10332: U-2R—first noted in 1973 while serving with the 100th SRW. Later assigned to the 9th SRW from 1976. Assigned to 1130th ATTG until the unit was disbanded.

68-10333: U-2R—first noted in 1970 while serving with the 100th SRW. Later assigned to the 9th SRW from 1976.

68-10334: U-2R—first noted in 1974 while serving with the 100th SRW. Last noted in March of 1975 and thought to be the aircraft that crashed in August of 1975.

68-10335: U-2R—first noted in 1979 while assigned to the 9th SRW. Last noted at Diego Garcia in April of 1979.

68-10336: U-2R—first noted in 1972 while serving with the 100th SRW. Later assigned to the 9th SRW from 1976. Has apparently been on bale to Lockheed for tests of new nose-mounted SLAR system. Modification entails major redesign of nose with significant increase in over-all length.

68-10337: U-2R—first noted in 1971 while serving with the 100th SRW. Later assigned to the 9th SRW from 1976.

68-10338: U-2R—first noted in 1973 while serving with the 100th SRW. Later assigned to the 9th SRW from 1976.

68-10339: U-2R—first noted in 1969 while serving with the 100th SRW. Later assigned to the 9th SRW from 1976. Converted under Navy contract to become U-2 EP-X testbed. Modifications to

Lockheed-California Company

Extraordinary wing flex is one of numerous distinctive characteristics illustrated by this photo of U-2CT, 56-6953. Elevated second seat is also shown to advantage, as is all-white color scheme. 56-6953 is the only one of the two U-2CT's built still being flown on a regular basis.

nose radome, wing pods, and lesser sensor system bays. Aircraft later was utilized in TR-1 equipment trials out of RAF Upper Heyford.

68-10340: U-2R—first noted in 1969 while serving with the 100th SRW. Later assigned to the 9th SRW from 1976.

68-10341: U-2R—nothing known.

68-10342: U-2R—first noted in 1975 while serving with the 100th SRW at Davis-Monthan AFB. No further information.

68-10343: U-2R—nothing known.

68-10344: U-2R—nothing known.

68-10345: U-2R—first noted in 1975 while serving with the 100th SRW. Later assigned to the 9th SRW from 1976. Was first U-2R to visit RAF Mildenhall when it staged through twice enroute to and from Akrotiri (January, 1975; and May or June of 1976). Was observed again in June of 1977, but has not been seen since.

68-10346: U-2R—nothing known, possibly not built.

68-10347: U-2R—nothing known, possibly not built.

Jim Goodall

An inflatable radome modification was tested on a U-2R during mid-1976. Radome, housing a classified directionaly radar system, was apparently a mylar-material coated with rubber. Zipper provided access to the antenna inside.

Roger Freeman via Chris Pocock

Most contemporary operational missions of a clandestine nature undertaken by members of the U-2 family are to gather ELINT. Excellent example of SIGINT/COMINT dedicated U-2R is 68-10339, seen taking off on mission out of RAF Mildenhall in England.

Lockheed-California Company

Immediately prior to delivery to Beale AFB, the first TR-1B, 80-1064, formates for photo session with company photo ship. Well-known Lockheed chief photographer Bob Ferguson took this excellent photo of number one TR-1 trainer.

This over-all flat black scheme, modeled by 68-10337, has been the standard paint scheme for this U-2 model almost from the day the first aircraft was rolled out. Only visible markings are red tail numbers.

U-2R, 69-10338, is seen at RAF Mildenhall in July of 1977. Note the Snoopy cartoon character wearing a leather flying helmet and flying his dog kennel.

U-2R, 68-10339, cruises serenely over California countryside during a short test hop out of Palmdale. Tube protruding from top of vertical fin is emergency fuel dump pipe.

68-10348: U-2R—nothing known, possibly not built.

68-10349: U-2R—nothing known, possibly not built.

68-10350: U-2R—nothing known, possibly not built.

68-10351: U-2R—nothing known, possibly not built.

68-10352: U-2R—nothing known, possibly not built.

68-10353: U-2R—nothing known, possibly not built.

80-1063: ER-2—effectively the aerodynamic prototype for the TR-1 series. Currently operated by NASA Ames following delivery on June 10, 1981.

80-1064: TR-1B—first TR-1B. Delivered to Beale AFB where it currently serves with the 9th SRW.

80-1065: TR-1B—second TR-1B. Delivered to Beale AFB where it currently serves with the 9th SRW.

80-1066: TR-1A—first TR-1A. Delivered to Beale AFB where it currently serves with the 9th SRW.

80-1067: TR-1A—second TR-1A. Delivered to Beale AFB where it currently serves with the 9th SRW.

80-1068: TR-1A—initially delivered to Beale and 9th SRW. Was seen at Offutt AFB in August of 1982, and was bailed back to Lockheed for the Farnborough show in England in September of 1982.

80-1069: TR-1A—initially delivered to Beale and 9th SRW.

The following U-2 registrations have been documented photographically or by observation. Unfortunately, it has not been possible to assign them for certain to any of the above serial numbers.

NASA 55741—comments concerning this "serial number" have been made elsewhere in this book.

NACA 320—first released photo of the U-2 in February of 1957. Almost certainly depicts prototype Agency aircraft with NACA markings air-

Variance in contrast between the numbers 103 and 40 give evidence that serial numbers of these aircraft are, indeed, changed at random.

brushed onto photo.

NACA 331—Agency aircraft seen at Lakenheath, England in 1956.

NACA 357(?)—number noted on an Agency U-2 that crashed on February 16, 1956. ''Piloted by 'NACA pilot number 357' '' according to Aviation Week & Space Technology in their May 16, 1960 issue.

NASA 405—seen on an all-black Agency U-2B operating out of Atsugi, Japan during 1959 and 1960.

NASA 432—seen on an all-black Agency U-2B operating out of Atsugi, Japan during 1959 and 1960. This aircraft was photographed by the Japanese press following a landing accident.

(NASA) 449—seen on the all-black Agency U-2B that crash-landed near Tokyo, Japan. This aircraft has also been referred to as ''NASA 360'' and is supposedly the aircraft that Gary Powers was in when he was shot down while flying over the Soviet Union

NASA 464—seen at Atsugi, Japan on January 7, 1960. Operated by the Agency and painted black overall.

55891—possibly aircraft 55-6689 (N-809X). Seen at Atsugi, Japan (?).

N-800X—seen at Van Nuys airport in November of 1965, during overhaul at Lockheed facility there. Converted from U-2B to U-2F.

N-802X—seen at Van Nuys airport in March of 1966, during overhaul at Lockheed facility there.

N-803X—U-2B indentified from Lockheed photos.

N-803X—natural metal U-2R identified from Lockheed phhotos—possibly prototype aircraft.

N-804X—seen at Van Nuys airport in November of 1965, during overhaul at Lockheed facility there. Converted from U-2B to U-2F.

N-806X(?)—U-2B/C seen with large ''super pods'' in place of more conventional slipper tanks.

N-807X—seen at Van Nuys airport in May of 1965 and March of 1966, during overhaul at Lockheed facility there. Converted from U-2B to

Nationalist Chinese U-2R is seen over Taiwan during descent to landing. Nationalist Chinese markings are barely visible to the rear of the extended airbrake.

Second TR-1A, 80-1067, cruises over southern California during a test flight out of Palmdale. This aircraft has since been delivered to Beale AFB where it has since entered service with the 95th SRS.

Departing Offutt AFB, Nebraska, U-2R 68-10338 heads skyward for a return mission to Beale AFB. The U-2R's initial rate of descent is comparable to the majority of the operational fighters in the present Air Force inventory.

During an early test flight, NASA's ER-2 cruises over the southern California desert. Aircraft had yet to be painted when photo was taken.

Following landing at Palmdale, main gear brake temperatures are checked by a Lockheed test crew. Note the extended spoiler on the top surface of the wing.

U-2F.

N-808X—seen at Van Nuys airport in April of 1965, during overhaul at Lockheed facility there. Converted from U-2B to U-2F

N-809X—U-2B identified from Lockheed photos.

N-809X—U-2R flown from Taiwan by both Agency and Nationalist Chinese pilots.

N-810X—U-2R identified from Lockheed photos.

320—Chinese Nationalist markings as seen in photos of U-2B/C wreckage on display in Peking in 1965.

3512—Chinese Nationalist markings as seen in photos of U-2B/C wreckage on display in Peking in 1965.

3514—Chinese Nationalist markings as seen in photos of U-2B/C wreckage on display in Peking in 1965.

3925—Chinese Nationalist markings as seen in photos of U-2R.

The following is an abbreviated chronology of operational U-2 modifications and the approximate dates they were incorporated:

1957—ejection seat and possible powerplant uprating through the incorporation of the J57-P-37A.

1957—air particle sampling scoop on the Q-bay lower hatch and nose intake for gaseous sampling.

1958—radar homing and warning (RHAW) and electronic countermeasures equipment (some reportedly built by Granger).

1958—J75-P-13 first introduced in U-2B.

1959—J75-P-13B first introduced in U-2B.

Just prior to its official roll-out ceremony at Palmdale, the first TR-1A, 80-1066, poses for the Lockheed chief photographer, Bob Ferguson. Note Skunk Works logo on hangar door to the rear of the aircraft.

1959—Large ventral antenna forward of the tail-wheel introduced. This antenna, looking very much like a ventral fin, was noted in several different forms and on several different aircraft.

1959—Long fairing on fuselage below trailing edge of port wing. Purpose unknown.

1962—first installation of air refueling system.

1962—HF radio housing atop fuselage.

1963—First minor modifications for carrier operation.

1964—Infra-red suppression device, known as a "sugar scoop" mounted on the bottom of the fuselage under the engine exhaust nozzle. This device effectively created a reduced "acceptance angle" for heat-seeking missiles.

1964—first major modifications for carrier operations added to U-2C. Consisted of retractable arrestor hook, minor changes to the main gear geometry, and wing tip skid extensions.

1964—extension of radio housing fairing.

1964—large multi-frequency scimitar jamming antennas ("rams horn" antennas) fitted for the first time.

1965/1966—extension of radio housing fairing along top of fuselage to base of vertical fin. This modification permitted transport of additional sensor system related items, and also permitted, in some aircraft, a more refined ARS configuration.

1968—flared intakes for improved performance at maximum cruising altitudes and lower susceptability to compressor stalls.

1975—square, aerodynamically refined fairing on lower hatch of Q-bay.

Bearing an early all-black paint scheme, U-2A 56-6953 is seen on display at Carswell AFB, Texas open house. Barely noticeable is the fact that this aircraft has the little-known extended tip skids.

Bearing the special British-mandated paint scheme, U-2C 56-6680 is put on display for a stateside airshow. This aircraft was placed in storage at Palmdale following removal from the operational Air Force inventory in 1981.

Though resembling the photo on page 67, this shot of HASP-equipped U-2A, 56-6715, was taken at a totally different time and in a totally different place. Somewhat more visible in this photo is the nose particulate sampling system exhaust port just ahead of the driftsight dome.

The loss of U-2C, 56-6700, over Winterberg, W. Germany was well-documented in newspapers around the world when it occurred on May 29, 1975. The pilot, Capt. Robert Rendleman, ejected and landed without injury.

Appendix B.
U-2 ACCIDENTS

The U-2, throughout its career, has been an extraordinarily demanding aircraft capable of being flown only the most proficient pilots. At cruising altitudes it is constantly operating in the sensitive "coffin corner" and during landing, it demands precise and perfectly accurate control. Couple these two important piloting considerations with the fact that the average full-scale mission lasts between seven and twelve hours (and sometimes significantly longer)—and that the pilot, during this period, is virtually immobilized in a rather cramped cockpit while wearing a partial or full-pressure suit and all the while breathing dry, pressurized liquid or gaseous oxygen (which prevents freezing problems), and it becomes apparent why the aircraft has a poor accident record.

The causes of the numerous U-2 accidents are varied. There were recorded instances of instantaneous loss of oxygen supply to the pilot, pilot physiological problems, destruction through enemy action, structural failures brought on by exceeding performance limitations at altitude and at landing approach speeds, powerplant failures, and in more than a few accidents, instances of poor piloting technique.

Interestingly, in a sizeable percentage of these accidents, the aircraft was found to have entered a classical flat spin before ground contact. Often, due to its low-q structure, the aircraft was found to have partially disintegrated during the descent.

In general, most of the more serious pilot-induced accidents seem to have taken place during the first few transitional flying hours. Novice pilots found the aircraft difficult to handle, particularly during landing, and stall/spin accidents from both high and low altitudes were not at all uncommon. The early model U-2's were substantially more difficult to fly than the late model aircraft, particularly at high altitude and during the final approach to landing. Late model aircraft, in fact, were designed to be more docile and their improved performance offered an expanded "coffin corner" envelope of some ten knots, versus the four to five knot margin in the early models.

Besides a basic need and economic rationale for the U-2, there is a third reason why the aircraft has twice gone back into production during its lifetime: the Agency and the Air Force have twice run out of airframes. Details of more than forty serious to fatal accidents can be documented, and there probably have been more.

What follows is a complete listing of all publicly documented U-2 accidents from the beginning of the program to the present:

DATE	LOCATION	PILOT
2/16/56	Arizona	Robert Everett
5/56	Groom Lake, Nevada	?
9/17/56	Kaiserlautern, Germany	Howard Carey
12/19/56	Arizona	?
4/57	Nevada	Robert Sieker
6/28/57	Laughlin AFB, Texas	Ford Lowcock
6/28/57	New Mexico	Lt. Leo Smith
9/26/57	Laughlin AFB, Texas	Col. Jack Nole
7/9/58	Laughlin AFB, Texas	Sqdn. Ldr. Chris Walker, RAF
7/10/58	Laughlin AFB, Texas	?
9/24/59	Fugisawa Airfield near Atsugi Airport near Tokyo, Japan	?
3/15/60	Saskatchewan, Canada	Capt. Roger Cooper
5/3/60	Sverdlovsk, Soviet Union	Gary Powers
7/13/60	Uvalde, Texas	Maj. Raleigh Myers
1/2/62	Picayune, Mississippi	Capt. Charles Stratton
3/2/62	Edwards AFB, California	Capt. John Campbell
9/9/62	East China	Col. Chen Wai Sheng
10/27/62	Cuba	Maj. Rudolph Anderson
11/63	China	?
11/20/63	Gulf of Mexico near southwestern tip of Florida	Capt. Joe Hyde
7/64	China	?
8/14/64	Boise, Idaho	Capt. Sheng Shi Hi
9/20/64	Davis-Monthan AFB, Arizona	Maj. Robert Primrose
12/19/64	Tucson, Arizona	Capt. Sheng Shi Hi
1/9/65	China	?
3/27/65	Tucson, Arizona	Capt. Fan Hung Ti
4/26/65	Boron, California	Buster Edens
2/25/66	Sequoia, California	Deke Hall
7/28/66	Bolivia	Capt. Robert Hickman
10/8/66	Bien Hoa, Vietnam	Maj. Leo Stewart
7/1/67	Louisiana	Capt. Sam Swart
9/9/67	China	?
4/2/68	China	?
5/21/68	Tucson, Arizona	Vic Milam
1/69	China	?
?/70	China	?
5/29/75	Winterberg, W. Germany	Capt. Robert Rendleman
8/15/75	Gulf of Siam	Capt. Robert Little
12/7/77	Nicosia, Cyprus	Capt. Robert Henderson
1/31/80	Oroville, California	Capt. Edward Beaumont

Appendix C.
UNIT HISTORIES

The following are abbreviated histories of the Air Force wings and squadrons to have operated the Lockheed U-2:

4080th SRW
Original unit activated on April 1, 1956 at Turner AFB, Georgia as the 4080th Strategic Reconnaissance Wing (Light). Moved to Laughlin AFB, Texas during February and April of 1957. Redesignated 4080th Strategic Reconnaissance Wing on June 15, 1963. Completed move to Davis-Monthan AFB, Arizona in July of 1963. Redesignated 100th Strategic Reconnaissance Wing on June 15, 1966. U-2 operations transferred to Beale AFB, California under control of 9th Strategic Reconnaissance Wing in March/April of 1976. 100th SRW designation transferred to Beale AFB to control two KC-135 squadrons.

4025 SRS
Activated on June 8, 1955, at Lockbourne AFB, Ohio as 4025th Strategic Reconnaissance Squadron (Light), but moved to Turner AFB, Georgia before receiving the RB-57D in May of 1956. Moved with the 4080th SRW (L) to Laughlin AFB, Texas in 1957. Deactivated on June 15, 1960, when the RB-57D was retired. Reactivated on July 1, 1965, at Davis-Monthan AFB as the 4025th Reconnaissance Squadron to control RPV activities (previously known as *Operation Lightning Bug.* Redesignated the 350th Strategic Reconnaissance Squadron on June 15, 1966. Deactivated in 1976 when all SAC RPV assets were transferred to TAC.

4028th SRS
Activated on May 1, 1956, and received first U-2 at Laughlin AFB, Texas on June 11, 1957. Redesignated the 4028th Strategic Reconnaissance Weather Squadron on June 13, 1957. Moved with the 4080th SRW to Davis-Monthan AFB in July of 1963. Redesignated the 349th Strategic Reconnaissance Squadron on June 15, 1966. Designation transferred in 1976 to a KC-135 squadron.

4029th SRS
Allocated to the 4080th SRW (L) upon activation, but never manned. Deactiveated in 1960. Reactivated in 1981 as the 4029th Strategic Reconnaissance Training Squadron under the 9th SRW at Beale AFB to control U-2/TR-1 training.

Operating Location 20
Redesignation of 100th SRW Operating Location (OL) 20 which controlled U-2 operations in Southeast Asia, and moved from Bien Hoa AB, Vietnam to U-Tapao Royal Thai Air Force Base, Thailand in July of 1970. Returned to the US in April of 1976 and became the operational U-2 squadron under control of the 9th SRW at Beale AFB. From 1976 to the present the unit has been designated the 99th Strategic Reconnaissance Squadron.

Appendix D:
BASIC OPERATING RULES OF THE LOCKHEED SKUNK WORKS:

Kelly Johnson's undeniable success as the designer of aircraft is due at least in part to his organizational abilities. For many years he has quietly promoted his Skunk Works operating philosophies, a summary of which is as follows:

1. The Skunk Works manager must be delegated practically complete control of his program in all respects. He should report to a division president or higher.

2. Strong *but small* project offices must be provided both by the military and industry.

3. The number of people having any connection with the project must be restricted in an almost vicious manner. Use a small number of good people (10% to 25% compared to the so-called normal systems).

4. A very simple drawing and drawing release system with great flexibility for making changes must be provided.

5. There must be a minimum number of reports required, but *important* work must be recorded thoroughly.

6. There must be a monthly cost review covering not only what has been spent and committed but also projected costs to the conclusion of the program. Don't have the books ninety days late and don't surprise the customer with sudden overruns.

7. The contractor must be delegated and must assume more than *normal* responsibility to get good vendor bids for subcontract work on the project. Commercial bid procedures are very often better than military ones.

8. The inspection system as currently used by ADP, which has been approved by both the Air Force and Navy, meets the intent of existing military requirements and should be used on new projects. Push more basic inspection responsibility back to subcontractors and vendors. Don't duplicate so much inspection.

9. The contractor *must* be delegated the authority to test his final product in flight. He can and must test it in the initial stages. If he doesn't, he rapidly loses his competency to design other vehicles.

10. The specifications applying to the hardware must be agreed to in *advance* of contracting. The ADP practice of having a specification section stating clearly which important military specification items will not knowingly be complied with and reasons therefore is highly recommended.

11. Funding a program must be *timely* so that the contractor doesn't have to keep running to the bank to support government projects.

12. There must be mutual trust between the military project organization and the contractor, with very close cooperation and liaison on a day to day basis. This cuts down misunderstanding and correspondence to an absolute minimum.

13. Access by outsiders to the project and its personnel must be strictly controlled by appropriate security measures.

14. Because only a few people will be used in engineering and most other areas, ways must be provided to reward good performance by *pay not based on the number of personnel supervised*.

Appendix E:
WING ASPECT RATIO DEFINED:

Perhaps the most important aerodynamic aspect of the U-2 is its high aspect ratio wing. Basically, aspect ratio is defined as the ratio of the average chord length to the over-all wingspan. The aspect ratio is a fineness ratio of the wing and this quantity is very important in determining the aerodynamic characteristics and structural weight. Typical aspects ratios vary from 35 to 1 for a high-performance sailplane, to 3.5 to 1 for a modern fighter and 1.28 to 1 for a flying saucer. Generally speaking, high aspect ratio wings are the most efficient and tend to generate their greatest lift coefficients at modest speeds. Structural limitations tend to limit the maximum speed potential of aircraft with high aspect ratio wings.

One of at least two U-2D's assigned to the 6712th Test Squadron at Edwards AFB, 56-6722 was the only U-2 to be configured for the unique HICAT mission.

YAKOVLEV YAK-26 *MANDRAKE*

The intrusion of the Lockheed U-2 into Soviet airspace prompted the Soviet Union, in the late 1950's, to initiate development of their own high-altitude-capable recce aircraft. Like the U-2, the initial design study was developed around an extant airframe, in this case that of the Yakovlev Yak-25. Unlike the U-2, however, this approach was carried through and the end result, the Yak-26 *Mandrake* (the Yak-26 designation remains tentative and, in fact, the majority of the Soviet aircraft authorities consulted by the author seem to feel that the designation Yak-25RD is more accurate), incorporated a virtually stock, though lightened, Yak-25 fuselage and associated tail surfaces and a totally new wing. Besides the new long span, high-aspect-ratio wing (the standard Yak-25 has a conventional swept wing of modest low aspect ratio), the Yak-26 was also reconfigured to be a single-seat aircraft and the space normally occupied by the back seat crew member in stock Yak-25's was allocated to sensor systems that included dedicated LOROP and long focal length lens cameras and ELINT equipment.

Yak-26's have been intercepted and photographed by allied aircraft on a number of occasions, though this data remains sensitive. Additionally, there have been a number of reports leaked revealing use of the aircraft during over-flight missions of China, India, and Pakistan.

The Yak-26's performance is comparable, in most respects, to that of the Martin RB-57D. Cruise is normally consummated at approximately 56,000', and as fuel is burned off and the aircraft becomes lighter, a drift up to 65,000' occurs. Range is probably around 2,500 miles and cruising Mach number is approximately .78. Normal loaded weight is just over 20,000 lbs. and the payload weight is estimated to be 650 lbs. Wingspan is approximately 71', length is approximately 51', and height is approximately 16'. The powerplants are two Tumansky RD-9 turbojets which burn a special kerosene fuel equivalent to JP-TS. The total number of *Mandrakes* built-up from older Yak-25's is unknown.

Aerofax, Inc. collection

At least one Yakolev "Mandrake" has been saved for posterity. Several years ago, this example was placed on display at the Gagarin Military Air Academy Museum at Monino in the Soviet Union. The "Mandrake" is thought to have been the direct result of the U-2's unparalleled intelligence gathering successes in the late 1950's.

PILOT REQUIREMENTS AND FLIGHT INSTRUCTION:

Pilot background and physical requirements for joining the U-2 program have varied considerably over the years since the inception of the program in the mid-1950's. Agency restrictions were significantly more defined than those currently in use and the psychological qualifications were definitely more demanding.

In general, the requirements dictated by the various services included a defined sitting spinal height dimension, a maximum weight and standing height, uncorrected vision, and no deleterious physical abnormalities (pilots were also screened specifically for pressure-suit compatibility and were run through a rigorous altitude chamber program to make sure they were pressure suit tolerant). Other requirements included a minimum of 1,500 hours total time or at least 1,000 hours in jets. Additionally, ratings were necessary in at least two different aircraft types, and a letter of recommendation from a commanding officer was required.

Training started with ground school. The classes were small and very informal. Pilots were taught powerplant operation and systems, how to use the autopilot, miscellaneous aircraft systems, and the sensors. Classes were usually equipped with detailed mock-ups and provided with instructors from the various companies.

Before flying the U-2, pilots were given introductory flight training in a Cessna U-3A/B. Two of these aircraft were used for the initial approach speed and pattern training flight test work primarily because they had dual yoke-type cockpit controls.

Taxi practice was the first thing a novice pilot was permitted to do with the actual aircraft. Most new U-2 pilots found the aircraft to be a real ground looper, particularly without the pogos in place.

Once the pilot was cleared for flight, he was basically on his own. Initially, there were no two-

Several Cessna U-3A's and U-3B's have been used by the Air Force as trainer and chase aircraft for the U-2. This particular aircraft, U-3A 57-5869, was used during most of the years the U-2 operated out of Davis-Monthan AFB.

The U-2CT's usefulness as a trainer has apparently come to an end with the removal of all early model U-2's from the Air Force inventory.

During a pilot's initial flights in the U-2, the pogos are left in place. This facilitates landing the aircraft which, without the pogos, can be a bit nasty during flare and touchdown.

Bob Birkett collection

seat training aircraft (U-2CT's) and a first flight was also a first solo. The pogos were retained during the first three flights and the power was restricted to 90%. Normal takeoffs called for a ground roll of about 400'. On the first few flights, a chase U-3 with an instructor pilot (i.p.) aboard, flew formation and monitored the piloting technique and aircraft configuration. During these first flights the i.p. allowed only a 2 knot deviation in airspeed.

Initially, pilots were given basic navigation and fuel balance problems. Landing approaches were low and the airspeed was closely monitored. The third flight was devoted to stall practice. On the fourth flight the pogos were pulled and the first maximum performance takeoff was undertaken (160-knots at 60 deg. angle of ascent).

On the fifth flight, a pressure suit was worn for the first time and the pilot was cleared to an altitude of 60,000' (Up to this point, conventional flight suits had been worn and the maximum altitude had been held to 30,000'). The sixth and final training flight was a maximum altitude flight, usually to 70,000' or more.

U-2R piloting qualification requirements were similar to those for early models with ground school being followed by 3 low altitude flights, and 3 high altitude flights.

The first landings were observed closely with one i.p. in a U-3 flying formation in the air, and another in a chase car following close behind on the runway. Altitude was called out by the chase car i.p. from 10' to ground level. A full stall was required to get the aircraft on the ground and it was mandatory that the zero-track landing gear be lined up perfectly with the centerline of the runway (the saying was, "keep the crack in your fanny lined up with the white stripe down the center of the runway").

Braking was a bit tricky, too, as falling off on one wing tip or the other would lower the drag coefficient on one tire and cause it to scrub—sometimes leading to a tire failure.

U-2 operations were generally supported by a physiological support van, two radio equipped chase cars, and a pick-up truck with a built-on ladder.

Once on operational duty, U-2 pilots could expect sixty day TDY's (with 30 day overlaps between pilots). Pilots were often away from home 200 to 280 days a year.

Ingressing and egressing the U-2 in either a partial- or full-pressure suit is not easily accomplished. Here, then-Secretary of the Air Force McLucas is ingressed for a demo ride to 70,000'. Note air-conditioning pipe for colling cockpit during preflight.

USAF via René Francillon

From certain angles, the U-2CT (56-6953) could give the impression of being a conventional single seat U-2C. Aircraft is shown making approach to Davis-Monthan AFB during training flight.

REFERENCES

Books:

EDWARDS — FLIGHT TEST CENTER OF THE USAF, John D. Ball, Duell, Sloan, Pearce, New York, New York, 1962

THE OBSERVER'S SOVIET AIRCRAFT DIRECTORY, William Green and Gordon Swanborough, Frederick Warne (Publisher's) Ltd., London, England, 1975

LOCKHEED AIRCRAFT SINCE 1913, René Francillon, Putnam & Company, Ltd., London, England, 1982

JANE'S ALL THE WORLD'S AIRCRAFT, 1982/83 edition, edited by John W. R. Taylor, Jane's Yearbooks, 1982

JANE'S ALL THE WORLD'S AIRCRAFT, 1979/80 edition, edited by John W. R. Taylor, Jane's Yearbooks, 1979

JANE'S ALL THE WORLD'S AIRCRAFT, 1974/75 edition, edited by John W. R. Taylor, Jane's Yearbooks, 1974

AIRCRAFT, ENGINES, AND AIRMEN, August Hanniball, The Scarcrow Press, Inc., Metuchen, New Jersey, 1972

AERODYNAMICS FOR NAVAL AVIATORS, H. H. Hart, Jr., Wm. C. Brown Company, Dubuque, Iowa 1965

U.S. MILITARY AIRCRAFT DESIGNATIONS AND SERIALS SINCE 1909, John Andrade, Midland Counties Publications, Leicester, England, 1979

OPERATION OVERFLIGHT, Francis Gary Powers, Holt, Rinehart and Winston, New York, New York, 1970

THE CRAFT OF INTELLIGENCE, Allen Dulles, Weidenfeld and Nicholson, 1963

WAGING PEACE, THE WHITE HOUSE YEARS 1956–1961, DWIGHT D. EISENHOWER, Doubleday, New York, 1965

THE PENKOVSKY PAPERS, Oleg Penkovsky, Doubleday, New York, New York, 1965

THE SHAPE OF WARS TO COME, David Baker, Patrick Stephens, England, 1981.

SECRETS OF ELECTRONIC ESPIONAGE, John M. Carroll, E.P. Dutton, New York, New York, 1966.

THE C.I.A. AND THE CULT OF INTELLIGENCE, Victor Marchetti and John Marks, Dell Publishing Co., New York, New York, 1974

STRATEGIC RECONNAISSANCE 1956–1976: A HISTORY OF THE 4080th/100th SRW, 100th Strategic Reconnaissance Wing, edited by Thomas J. Doubek, Taylor Publishing Company, Dallas, Texas, 1976

LIQUID HYDROGEN AS A PROPULSION FUEL, 1945–1959, John L. Sloop, National Aeronautics and Space Administration, Washington, D.C., 1978

STRATEGIC AIR COMMAND, David A. Anderton, Charles Scribner's Sons, New York, New York, 1975

LIGHTNING BUGS AND OTHER RECONNAISSANCE DRONES, William Wagner, Aero Publishers, Inc., Fallbrook, California, 1982

THE U.S.A.F. IN SOUTHEAST ASIA; THE ADVISORY YEARS TO 1965, Robert F. Futrell, Office of Air Force History, 1976

RECONNAISSANCE HANDY BOOK FOR THE TACTICAL RECONNAISSANCE SPECIALIST, McDonnell Douglas Corporation, St. Louis, Missouri, no date

THE SOVIET ESTIMATE, U.S. INTELLIGENCE ANALYSIS & RUSSIAN MILITARY STRENGTH, John Prados, The Dial Press, New York, New York, 1981

AERIAL RECONNAISSANCE, THE 10TH PHOTO RECON GROUP IN WORLD WAR II, Tom Ivie, Aero Publishers, Inc., Fallbrook, California, 1981

THE CUBAN MISSILE CRISIS, edited by Robert A. Divine, Quadrangle Books, Inc., Chicago, Illinois, 1971

THE HISTORY OF THE U.S. AIR FORCE, David A. Anderton, Crescent Books, New York, New York, 1981

SUITING UP FOR SPACE, THE EVOLUTION OF THE SPACE SUIT, Lloyd Mallan, The John Day Company, New York, New York, 1971

MANUAL OF COLOR AERIAL PHOTOGRAPHY, edited by John T. Smith, Jr., and Abraham Anson, American Society of Photogrammetry, 1968.

MARCO POLO IF YOU CAN, William F. Buckley, Jr., Avon Books, New York, New York, 1983

THE X-PLANES, X-1 to X-29, Jay N. Miller, Specialty Press, Osceola, Wisconsin, 1983

EVIDENCE IN CAMERA, THE STORY OF PHOTOGRAPHIC INTELLIGENCE IN WWII, Constance Babington Smith, Chatto and Windus, London, England, 1958

DIE DEUTSCHEN FLUGZEUGE 1933–1945, Karlheinz Kens and Heinz J. Nowarra, J.F. Lehmanns Verlag, Munchen, Germany, 1977

BALLOONS AND AIRSHIPS, Lennart Ege, MacMillan Publishing Co., Inc., New York, New York, 1974

AEROSPHERE 1939, Glenn D. Angle, Aircraft Publications, New York, New York, 1940

B-57 CANBERRA AT WAR, Robert C. Mikesh, Charles Scribner's Sons, New York, New York, 1980.

THE ARMY AIR FORCES IN WORLE WAR II, Vols. 1 to 7, Wesley F. Craven and James L. Cate, The University of Chicago Press, Chicago, Illinois, 1964

THE UNITED STATES AIR FORCE IN KOREA, 1950-1953, Robert F. Futrell, Duell, Sloan, Pearce, New York, New York, 1961

Miscellaneous Publications:

ENGINE LISTINGS MANUAL, Prepared by Marketing Support & Data Management Section, Marketing Department, Pratt & Whitney Aircraft Group, United Technologies, 1976

AF(C)-1-1 FLIGHT MANUAL, MODELS U-2C and U-2F AIRCRAFT, May 10, 1967/changed October 15, 1968.

CASE HISTORY OF THE B-57 (CANBERRA) AIRPLANE, AUGUST 1950–JUNE 1953, Helen W. Schulz, Historical Division, Office of Information Services, Air Materiel Command, Wright-Patterson AFB, April, 1954

HISTORY OF THE B-57 AIRPLANE, JULY 1953–JANUARY 1958, Volume 1, Text, Frederick A. Alling, Historical Division, Office of Information Services, Air Materiel Command, Wright-Patterson AFB, September, 1958

HIGH ALTITUDE PERSPECTIVE, Airborne Missions and Applications Division, NASA Ames Research Center, Moffett Field, California, 1977

DEDICATED TO PEACE, 4080th Strategic Wing unofficial ten-year history, 1966.

Lockheed Press Releases LA3583-107 and LA4957

PILOTS CONDENSED CHECKLIST, MODEL U-2A AIRCRAFT, June 15, 1965, Changed December 20, 1965

U-2 INVESTIGATOR'S HANDBOOK, VOLS. 1 & 2, NASA Airborne Instrumentation Research Project, Applications Division, August, 1978

Magazines

AIR FORCE
    January, 1976: Learning To Land The U-2
    June, 1979: Jane's Supplement
    April, 1977: Flying The U-2

AIRMAN
    September, 1978: Where The High Flyers Go
AIR PICTORIAL
    July, 1956: Mystery Machine
AIREVIEW
    April, November, December, 1959
AIR UNIVERSITY REVIEW
    March/April, 1982: An Approach to Reconnaissance Doctrine

AMERICAN HERITAGE
    October, 1977: The Time Of The Angel: The U-2, Cuba, And The C.I.A.
    (Month unknown) 1977: The U-2 Story
AVIATION JOURNAL
    October, 1979

AVIATION WEEK & SPACE TECHNOLOGY
    May 16, 1960: SAC U-2 Fleet; Wreckage Displayed; Soviet Missile Command; Extreme Cleanness, Manufacturing Care Mark U-2; Soviets Exploit U-2, Boast of Strength; U-2 Developmental And Operational Chronology
    May 23, 1960: Low Volatility Fuel Use In U-2 Lightweight
    May 30, 1960: U-2 Carried Inertial Guidance System
    October 24, 1960: NASA Reports Confirm 75,000' U-2 Altitude
    September 25, 1961: *Discoverer* Becomes Satellite Test Bed
    September 17, 1962: Chinese U-2's Seek Nuclear, IRBM Data
    (Date unknown) 1973: SAC U-2's Modified For Fallout Sampling
    January 29, 1973: Lockheed To Flight Test U-2 For Navy Surveillance Role
    July 11, 1977: USAF Picks Lockheed Team To Develop Targeting System
    June 16, 1980: Strategic Air Command To Form New Training Unit; Role Of U-2 High-Altitude Surveillance Aircraft to Be Expanded
    July 28, 1980: Most Recent Eruptions Draw Large Crowds
    September 29, 1980: Sensor Key In Missile Warning System
    October 29, 1979: U-2 Collection Believed To Be Dust Of Comet
BUSINESS WEEK
    June 4, 1960: How High The Spy?
ESQUIRE
    May, 1966: Going To See Gary
FLIGHT INTERNATIONAL (FLIGHT)
    June 1, 1956: (Title unknown)
    January 26, 1980: Egyptians Exercise With AWACs
    January 12, 1980: High-Flier Detects Galaxy Cluster
    February 9, 1980: Readiness Key To 1981 Budget
    March 8, 1980: TR-1 And KC-10 Procurement Increased
    May 7, 1983: New Life For The Dragon Lady
FLYING
    June, 1980: Dragon Lady 13 Miles Up
FLYING REVIEW INTERNATIONAL
(RAF FLYING REVIEW)
    August, 1960: U-2: Facts (and Fiction)
    February, 1966: A Watch From The Sky—Overhead Reconnaissance
LOCKHEED HORIZONS
    Second Quarter, 1966: Clear Air Turbulence
MODEL AIRPLANE NEWS
    March, 1968

NEWSWEEK
    May 16, 1960: The Flight Of The U-2
    February 12, 1968: Where Are They Now?
    February 28, 1977: The Sting's The Thing; The High-Spying U-2
PARADE
    October 15, 1978: U-2 Renewed

It is extremely difficult to differentiate between U-2R's and TR-1A's when the latter is devoid of its super pods. Second TR-1A, 80-1067, is seen during test hop over southern California.

ROLLS ROYCE MAGAZINE
   September, 1982: Taking The Record Beyond 60,000 Feet
SPACEFLIGHT
   November/December 1980; Tests Of The SS-6 *Sapwood* ICBM
TIME
   April 7, 1980: Spying From On High
U.S. NEWS & WORLD REPORT
   April 19, 1976: When U-2 Flies A Mission of Mercy

WESTERN AVIATION, MISSILES, AND SPACE
   February, 1961: The U-2 Today Scores Short-Cuts To Space With Its Long, Lonely Flights
   (Date unknown); The U-2 Today Scores Short Cuts To Space With Its Long, Lonely Flights
WINGS/AIRPOWER
   June, 1983: High Flight, pt. 1
   July, 1983: High Flight, pt. 2

Miscellaneous:

THE U-2 STORY, 1978 lecture by Kenneth W. Weir, Lockheed Corp.
Los Angeles Times
   February 12, 1973: U-2 May Do Ocean Surveillance
Baltimore Sun
   May 19, 1960: Reds Print Paperback On U-2 Case
   July 11, 1960: 3 U-2 Planes Moved Out, Japan Says
Empire News
   August 31, 1960: Was There A Leak On U-2 Trip?
Austin American-Statesman
   December 8, 1977: U-2 Pilot Dies In Takeoff Crash

Marysville Appeal-Democrat
   May 2, 1960: Crashed U-2 To Be Displayed

Philadephia Inquirer
   August 5, 1960: Russia Overflown 7 years Before U-2
San Francisco Inquirer
   February 1, 1980: Spy Plane In Trouble
Wall Street Journal
   October 13, 1980: The Skunk Works: Hush-Hush Projects Often Emerge There
Washington Post
   May 11, 1960: U-2 Spy Data Printed In 1958
   May 15, 1968: U.S. May Lose Base In Pakistan
   May 20, 1968: Good Riddance
   May 22, 1960: 'Inside Story' Of U-2 Tells Of Big New Red Missiles
   May 28, 1960: U-2's Flew Over China, Reds Claim
   August 7, 1960: Light Punishment For Powers Seen
   May 22, 1983: Air Force, Citing Costs, Seeks to Cancel Projects
   ?, 1983: A Super Flying And Spying Machine

Playground Daily News
   May 9, 1976: Eglin Tests U-2 In Climatic Lab
Chicago Tribune
   June 4, 1960: U-2 Jet Lost In Red China, Canadian Says
St. Louis Post Dispatch
   July 18, 1960: Army Counsel Cites U-2 Flights' Value
MILITARY SPECIFICATION, FUEL AIRCRAFT TURBINE AND JET ENGINE, THERMALLY STABLE, MIL-F-25524A (USAF), October 4, 1956 (Superceding MIL-F-25524) USAF, February 3, 1956

Lockheed Report #9732, March 4, 1954: CL-282
A TRIBUTE TO CLARENCE L. "KELLY" JOHNSON, Script for Lockheed Corporation, AIAA meeting, 1978

Christian Science Monitor
   May 17, 1960: Spy Program Juggled By U.S.: Soviet Space Shot
   May 18, 1960: U-2 Incident Spurs Space-Law Studies
HASP SPECIAL REPORT ON HIGH ALTITUDE SAMPLING PROGRAM, Maj. Albert K. Stebbins, Radiation Division, Defense Atomic Support Agency, Washington, D.C., June 1, 1960

Friends and noted authorities on several of Lockheed's most esoteric recce aircraft, Chris Pocock, John Andrews, and René Francillon, made rather serious contributions to this book by sending the author their respective sizeable files of both published and unpublished papers and reference documents. These items covered every facet of the U-2 program and proved critical to the accurate history and technical details this book contains. This generosity is deserving of special mention.

Interviews:

John Seaberg, "Deke" Hall, Bob Schumacher, Ben Rich, Don Webster, Bob Birkett, Bob Danielson, John Andrews, Jim Goodall, Ray Goudey, and Chris Pocock.

A FINAL WORD

As this book goes to press, the production future of the TR-1A has come into question. The Air Force, in an austerity measure of some modesty, has proposed dropping several major items from its research and procurement programs, including the TR-1A. The future of these cuts is in some doubt, but it does appear, as of this writing, that the U-2 may have at long last come to the end of its production road.

Lockheed-California Company

INDEX